Twentieth-Century Poetry and the Visual Arts

The emergence of photography and film in the twentieth century helped to create a shift from a culture of words to a culture of images. Since then, the question of how literature engages the visual arts has become a key question for literary studies. This extended treatment of the poetic representation of visual art examines a wide range of figures, from W. B. Yeats and Marianne Moore to Anne Sexton and Ted Hughes. Elegantly and persuasively written, the study also contains a rich sample of images that allows readers to see the same works these poets were addressing. By investigating the complex, changing relations between twentieth-century poetry, visual art, and audience, it considers the way in which poetic responses to visual art place the lyric firmly within the social world. For those interested in the interplay between poetry and visual art, this will be essential reading.

ELIZABETH BERGMANN LOIZEAUX is professor of English at the University of Maryland, College Park.

Twentieth-Century Poetry and the Visual Arts

ELIZABETH BERGMANN LOIZEAUX
University of Maryland, College Park

CAMBRIDGE
UNIVERSITY PRESS

CAMBRIDGE UNIVERSITY PRESS
Cambridge, New York, Melbourne, Madrid, Cape Town, Singapore, São Paulo, Delhi

Cambridge University Press
The Edinburgh Building, Cambridge CB2 8RU, UK

Published in the United States of America by Cambridge University Press, New York

www.cambridge.org
Information on this title: www.cambridge.org/9780521887953

First published 2008

Printed in the United Kingdom at the University Press, Cambridge

A catalogue record for this publication is available from the British Library

Library of Congress Cataloguing in Publication data
Loizeaux, Elizabeth Bergmann.
  Twentieth-century poetry and the visual arts / Elizabeth Bergmann Loizeaux.
    p.   cm.
  Includes bibliographical references and index.
  ISBN 978-0-521-88795-3 (hardback)
  1. American poetry – 20th century – History and criticism.   2. English poetry – 20th
century – History and criticism.   3. Art and literature – United States – History – 20th
century.   4. Art and literature – Great Britain – History – 20th century.
  5. Ekphrasis.   I. Title.
  PS 310.A76L65   2008
  811′.509–dc22   2008027112

ISBN 978-0-521-88795-3 hardback

For Bill and Emma,
and in memory of Anna

Contents

Illustrations

Acknowledgments

I would like to thank the University of Maryland, College Park General Research Board for its support in the writing and publishing of this book, and my colleagues in the English Department of the University of Maryland for providing such a warm and lively intellectual community.

This book has come about with the sustained help and generosity of many colleagues and friends. For their conversation and acute readings of drafts that made this a better book, I thank John Auchard, Jonathan Auerbach, Marsha Bryant, Richard Cross, Neil Fraistat, Jeff Hammond, Ted Leinwand, Bob Levine, Lucy MacDiarmid, Catherine Paul, Susan Rosenbaum, Norma Tilden and the two anonymous readers at Cambridge University Press. Little did I know when I walked into George Bornstein's seminar on modern poetry at the University of Michigan that I was about to receive a lifetime guarantee of encouragement, support and friendship, for which I continue to be grateful. My thanks also to Rose Ann Cleveland, Joan Goldberg, Ivy Goodman, Eric and Rochelle Mayer, and Pam Wessling for their sustaining friendship. Friends from the inception of this project in England years ago have been more important than they know: John Haffenden, Mick Hattaway, Michael Leslie, Jeanne Martin, Derek Roper and Claire Tylee. Thanks also go to my students: Cameron Bushnell, whose unpublished paper suggested a way into Moore, and Magdelyn Hammond, whose hunting in the archives contributed so substantially to the chapter on Ted Hughes. No one could wish for a more responsive and intelligent research assistant than Natalie Prizel, whose help was invaluable during the final stage of this project. Chapter 2 is dedicated to the late Herbert Barrows with whom I first read Auden.

For their willingness to give of their personal and professional help, I thank Lisa Baskin, W. D. Snodgrass, Michael Basinski (Special Collections, State University of New York at Buffalo), Stephen Enniss (Manuscript, Archives and Rare Books Library, Emory University), L. Rebecca Johnson Melvin (Rare Book and Manuscript Library, University of Delaware) and Tara Wenger (Harry Ransom Humanities Research Center, University of Texas at Austin). Thanks also to the editorial staff at Cambridge University Press, especially Ray Ryan and Paul

Stevens, and to production manager Jamie Hood and copy-editor Robert Whitelock.

To my parents, Carl and Elizabeth Bergmann; my siblings, Fritz, Ann and Bill, and their spouses and children; and to Jean and the late Jack Loizeaux, Chris and Meg and their spouses and children, my gratitude for their loving patience and interest.

I dedicate this book to my husband Bill and my daughter Emma who know how much of it is really theirs; and to my daughter Anna Seaver Loizeaux whose joy and courage during her short life continue to teach and amaze.

For permission to quote unpublished letters from W. D. Snodgrass to Anne Sexton: W. D. Snodgrass; and Harry Ransom Humanities Research Center, The University of Texas at Austin.

For permission to quote from a letter from Anne Sexton to W. D. Snodgrass: W. D. Snodgrass Papers, University of Delaware Library, Newark, Delaware.

For permission to quote from unpublished letters from Ted Hughes to Leonard Baskin in the Leonard Baskin Collection, British Library, London: The Estate of Ted Hughes.

For permission to quote from unpublished letters by Leonard Baskin and to reproduce images of his work: The Estate of Leonard Baskin. © Estate of Leonard Baskin; and the Ted Hughes Collection, Manuscript, Archives, and Rare Book Library, Emory University.

For permission to quote from unpublished editorial correspondence from George Nicholson and Michael Loeb to Leonard Baskin in the Leonard Baskin Collection, British Library, London: The Penguin Group, USA.

Parts of Chapter 1 (on Durcan) and Chapter 4 (on Hughes's and Baskin's *Cave Birds*) were published in "Ekphrasis and textual consciousness," *Word & Image* 15.1 (January, 1999), pp. 76–96. Material in Chapter 4 also appeared in "Reading word, image and the body of the book: Ted Hughes's and Leonard Baskin's *Cave Birds*," *Twentieth Century Literature* 50.1 (Spring, 2004), 18–58.

Elizabeth Bergmann Loizeaux has paid the visual creators of the Design and Artists Copyright Society for the use of their artistic works.

Introduction. The engaging eye: Ekphrasis and twentieth-century poetry

You are worried that you don't write?
Don't be. It's the tribute of the air that
your paintings don't just let go
of you. And what poet ever sat down
in front of a Titian, pulled out
his versifying tablet and began
to drone? Don't complain, my dear,
You do what I can only name.

(Frank O'Hara, "To Larry Rivers," 1955)[1]

Admire, when you come here, the glimmering hair
Of the girl; praise her pale
Complexion. Think well of her dress
Though that is somewhat out of fashion.
Don't try to take her hand, but smile for
Her hesitant gentleness.

(W. D. Snodgrass, "VUILLARD: 'The Mother and
Sister of the Artist,'" 1960–1961)[2]

This book takes up one prominent aspect of twentieth-century poetry's varied and intense involvement with the visual arts: ekphrasis, the poem that addresses a work of art. Specifically, this book is about the social dynamics of ekphrasis; about the complex, changing and various relations among poet, work of art, and audience that structure the ekphrastic poem; and about how ekphrastic poetry, by means of those relations, opens the lyric into a network of social engagements within and across the boundaries of the poem. The book began in a fascination with the workings of modern ekphrasis and with a question: Why did so many modern poets, with such attention and such conflicted self-consciousness, turn to painting and sculpture as subjects for their poems? Why does this subgenre of the lyric occur so frequently in Anglo-American poetry in the twentieth century, used by so many poets, often repeatedly and to produce their best work? From W. B. Yeats's "Leda and the Swan," "The Municipal Gallery Re-visited" and "Lapis Lazuli," through W. H. Auden's "Musée des

Beaux Arts," Marianne Moore's "Sea Unicorns and Land Unicorns" and William Carlos Williams's "Pictures from Brueghel," to Robert Lowell's "For the Union Dead," Adrienne Rich's "Mourning Picture," Thom Gunn's "In Santa Maria del Popolo," John Ashbery's "Self-Portrait in a Convex Mirror" and Rita Dove's "Agosta the Winged Man and Rasha the Black Dove," poets across the stylistic spectrum turned to ekphrasis to write some of the finest and most important poems of the twentieth century. Well-exercised in the first half of the century by Pound, H. D., Stein and Stevens as well, ekphrasis boomed in the second half: Ted Hughes, Sylvia Plath, Lawrence Ferlinghetti, Frank O'Hara, Denise Levertov, James Merrill, Seamus Heaney, Yusef Komunyakaa, Jorie Graham, Mark Doty. Nearly every poet has turned at least once, many again and again, to painting and sculpture, and to the genre that stages their interaction. J. D. McClatchy hardly exaggerated when he observed that "for most [twentieth-century] poets paintings are primal, as 'real' as the bread and wine on the table, as urgent as a dying parent or concealed lover in the next room."[3] Wallace Stevens compared the relation between poetry and painting to that necessary dialogue between our inner and outer worlds: "The world about us would be desolate except for the world within us. There is the same interchange between these two worlds that there is between one art and another, migratory passings to and fro, quickenings, Promethean liberations and discoveries."[4] "Picture-making is the air I breathe," said Paul Durcan.[5]

If the record of ekphrastic production can be a measure, images are more urgent in the twentieth century than ever before. The intimacy and necessity McClatchy identifies pervades modern ekphrasis, the "quickenings" of love and friendship, the "passings to and fro" of a life-sustaining connection among artists. "I am alone on the surface/ of a turning planet. What// to do but, like Michelangelo's/ Adam, put my hand/ out into unknown space,/ hoping for the reciprocating touch?" asked R. S. Thomas, himself looking to Michelangelo.[6] As in O'Hara's "To Larry Rivers" above, direct address to the artist registers that connection in many modern ekphrases, companionable, contentious, desiring, admiring: "and all the while you knew/ what you dared to acknowledge only in oils," says Richard Howard to Henri Fantin-Latour; "Can you stand it,/ Francesco? Are you strong enough for it?" Ashbery asks Parmagianino; "You were more interested/ in her swinging baroque tits/ and the space between her thighs/ than the expression on her face," Vicki Feaver accuses Roger Hilton.[7]

The twentieth century's various pan-arts avant-gardes and their multi-disciplinary manifestos (Dada, vorticism, futurism, surrealism) speak to this energizing banding together, as do the circles of artists and writers like the one that gathered in the 1910s around Alfred Stieglitz's 291 gallery, or around Walter Arensberg and Alfred Kreymborg's journal *Others*, or in Stein's Paris apartment, or, in the fifties, as the New York School: "We were restless and constrained, closely allied to the painters. Impressionism, Dadaism, surrealism applied to both painting and the poem," commented Williams.[8] This sense of shared goals points to one of the many varied and interconnected ways the engagement with the visual arts tells in the work of poets. As Marjorie Perloff and others have documented, poets and artists, working off of and with each other, jointly developed ideas and strategies for confronting modernity.[9] Analogy frequently provided a way of fruitfully taking those strategies into the different arts. Yeats turned to the later Pre-Raphaelites for the "picture" that he hoped would save him from the sin of Victorian poetic abstraction.[10] Imagism developed by implicit analogy to the visual arts in desiring the instantaneous revelation the visual image is thought to have: "that which presents an intellectual and emotional complex in an instant of time."[11] Abstraction, itself, as Charles Altieri has argued, would later become a goal that the poets worked by analogy to painting.[12] More materially, poets and artists collaborated with each other, producing imagetexts of many kinds, as we'll see in Chapter 5 on Ted Hughes's and Leonard Baskin's collaboration. Reference and allusion to the visual arts abound, as in *The Cantos*, for example. Concrete or shaped poems reappeared as a viable poetic model. And in prose, twentieth-century poets wrote frequently about art and artists in numerous essays and reviews: Yeats on the Pre-Raphaelites, Pound on Henri Gaudier-Brzeska, Auden on Van Gogh, Elizabeth Bishop on Gregorio Valdes, Ted Hughes on Leonard Baskin, Frank O'Hara on Jackson Pollock, Mark Strand on Edward Hopper.[13] As the engagement with a work of art, ekphrasis often contains or is intertwined with all of these verbal–visual relations

Why, among the arts, such interest in images in particular as subject matter for poems? This book will suggest a number of reasons, but two, I think, predominate. First, poets, like the rest of us, look at images because they are everywhere. The widespread presence of ekphrasis in twentieth-century poetry can be understood as both a response to and a participant in what W. J. T. Mitchell has called "the pictorial turn" from a culture of words into a culture of images that began in the late nineteenth century with the advent of photography and then film, and has accelerated since the mid twentieth century with the invention of television and, now, digital media.[14] Excited – and haunted – by a sense of images' increasing power in western culture, poets have taken up ekphrasis as a way of engaging and understanding their allure and force. With the founding of public art museums, beginning in the late eighteenth century and increasing through the twentieth (the Louvre in 1793; the National Gallery, London in 1824; the Metropolitan Museum in New York in 1880; MoMA in 1929; the National Gallery, Washington in 1941), works of art have become readily available, and sometimes popular with a large public, as the blockbuster exhibitions of the late twentieth century attest. Photographic reproductions on postcards, posters, exhibition catalogues and, most recently, websites – constituting what André Malraux called a "museum without walls" – have helped make works of art vital participants in visual culture.[15]

At the heart of twentieth-century ekphrasis is this growing familiarity of works of art among a broad reading public. Poets write on a Van Gogh or Brueghel or Monet or Hopper aware that those works are available to the eye and the mind's eye of an audience. As I'll argue in Chapters 2 (Brueghel) and 3 (Van Gogh), ekphrasis has both increased and tapped the cultural currency of the images it engages, and helped shape the debate about them. When Anne Sexton writes on Van Gogh's *The Starry Night*, for example, she appeals to wide-spread familiarity with the image and enters into the popular debate about madness and artistic genius that centered on Van Gogh. Paul Durcan's 1991 volume of poems on the collection of the National Gallery of Ireland rose to the top of the best-seller list and sold 20,000 copies in Dublin in two months. There's an audience beyond the usual poetry readers interested in a poet's take on images, and not just in Ireland.

Along with the deep pleasure and the sense of excitement and possibility for poetry in being involved with images comes the nagging sense that pictures have something that words do not – and an underlying fear that the power to shape culture is passing from one medium to another. Modern poems on works of art are fraught with mixed emotions about images. McClatchy's sense of painting as a dying parent or concealed lover gets at a complex, ambivalent feeling that the visual arts are an intimate, pressing bodily presence in the next room. Ekphrasis is an emphatically deictic mode: "Here," says Snodgrass above, indicating how tightly the space of the painting binds to his own. "See," "Look" are frequent imperatives of the pointing poet. From early Pound and the imagists to the post-language poets, poets have seen in works of art an immediacy, a presence, a "hereness" that they have wanted for words, but that they suspect words can only gesture toward. "The writer will always envy the

painter," said James Merrill in "Notes on Corot."[16] When Seamus Heaney
set out to collaborate with photographer Rachel Giese on *Sweeney's Flight*
(1992), he confessed he feared a "misalliance of some sort between the
impersonal instantaneous thereness of the picture ... and the personal,
time-stretching pleas of the verse."[17] The word might be shown up as a
beggar for the audience's attention, having to start from a disadvantaged
position as symbolic and non-objective statement. No amount of talk
about the illusion of the natural sign in painting, about images as semiotic
systems too, or about writing as itself visual and material, can do away with
the suspicion that the image participates in the physical world and/or can
give access to it in a more direct, less mediated way than language. Modern
painting's emphasis on its own materials and making, which could make
painting seem more like writing, did little to banish the persistent sense
among many ekphrastic poets that painting still has more presence in the
world than words. As Frank O'Hara said so wistfully to Larry Rivers, "You
do what I can only name."

The second major reason for the prevalence of ekphrasis in twentieth-
century poetry arises from the particular resources of the genre itself,
beginning with its given structure. Writing on a work of art differs from
writing on a natural object in that the work of art constitutes a statement
already made about/in the world. As the staging of the relation between
words and images, poet and artist, ekphrasis is inherently dialogic. What
Mary Ann Caws calls the "afterness" of ekphrasis, which sometimes
translates as a sense of belatedness, is also the fundamental relatedness of
ekphrasis.[18] The ekphrastic poet always responds to someone else's work.
The poet who would write on a work of art, says James Merrill, must
"listen for its opening words."[19] Ekphrasis is a mode of poetry that, by its
very nature, opens out of lyric subjectivity into a social world. In the
twentieth century, it has been one means of making the lyric, the dominant
poetic mode, more flexible; of expanding lyric subjectivity into a field that
includes at least one other, the artist/work of art, with a third always
present and sometimes active in the exchange, the audience. What we
might call the "ekphrastic situation" – the poet engaging the work of art
and representing it to an audience – contains at least three participants. In
arguing for the key role of the Victorian "literature of art" in the transition
from Romanticism to modernism, Richard Stein pointed to the dynamics
this triangle introduced into the lyric: "the writer now mediates between
an external object, an acknowledged personal perspective on it, and a felt
need to create a new public context of values."[20] The importance of the
audience's role to a revitalized poetry became increasingly important in the

twentieth century as poetry further lost popular readership and its significant social role. Ekphrasis engages the reader: "The reference to a second art gives a new and important role to the reader-spectator, who shares the writer's contemplation of an external artifact."[21] Randall Jarrell prompted the readers of "The Knight, Death, and the Devil," on Dürer's engraving of the same name, to compare "the details of the poem with those of the picture," to engage in the conversation of interpretation.[22] W. D. Snodgrass, above, gives his readers "instructions" for visiting the scene in Vuillard's disturbing portrait of his mother and sister. The opening of the lyric field into a social realm thus happens along two lines – the poet's relation with the artist/work of art and his relation to his audience – and in the interaction among the three.

Richard Wilbur's "A Dutch Courtyard" (1947), a witty send-up of the ekphrastic situation, exposes the urgency of the social relations inherent in ekphrasis and suggests what the stakes can be:

A Dutch Courtyard

What wholly blameless fun
To stand and look at pictures. Ah, they are
Immune to us. This courtyard may appear
To be consumed with sun,

Most mortally to burn,
Yet it is quite beyond the reach of eyes
Or thoughts, this place and moment oxidize;
This girl will never turn,

Cry what you dare, but smiles
Tirelessly toward the seated cavalier,
Who will not proffer you his pot of beer;
And your most lavish wiles

Can never turn this chair
To proper uses, nor your guile evict
These tenants. What surprising strict
Propriety! In despair,

Consumed with greedy ire,
Old Andrew Mellon glowered at this Dutch
Courtyard, until it bothered him so much
He bought the thing entire.[23]

Figure 1 Pieter De Hooch, *A Dutch Courtyard* (1658/1660).

At the heart of this self-ironic "ars ekphrasis" is a triangular set of social relations: between the speaker/poet and the figures depicted in De Hooch's seventeenth-century Dutch genre scene (Fig. 1); between the speaker/poet and De Hooch, whose painting seems to invite the viewer in with its ordinary domestic scene of people talking and laughing and its perspective lines opening the space of the picture into ours (see how the floor extends to include us); and between the speaker/poet and his audience/fellow viewer (the "us"). The poem revolves around how the parties involved conduct their relations: not well, in Wilbur's scenario. This ekphrastic poet has a grievance: "This girl will never turn,// Cry what you dare, but smiles/ Tirelessly toward the seated cavalier,/ Who will not proffer you his pot of beer." The figures in De Hooch's scene refuse entry to the party, despite the invitation the painting seems to offer.

So, out of the ekphrastic situation, the simple, "blameless fun" of looking at pictures, balloon big issues of life and art. The ekphrastic poet, the poem implies, comes to the painting seeking friendship, fun, a little flirtation: in short, connection to others in a world that seems warmer and more certain than his own, only to find it indifferent to him. "That simpler world from which we've been evicted," is how Sassoon similarly described the scene in an English landscape.[24] This is the cry of nostalgic modernity, uttered with all the shock of the new in Sassoon's case, satirized, though acknowledged, in Wilbur's. With one foot often in the past, ekphrasis can thus dramatize in social terms the relation of the present to the past in an age in which that past seems to beckon, only to turn its back.

Looking is not, never has been, ethically neutral, and ekphrasis stages relations lived under that fact.[25] Wilbur's poem tackles directly this underlying condition of ekphrasis. Whether looking serves truth out of which right action grows or is proprietary and invasive (itself an act of transgression) troubles the moderns: "What wholly blameless fun," Wilbur mocks our willfully innocent desire to look.[26] Ethically charged, too, is the collecting that begat the modern art museum out of which this and most modern ekphrases come. With the poem's language of property, Wilbur tests the relation between art and material possession which his choice of ekphrastic object reinforces: Dutch genre scenes such as De Hooch's were painted for a booming art market in a newly independent country of merchants and farmers, eager to exercise their buying power and to have their national identity reflected and validated in paint. Acutely aware of his situation both physically (in the National Gallery in Washington, DC) and ethically, Wilbur knows that he and Mellon (the Gallery's founder) are allied in the "greedy ire" with which they set out to possess the object of desire.

"A Dutch Courtyard" plays to the hilt the gendering of poet and work of art that has been taken as a hallmark of ekphrasis by recent commentators: the observing male poet gazing on the feminized image and wanting his way with her.[27] Mellon and Wilbur are outrageously, stereotypically, male, intent on seducing and finally possessing the resolutely independent females in the image, and the recalcitrant feminized image. The "guile" and "lavish wiles" Wilbur deploys in his pursuit include this poem's showily deft quatrains and clever rhymes. They mock the poet's doomed efforts. Ekphrasis thus opens the charged terrain of twentieth-century gender struggles. The gender dynamics of the ekphrastic situation so evident in "A Dutch Courtyard," is, I will argue, questioned, reversed and differently written in significant ways in twentieth-century ekphrases, especially those by women.

Wilbur's poem also plays up the self-reflexive nature of ekphrasis: writing on a work of art becomes a way of looking sideways at poetry. "A Dutch Courtyard" dramatizes the relation of the poet to his materials, laying bare and thematizing, again in social terms, what the poet does with the objects he contemplates, and how those objects respond. Wilbur's gallery-goer/poet is caught between resistant material and his own desire to "make" something of it. If we as readers consult the originating images (sometimes even presented to us on the page with the poem), ekphrasis often allows us to see for ourselves how the poet has treated his subjects.

Ekphrasis occurs early, middle and late in the century, and crosses the stylistic spectrum. I want to suggest that the prevalence of ekphrasis indicates continuous and ongoing efforts across the century to break open the possibilities of lyric poetry. In his influential account of the transformation of modern to contemporary American poetry (1984), James Breslin located an "opening of the field" of poetry in the work produced in the 1950s by five loose groups exemplified by Allen Ginsberg (Beats), Robert Lowell (confessionals), Denise Levertov (Black Mountain), Frank O'Hara (New York School) and James Wright (Deep Image): "with the shattering of the hermetically sealed autotelic poem, American poetry broke open to the physical moment – the literal, the temporal, the immediate."[28] Breslin talks in terms of a mid-century "breakthrough" from fixed forms to open, processual free verse that exposes the material nature of language. But the desire to open the field of the lyric poem (never so enclosed or monolithic as Breslin represents it, in any case) crosses the stylistic divide he constructs and is pursued by other means as well. It lies behind the prevalence of ekphrasis. In focusing on a work of art, ekphrasis, by its very nature, does what Breslin's shattered autotelic poem does, "acknowledge[s] an immediate external reality that remains stubbornly other."[29] The ekphrastic poem is all about that otherness, and about how one engages it. While Richard Wilbur, with his persistent formalism, represents what Breslin's postwar American experimenters supposedly break through from, "A Dutch Courtyard" nevertheless shows Wilbur dramatizing, and accepting, the otherness of an irrefutable external reality as vigorously as those who looked to formal experimentation to accomplish that end. The desire to take such otherness into the self, to obliterate its difference, is precisely what Wilbur's poem mocks, and refuses. His self-consciously displayed rhymes are less a mark of detached wry urbanity, as Wilbur's rhymes are usually understood, than a calling of attention to the poet in the process of attempting to fold the strangeness of the picture into "poetry," an attempt that cannot succeed.[30] What Wilbur identifies with ironic primness as the painting's "surprising strict/ Propriety," John Ashbery calls more casually "This otherness, this/ 'Not-being-us.'"[31] Although ekphrasis has had certain forms associated with it (primarily the sonnet), it is not itself a form, but a rhetorical situation and a set of practices and tropes that offer non-prescriptive possibilities for exploring that situation. Ekphrasis is, thus, not easily drafted into arguments pitting formalists against avant-gardists. Examples of it are routinely cited by critics across the range of poetic tastes.[32]

The inherently social dynamics of ekphrasis and its possibilities for polyvocality made it especially attractive to a postmodernism alive to the multiplicity of the lyric subject and to racial, ethnic and gender differences. Art historian Michael Fried's analysis of the rise of minimalist art in the 1960s is relevant here. In his famous 1967 essay "Art and objecthood," Fried argues that minimalist art (or, as he prefers, "literalist" art), as exemplified by the sculpture of Donald Judd and Robert Morris, is "theatrical" in that "it is concerned with the actual circumstances in which the beholder encounters literalist work."[33] It understands the work of art as an object and is principally concerned with the relation of the beholder to that object: "the experience of literalist art is of an object *in a situation –* one that, virtually by definition, *includes the beholder.*"[34] For Fried, the theatrical is a matter of "experience, conviction, sensibility."[35] While the object of contemplation in ekphrasis is rarely the minimalist object with which Fried is concerned, ekphrasis itself might be understood as displaying this theatrical sensibility in its basic staging of the encounter. If minimalist theatricality speaks to and expresses a widespread sensibility in the second half of the century, the proliferation of ekphrasis can be seen as evidence and expression of that sensibility.[36]

Whereas Fried's analysis leads him to see a sharp opposition between the modernist (non-theatrical) and the postmodern (at least as exemplified by theatrical literalist art), the study of ekphrasis suggests threads of continuity and connection. Efforts to distinguish a postmodern ekphrasis in opposition to a modernist ekphrasis tend to occlude the record of relation across the century. Marianne Moore's ekphrastic practice – wry, disruptive, interrupted – may have more in common with Ashbery's than with Yeats's, and Yeats's is more various and less iconically monumental than it is commonly represented as being (see "Leda and the Swan" [1925] and "Michael Robartes and the Dancer" [1920], for example). Ekphrasis' postmodern development leads back through the moderns to the nineteenth century. The study of ekphrasis, then, suggests a view of twentieth-century poetry in which postmodernist practice built on certain aspects of modernism even as it diverged from others, and in which modernism displays tendencies and features later associated with postmodernism.[37]

The study of ekphrasis also argues for a view of twentieth-century poetry in which the crossings of national boundaries are freer and more open than the structure of critical discussion often indicates. Twentieth-century poetry in English has always fit uncomfortably into the national divisions that have characterized academic study of it, and the very nature of ekphrasis pushes at those boundaries. Twentieth-century ekphrasis is an international phenomenon that invigorated American poetry, as in the examples of Wilbur and Ashbery above, as well as English poetry (as in Thom Gunn's signature early poem "In Santa Maria del Popolo") and, especially, Irish poetry in works from Yeats through Heaney, Mahon, Boland and Muldoon. (And this is to say nothing of ekphrases in other languages.) Further, those drinkers in Wilbur's poem present a challenge not just because they belong to another medium and time, but also because they are of another culture: the courtyard, the title emphasizes, is Dutch. Ekphrasis often stages an engagement with the foreign. It thus became a means of international modernism and of the continuing globalization of poetry. While the crossings this book explores are primarily (though not exclusively) between western cultures, one might fruitfully look at ekphrases in which English-speaking poets from Yeats, Pound and Moore onwards address the art of eastern cultures in an engagement that will inevitably intensify with growing western awareness of other cultures.

The "otherness" of the ekphrastic object and how language responds to it have been the central focus of the critical interest in ekphrasis that surfaced in the 1950s and has developed in the past fifteen years into a small theoretical industry. While hardly a household word, "ekphrasis" in a recent Google search nevertheless yielded an astonishing 7,400 results. Should you wish to read up on it, Amazon.com offers 304 entries. As a concrete instance of the relations between words and images, ekphrasis has featured prominently in efforts to articulate a sufficiently rigorous interdisciplinary practice, one that does not depend on vague comparisons between the arts or on grand historical/stylistic generalizations (e.g., "the Baroque"), but on particular occasions of interaction.[38] Propelled by a poststructural focus on representation and by the proliferation of ekphrastic practice, recent discussion of poetic ekphrasis developed through the 1980s from John Dixon Hunt's provocative essay that first categorized varieties of ekphrastic relations (1980); through Wendy Steiner's semiotic study of modern literature and the visual arts in *The Colors of Rhetoric* (1982), the founding of the journal *Word & Image* in 1984 and W. J. T. Mitchell's ideological reading of images in *Iconology: Image, Text, Ideology* (1986); to, in the early 1990s, a series of important theoretical and historical works on ekphrasis: Murray Krieger's *Ekphrasis: The Illusion of the Natural Sign* (1992); James Heffernan's essential survey of the genre and its tropes, *Museum of Words: The Poetics of Ekphrasis from Homer to Ashbery* (1993); W. J. T. Mitchell's *Picture Theory*, which includes his influential essay "Ekphrasis and the other" (1994); Grant Scott's *The Sculpted Word: Keats, Ekphrasis, and the Visual Arts* (1994); and John Hollander's anthology of ekphrases with extensive commentary, *The Gazer's Spirit* (1995).[39]

A surprisingly modern development in critical terminology, the definition of ekphrasis as a subgenre of the lyric arose in concert with this critical interest: in the midst, in other words, of its increasing presence in the landscape of twentieth-century poetry and in response to the increasing critical interest in the relations between words and images.[40] "Ekphrasis" (from the Greek *ek*, "out" and *phrazein*, "to speak") began life in the first centuries CE as a rhetorical term for a vivid description that would bring persons, places, things, ideas and, sometimes, actions to the mind's eye of an audience. Focused on a particular kind of description rather than specific subject matter, the early definitions of "ekphrasis" mention "statues or paintings" only as possible objects, and then by the way. It wasn't until the nineteenth century that works of art as objects of classical ekphrasis became critically prominent, and not until 1955 when Leo Spitzer defined "ekphrasis" as "the poetic description of a pictorial or sculptural work of art"[41] that the term came into use in English and Comparative Literature studies and to be limited to works of art and to poems. Several years later, Jean Hagstrum argued for the term "iconic" to designate poems describing works of art, and thereby emphasized the qualities of mimetic vividness as central to the tradition.[42] Along with this increasing interest, ekphrasis acquired its modern history in a poetic tradition stretching back through Rossetti's sonnets on pictures and Keats's "Ode on a Grecian Urn" to the neo-classical poets, Shakespeare and, finally, Homer's description of Achilles' shield. The view of that tradition has since come to distinguish notional ekphrasis (John Hollander's term for representations of imagined works of art)[43] like Homer's and Keats's, from representations of real works that, if they have survived, we can go back to and consult. In the 1980s, as art history came under the influence of poststructuralism and began to make itself new, in part by questioning its own representational practices, "ekphrasis" took on a related life in art criticism. Although still associated primarily with poetry in literary studies, in the past fifteen years it has come to mean more generally, in James Heffernan's well-rehearsed phrase, "the verbal representation of visual representation."[44] "Ekphrasis" might refer to passages of prose fiction as well as poems, and to other kinds of writing about art, such as exhibition catalogue entries. Retrospectively, art historians have elaborated a tradition of ekphrastic artwriting (the term is David Carrier's) traceable back to Vasari's *Lives of the Painters.*[45]

While maintaining this wider sense of ekphrasis that reminds us of poetry's relation to other forms of writing, this study deals with ekphrasis as a poetic genre and with the tropes and conventions twentieth-century poets inherited from a long line of poetic predecessors and transformed for their own uses. In addition, I want to recover something of the classical sense of ekphrasis as the description of a process. Theon lists "actions" as among the subjects of ekphrastic description, distinguishing classical ekphrasis (so often depicting battles) from the modern ekphrasis of objects. While "actions" in general clearly fall outside the range of ekphrasis in its modern usage, the acutely self-reflexive nature of much modern ekphrasis shows in the many poems focusing on the creation of the work of art (which the poem may describe, but not necessarily.) The origin of such "ekphrases of creation" can be found in Homer's description of Achilles' shield, which is framed by and periodically reverts to Hephaestos' making of it. It often takes the form of the poet addressing the artist and asking him to create a work of art according to the specifications set out in the poem.[46] Modern ekphrases of creation tend to focus more specifically on the process and challenges of artistic creation, including the ethical implications of being an observer. This book deals in detail with one such poem (Rita Dove's "Agosta the Winged Man and Rasha the Black Dove") and refers to others.

W. J. T. Mitchell's essay "Ekphrasis and the other" has been the most fruitful and persuasive theorization of ekphrasis. The power of Mitchell's argument lies in his perception of the inherently social nature of ekphrasis: a perception, as is clear by now, central to the arguments I wish to make in this book. Mitchell locates our fascination with ekphrasis in its dramatic confrontation of words and images, whose differences are deeply embedded in western discourse about the arts, famously articulated by Gotthold Lessing in *Laocoön* (1766). Attached to Lessing's basic distinction between poetry as a temporal art ("articulated sounds in time") and painting as a spatial art ("figures and colors in space") are a shifting host of associated attributes: image as bodily, present, replete, still, silent, natural, and feminine; and word as abstract, rational, active, eloquent, and male.[47] Semantically, there is for Mitchell "no essential difference between texts and images": images can tell stories and make arguments, too.[48] But our investment in their difference is deep-seated and, as he argued in *Iconology* (1986), ideologically founded in maintaining and patrolling boundaries of various kinds, including those between states and those between the sexes.[49] "The 'otherness' we attribute to the image–text relationship," Mitchell comments, "takes on the full range of possible social relations inscribed within the field of verbal and visual representation."[50]

As this summary suggests, at the center of the ekphrastic relationship, for Mitchell, is Leonardo's *paragone*, the contest of the arts. In ekphrasis, he argues, language tries to overcome the image, to best it, to turn it to its own needs: "Ekphrastic poetry is the genre in which texts encounter their own semiotic 'others,' those rival, alien modes of representation called the visual, graphic, plastic, or 'spatial' arts."[51] "Ekphrasis," says James Heffernan, following Mitchell, "is a literary mode that turns on the antagonism . . . between verbal and visual representation,"[52] between the still, fixed world of the painting and the active, mutable world of the viewer, an antagonism we see so comically developing, and mocked, in "A Dutch Courtyard." Another way of framing this is to consider the challenge the image issues to the ekphrastic poet: the poem must at least equal the image if it is not to be "mere" addendum, caption, decoration. Highly self-reflexive, the "workings" of ekphrasis reveal the processes of its own making; ekphrasis, argues Mitchell, "expose[s] the social structure of representation as an activity and a relationship of power/knowledge/desire – representation as something done to something, with something, by someone, for someone."[53]

By locating ekphrasis in the wider, charged discourse of the arts, and situating that discourse historically, this view of ekphrastic representation as paragonal contest has moved interart discussions beyond vague historical comparisons between the arts and a cheerful view of them as amiable sisters. Tracing the genealogy of ekphrasis from Homer, Virgil and Dante through Chaucer, Spenser and Shakespeare, to Wordsworth, Keats and Byron, then Auden, Williams and Ashbery, James Heffernan's *Museum of Words* turns Mitchell's work to demonstrating "a struggle for dominance" played out in the ekphrastic arena in terms primarily of gender and of "representational friction" that shows up the differences among the arts in representational power.[54] Mitchell has been especially helpful in exposing the gendering of ekphrasis, the extent to which the language of seduction and rape guides the terms by which word approaches image (a subject to which Heffernan devotes a chapter). Important work by Grant Scott has used Mitchell to renovate our view of the most important Romantic ekphrastic poet, Keats.[55]

Mitchell's paragonal model has been less satisfying, however, when it comes to understanding, or even recognizing, such modest, and profound, feelings as companionship or friendship, the terms in which poets often describe their ekphrastic motives. It has been difficult to move beyond the appealing drama of *paragone*, with its plot of conflict and uncertain victory. But under its lens every ekphrastic relationship looks like linguistic appropriation, every gesture of friendship like co-option, every expression of admiration a declaration of envy by the word for the unobtainable power of the image. "Familiarity" was the term Gertrude Stein used to describe her growing relationship to oil painting: " . . . and I like familiarity. It does not in me breed contempt it just breeds familiarity. And the more familiar a thing is the more there is to be familiar with. And so my familiarity began and kept on being."[56] "I speak to these sculptures, wood prints, and paintings as I would to a friend over coffee or champagne," said Ntozake Shange, explaining the poems of her 1987 ekphrastic collection *Ridin' the Moon in Texas*.[57] Cole Swensen understands her persistent fascination with ekphrasis as "a way to spend more time with those paintings."[58] These three statements speak to a complicated sense of the ekphrastic relation that can be neither adequately explained as paragonal, nor discounted as naive or disingenuous or even productively blind. We are right to be wary of cheerful professions of sisterhood – antagonism and competition do inform much ekphrasis – but it repays us to take seriously the sense of a shared world these comments depict. W. S. Graham addresses the painter Peter Lanyon with poignant directness, speaking the need for sympathetic company that suffuses much modern ekphrasis:

Give me your hand, Peter,
To steady me on the word . . .
Uneasy, lovable man, give me your painting
Hand to steady me taking the word-road home.
                    ("The Thermal Stair," 1970)[59]

While ekphrasis depends on the difference between word and image and can stage their representational contest and opposition, it also stages relations across difference. Otherness is not always "rival," even when it is "alien."[60]

One aim of this study is to broaden the range of relations we see at play in ekphrasis and to recognize the intertwined and various nature of the ekphrastic response, how contest melts into (and can be part of) friendship, how feelings deepen and shift focus in the course of engagement, how a work of art that promises refuge from the world ends up sending the poet back out into it. This book emphasizes the psychological and emotional dynamics at play in any given ekphrastic situation. While the stillness of the work of art is an important trope of ekphrasis, it is not necessarily a characteristic of the ekphrastic poem. In this sense my understanding of ekphrasis differs from that expressed in Jean Hagstrum's use of the term "iconic" and from Murray Krieger's seminal exploration of ekphrasis as the basic impulse of all poetry for the still moment of the visual arts. Krieger works from Lessing's distinction between the temporal and spatial arts to characterize ekphrasis as a desire for the "natural sign," the effort of language to get for itself, via description and other devices, the presence of the visual arts. Ekphrasis, according to Krieger, "craves the spatial fix," though "it retains an awareness of the incapacity of words to come together at an instant (*tout à coup*), at a single stroke of sensuous immediacy, as if in an unmediated impact."[61] Ekphrasis can and sometimes does ask "for language – in spite of its arbitrary character and its temporality – to freeze itself into a spatial form," as Krieger argues.[62] Yet the very structure of ekphrasis encourages poems that emphasize the dynamic interplay of the perceiving, thinking, feeling poet, the work of art and the audience. Even in Keats's "Ode on a Grecian Urn," which so firmly established the "stillness" of the work of art, the speaker's relationship to the urn evolves over the poem's course: it moves in and out of identity and difference, empathy and distance.[63] The different kinds of questions the speaker asks, the mounting of question on question (as many as seven in a row) constitute the trying on of different conversational approaches, grasping for a ground of engagement. In refusing to answer the questions and so divest the urn of its troubling mystery, Keats keeps the issue of the relationship between poet and urn open, alive, and at the center of the poem. In twentieth-century ekphrasis, the poem often stages this kind of shifting relation to the work of art. Ekphrasis plays a role in the development of modern poetry as Stevens described it: "The poem of the mind in the act of finding/ What will suffice."[64] In Wilbur's "A Dutch Courtyard," the speaker's frustration with the still image's refusal to do its share thematizes the centrality of dynamic engagement to ekphrasis. Even description, which has often been posed as the still counterpoint of narrative movement, inevitably traces a process of accumulating detail, of looking harder, of coming-to-know by seeing. And we shouldn't forget that the relation between speaker and audience can shift and develop, too. Wilbur's ekphrastic poet begins in the shared activity of looking at pictures ("us"), but soon, under the accumulating pressure of his complaint, "us" becomes a "you" onto whom he projects his own frustration: "This girl will never turn,// Cry what you dare, but smiles/ Tirelessly toward the seated cavalier,/ Who will not proffer you his pot of beer." "You" may be a generalized, colloquial "one," but there's difference and distance between "us" and "you." This book is less concerned with ekphrasis as the genre that tries to imitate the image or the still presence of the work of art and more with ekphrasis as the genre that negotiates a relation to that other. This sense of ekphrasis returns to the act of communication inherent in its Greek roots: *ek* and *phrazein*, to speak out.

The poet's response to a work of art is born of/into a context alive with other responses. What Bakhtin said about the dynamic relation between discourse and its object in the novel well applies to the ekphrastic situation in poetry:

... between the word and its object, between the word and the speaking subject, there exists an elastic environment of other, alien words about the same object ... any concrete discourse (utterance) finds the object at which it was directed already as it were overlain with qualifications, open to dispute, charged with value, already enveloped in an obscuring mist – or, on the contrary, by the "light" of alien words that have already been spoken about it. It is entangled, shot through with shared thoughts, points of view, alien value judgments and accents. The word, directed toward its object, enters a dialogically agitated and tension-filled environment of alien words, value judgments and accents, weaves in and out of complex interrelationships, merges with some, recoils from others, intersects with yet a third group.[65]

As in the many ekphrases on Brueghel (discussed in Chapter 2), and in Anne Sexton's and W. D. Snodgrass's responses to Van Gogh's *The Starry Night* (Chapter 4), ekphrases often carry on exchanges with other ekphrases (as well as with art-historical commentary) as both engage the work of art: a poet represents the work of art in response, in other words, not just to the work of art but to other representations of it, and in so doing crafts an "answer" to those implicit members of the audience. Ekphrases sometimes also record those other representations of the work of art, usually by importing into the poem the words of other commentators, diffusing the representational authority, multiplying the representing subject, opening up within the field of the single poem a variety of responses. Ekphrasis thus participates in the development of the modern polyvocal poem. When ekphrasis rises out of collaboration, artist and poet are often in literal conversation, creating in response to each other. Mary Ann Caws recently described how seeing Bernini's *Saint Theresa in Ecstasy* began a series of connections (starting with a poem by Crashaw) that opened a community of viewers seeing and saying:

A poem by Richard Crashaw about that wounding sends us straight back to Gerhard Seghers's painting on the same subject, and when Susan Stewart starts in on Saint Theresa's foot, in her recent *Poetry and the Fate of the Senses* (190), I feel afresh in a community of not just readers but also viewers.[66]

Since the early 1980s, in a series of books charting an expanded art history, Mieke Bal has argued for visual interpretation as a field filled with multiple and varying responses across time and across viewers.[67] Although my study does not pursue the narratological and semiological route Bal takes "beyond the word–image opposition," it aims at a similar sense of word–image relations she describes: a multiplication of points of view and a concept of the power of viewing "not as a monolith ... but rather a set of relations" that result in a "more complex and volatile arena" of interaction.[68]

As this suggests, ekphrasis is deeply entwined in its context. There are good reasons for looking at ekphrasis on its own (as most theoretical considerations of the genre do and as I will at times in this book), not the least of which are to see better what happens in it, and to reduce the overload of information that is a real and serious problem in interdisciplinary study – what Caws calls the "stress" of verbal–visual reading. In practice, however, ekphrasis is created and operates within a whole network of textual and social relations that open out of and into the relation of word and image, self and other, and audience. This study thus reads ekphrasis in a variety of contexts: Yeats, Durcan and Auden in the art museums of Dublin and Brussels in times of political instability; Moore and Rich forging a twentieth-century American feminism through ekphrasis; Snodgrass and Sexton in the cultural conversation during the 1960s and 1970s about confessionalism, artistic genius and suicide; Ted Hughes and Leonard Baskin pursuing a verbal–visual collaboration critiquing western dichotomizing and spurred by the modern fine press movement and the modernist *livre d'artiste*; Rita Dove among debates about African American culture in the 1980s; and ekphrases by all these poets in conversations among poems within the poetic volume itself.

Although discussions of ekphrasis have tended to rely on a concept of verbal representation as transparent window on the word–image dynamic, the circumstances of its production (as museum catalogues or in collaborations that result in limited-edition books, for example) often foreground the semantic value of the material nature of texts (paper, type face, shape, size, color, layout, decorations, illustrations, arrangements of contents, methods and means of distribution).[69] Ekphrastic poems are often resocialized in especially radical ways as they go from, say, a limited edition distributed to friends, to a volume of poems, to wall copy in a museum exhibition, as Yeats's "The Municipal Gallery Re-visited" did. Always there is the issue of whether the poem appears with its images. Chapters 5 (on Ted Hughes's and Leonard Baskin's *Cave Birds*) and 6 (on Rita Dove's *Museum*) focus specifically on the textual history, process of production, and organizational and material characteristics of ekphrasis, but throughout I've tried to keep an eye on the textual condition as inseparable from the social network in which ekphrasis works.

The set of practices and tropes with which modern poets negotiate the ekphrastic situation derives primarily from the nineteenth century when ekphrasis began to find a significant place in Anglo-American poetry with Shelley, Wordsworth, Byron, Browning and, especially, Keats and Rossetti. It grew from roots deep in the seismic cultural changes of the nineteenth century, particularly the growing institutionalization and democratization of visual culture represented by the invention of the public art museum, and the mass production of images. Before turning to specific examples of ekphrasis in context in the following chapters, I'd like here to sketch broadly a poetics and genealogy of modern ekphrasis by looking at some of the major means by which modern poets conduct the relation of words and images, and some of the ways those means are used to extend, develop and rework twentieth-century approaches to images in ekphrasis. I have hung this discussion on six tropes or practices.

Eternal stillness. When Yeats, looking at a Hellenistic bas-relief reproduced in Elie Faure's *History of Art* (1921), opened "Leda and the Swan" (1925) with "A sudden blow: the great wings beating still," he tapped the most common trope of ekphrasis, the stillness of the work of art.[70] Carrying its interrelated double senses as adjective and adverb ("not moving" and "enduring"), this "still" is born of the idea introduced by the early nineteenth century's nascent museum age that works of art might be preserved for posterity. Keats's "Ode on a Grecian Urn" (1819), that benchmark of ekphrasis for modern poets and critics alike, promoted what Heffernan calls the "ideology of transcendence" by posing mortal "breathing human passion" that "leaves a heart high-sorrowful and cloy'd" against the perfect potential of the urn's frozen figures, the love "For ever warm and still to be enjoy'd."[71] Death and eternity are the double edges of the promise the work of art holds out to the suffering, desiring Keats: to be stilled into art in exchange for still being. For twentieth-century poets, Keats's desire for the still timelessness of the work of art intensifies in the face of an accelerated, mechanized world in which all seems ephemeral and in motion. Stillness is often associated with calm in the midst of modern psychological and political chaos: "Only the little/ town ... still/ stands calm" observes Snodgrass of Van Gogh's *The Starry Night*.[72] To hold something still, and external to the self, is the impulse of imagism. "Is" abounds in ekphrasis.

Keats's deep ambivalence about the price paid for the work of art's timelessness ("never, never canst thou kiss")[73] registers less in modern ekphrasis than skepticism, born of modernism's keen awareness of the materiality of the work of art, that art could ever be timeless. The Elgin marbles were, after all, fragments, evidence that "all things fall." Stillness for the moderns is poised on the edge of destruction whose imminence shows, for example, in the "accidental crack or dent" in Yeats's lapis lazuli and the "faces" that "crack" in Lowell's Rembrandts.[74] Art may stay destruction – "desolation, stalled in paint, spares the little country," writes Sylvia Plath of "the lower right hand corner" of Brueghel's *The Triumph of Death*[75] – but as "stalled" suggests, only temporarily. There is little sense in modern ekphrasis of the sublimity of ruins that exists in Keats's "On Seeing the Elgin Marbles" or Shelley's "Ozymandias."

That the work of art may prove not still is one of the excitements of ekphrasis: what if that girl in the Dutch courtyard were to turn? When combined, as it often is, with the female gendering of the work of art in ekphrasis, the moving image can exert her power over the typically male viewer, sometimes rising up and speaking. In Shelley's unfinished "On the Medusa of Leonardo da Vinci, in the Florentine Gallery" (1819) – the other Romantic ekphrasis most often invoked in discussions of the genre – the Gorgon's severed head stills the viewer: she "turns the gazer's spirit into stone."[76] In the hands of twentieth-century feminist poets (male and female), images of/as still silent women may speak and move to reclaim some of their own, as in Lisel Mueller's "A Nude by Edward Hopper" and Adrienne Rich's "Mourning Picture." Gender dynamics of ekphrasis are thus reversed as the genre is put to explicitly social use. The trope is also troubled by a growing consciousness of what the colonizing gaze has done to "primitive" life. Rita Dove's fossilized "Fish in the Stone," emblem of the anthropological approach to "others," "would like to fall/ back into the sea": "He is weary/ of analysis, the small/ predictable truths./ He is weary of waiting/ in the open,/ his profile stamped/ by a white light."[77]

Into history. The transcendence of the work of art is also modified in modern ekphrasis by a greater sense of the work of art as historical. For many moderns it's not so much that painting and sculpture take the poet out of history, but that they take the poet into history. The work of art makes the past present and immediate. "This past/ Is now here: the painter's/ Reflected face, in which we linger," John Ashbery says, looking at Parmigianino's *Self Portrait in a Convex Mirror.*[78] The presence of the work of art, made in the past and perhaps depicting the past, opens a space in which present and past co-exist, become, indeed, blended as Ashbery's deictic "this past" suggests. The work of art can function as a portal and as a place of contact. Although he calls the urn "Attic shape," Keats hardly registers the kind of historical consciousness we find in much modern ekphrasis.[79] For the moderns, ekphrasis offered a means of getting into the brief lyric what Pound called the "poem including history."[80] We have tended to think of such poems as long (*The Cantos, The Waste Land, Paterson,* for example). Ekphrasis might satisfy the age's desire to make the past present by including history in the lyric as well.

As a poem on an artifact, ekphrasis is especially suited to probing the modern idea of history as constructed. In Robert Lowell's sonnet "Sir Thomas More," for example, the opening words, "Holbein's More," make plain that Lowell understands the 1527 portrait of More in the Frick Collection in New York to be, above all, the creation of the artist.[81] As he says a couple of pages later in "Charles V by Titian," "the true Charles, done by Titian, never lived."[82] The history that modern ekphrasis opens up is history as made by the artist and re-made by the viewer/poet.

In the museum. One of the distinguishing features of twentieth-century ekphrasis is that it is fully born of the museum age. Like many modern ekphrases, Wilbur's "A Dutch Courtyard" displays a high degree of awareness, even anxiety, about the place of viewing, and ambivalence about the very foundations of public museums. The invocation of Andrew Mellon at the end suddenly opens a window on the poem's situation: the poet is standing in the National Gallery in Washington and has been taken up, not by the transcendence of the work of art, but by its material provenance, probably inscribed then, as it is now, on the wall plaque: "Andrew W. Mellon Collection." In modern ekphrases, the museum is both the temple of art, a place of transcendent aesthetic experience (encouraged by the architecture of many museums, derived as it is from temples), and an institution founded on the material ambitions of an industrial elite. Robert Hayden found in Monet's waterlilies "illusive flesh of light/ that was not, was, forever is" at the same time that Lawrence Ferlinghetti wryly observed: "Monet never knew/ he was painting his 'Lilies' for/ a lady from the Chicago Art Institute/ who went to France and filmed/ today's lilies/ by the 'Bridge at Giverny'/ a leaf afloat among them."[83]

As James Heffernan argues, the museum practice of displaying works isolated for contemplation with plenty of space around them helped generate the individuated ekphrastic poem as we know it, separated from the narrative context in which it had been embedded in epic.[84] Museums, however, also gave rise to the idea of the series, of works of art arranged in a meaningful sequence. Ekphrasis thus is part of the story of the modern poetic sequence and of the modern poetic volume.[85] Such very different collections as William Carlos Williams's *Pictures from Brueghel and Other Poems* (1962), Robert Lowell's *History* (1973), Lawrence Ferlinghetti's *When I Look at Pictures* (1990), and Rita Dove's *Museum* (1983) arrange series of ekphrases (some mixed with other kinds of poems) in a museum display.[86] *History*, for example, evokes the historical museum display, with people and events named, set in chronological order and framed in white space around the picture-shaped sonnets, like so many paintings in a gallery.

Narrative. One of the most powerful impulses in ekphrasis has been to deliver the story out of the single moment so often depicted in western painting or sculpture. The impulse to tell what's happening persists in twentieth-century ekphrasis. Narrative has been seen as language's way of distinguishing itself from the image, of doing what the image can't. In twentieth-century ekphrasis, the fact that museum-going is the way we now most often see art in the flesh shapes the narrative impulse of ekphrasis. While Rossetti's sonnets are self-consciously structured by a systematic tour of the image to unpack the iconographic and narrative content of its moment, Auden's "Musée des Beaux Arts," Yeats's "The Municipal Gallery Re-visited" and Irving Feldman's sequence "All of Us

Here," for example, narrate the experience of encountering images in a museum.

The tutelary function. The tutelary function When the urn speaks in high philosophical and aphoristic terms, Keats taps the common tutelary function of ekphrasis present in the tradition since Philostratus tutored his young charge by showing him the family art collection. Whether the urn speaks the whole sentence ("Beauty is truth, truth beauty, – that is all/ Ye know on earth, and all ye need to know") or only the opening chiasmus,[87] the image has a lesson that ekphrasis delivers. One might trace a line from Philostratus, to what Wordsworth learned from Beaumont's painting of Peele Castle about withstanding the storms of personal misfortune, to Auden finding in the Old Masters lessons in how to think about human indifference to suffering.[88] Spurred by the increasing emphasis art museums placed on their educational missions (the idea that looking at pictures serves to educate a people), poets from Yeats, Marianne Moore and Auden to Adrienne Rich and Rita Dove take up the tutelary function of ekphrasis with firmness: "How this tart fable instructs/ And mocks!" exclaims Plath looking at Klee's etching *Jungfrau*.[89] Lowell calls "Holbein's More" "my patron saint."[90]

As the many protests to Auden's didactic voice in "Musée" suggest, however, for the moderns the truth art speaks is ringed round with a sense of the limits of the artist's vision and of the truth-telling potential of art. Twentieth-century poets are keenly aware that the work of art is made according to the peculiar vision of the maker. So in twentieth-century ekphrasis there is a heightened emphasis on the provisional nature of the truth pictures convey, just as there is about the history it tells: "According to Brueghel," "As Parmigianino did it" open two of the best-known twentieth-century ekphrases.[91] There is a wariness, too, of the viewer's ability to see "right," and of the illusion-making nature of art that further complicates the difference between "seem" and "is": of the ships in "Large Bad Picture," Bishop comments, "It would be hard to say what brought them there";[92] "In Goya's greatest scenes we seem to see," says Ferlinghetti.[93] The didactic strain of ekphrasis thus sits side by side with the strong anti-didactic strain bred in suspicion of Victorian moralizing, fed by surrealism, and bolstered by postmodern skepticism of universalizing of any sort.

Talking pictures. When the urn speaks out at the end of the "Ode," Keats takes advantage of the ekphrastic convention of prosopopoeia, the envoicing of the silent image, the most radical means ekphrasis has at its disposal to animate the still, silent image into speech. Prosopopoeia makes poetry what Simonides of Ceos said it should be in his classic statement of the sister arts tradition: "painting is mute poetry and poetry a speaking picture."[94] Twentieth-century poets, especially in the second half of the century, often speak through/as a figure in painting or sculpture: "I have closed my brief-case, dropped my/ pick," says the laborer taking a tea-break in Thom Gunn's poem on a photograph by Ander Gunn;[95] "I am Effie," declares the girl in Adrienne Rich's poem on Edwin Romanzo Elmer's *Mourning Picture*.[96] One might understand prosopopoeia as part of the history Carol Christ traces of Victorian and modern efforts to get out of the confines of Romantic lyric subjectivity by objectifying personality in a speaking voice not the poet's own.[97] Twentieth-century prosopopoeia in ekphrasis participates in the development of the dramatic monologues of Browning and Tennyson into the masks and personae of Yeats, Pound and Eliot and the postmodern concept of the poetic self as multiple and staged. In ekphrastic prosopopoeia, the speaking voice is not only objectified, but also embodied (in the image), making a double anchor in the world outside the poet. But prosopopoeia can also be understood as the collapse of subject and object, the inhabiting of another body and voice by the poet, equally an objectification and an exercise of empathy. As a closing of the gap between poet and image, prosopopoeia can be seen variously as the most hegemonic of moves (language taking over the image, inhabiting it) or as the most altruistic (language liberating the frozen image to tell its story). Whether and how one can speak for others gets to the center of the ethical questions ekphrasis raises.

The chapters that follow offer an interconnected set of culturally situated readings of ekphrasis that argue for ekphrasis as dynamic, as driven by its negotiation with others of various kinds, and as socially engaged and contingent. Working up out of a few specific examples, with reference to many more, they demonstrate how the relations between poet, painting and audience that constitute the ekphrastic poem open the lyric into a social realm in which the poem participates. Interacting with and building upon one another, the chapters, in the aggregate, map out a complex of issues and questions that arise from ekphrasis so considered. Although I begin with Yeats and end with Dove, the chapters are not arranged to make a chronological argument. Rather, they highlight major sites of ekphrastic encounter and major categories of "otherness" with which twentieth-century ekphrasis negotiates in representing the work of art: death and the dead (history), culture and nationality, gender, and race. These categories are more often than not intertwined with each other. Chapters that show how the imagined exchanges of ekphrasis' representational triangle open the lyric into a social world frame those that show those exchanges radically literalized in ekphrastic conversation and collaboration (Chapters 4 and 5). All show ekphrasis actively engaged in social, political and cultural debates. The book begins and ends in the two major sites of ekphrasis: the museum where ekphrasis originates (Chapters 1 and 2) and the poetic volume where it most often meets its audience (Chapters 5 and 6).

Chapters 1 and 2 establish the foundation of modern ekphrasis in the museum and in the experience of museum-going. Chapter 1, "Private lives in public places: Yeats and Durcan in Dublin's galleries," examines the function – and the fruitfulness – of the museum as setting in twentieth-century ekphrasis, taking as examples two ekphrastic encounters with Dublin museums, some sixty years apart: Yeats's "The Municipal Gallery Re-visited" (1939) and Paul Durcan's collection *Crazy About Women* (1991). Drawing on work by museum critics Carol Duncan and Philip Fisher, it shows Yeats and Durcan literally writing the scripts that define the national culture the public art museum stages, and thereby participating in the creation of a culture of images. Ekphrases in the museum have drawn on the museum's ambiguous, liminal space in which the living and the dead, the sacred and the secular, and the public and the private, intermingle. In writing ekphrases that ply the especially troubled intersection of public and private in the museum (private collections opened to the public, a public space for private meditation, publicly displayed works of art drawn into the personal lives of viewers), Yeats and Durcan explore one of the central problems of the lyric itself.

Chapter 2, "Bystanding in Auden's 'Musée', " continues in the museum, considering its role in Auden's great meditation on the ethics of looking in an age of violence. Turning questions most familiarly posed about photography onto the issue of looking in the museum, this chapter considers how the ekphrastic dynamic provided twentieth-century poets a way of exploring the ethical implications of being bystanders, that "modern fate" as M. L. Rosenthal called it.[98] Chapter 3, "Women looking: The feminist ekphrasis of Marianne Moore and Adrienne Rich," takes up the gendering of ekphrasis by asking what happens when women write it. Beginning to sketch out a place for women in the tradition of ekphrasis, it explores the differing ways Moore and Rich put ekphrasis to feminist use, rewriting the social and epistemological dynamics implied in the notion of an active, masculinized word and a passive, feminized image. With irony and indirection, Moore instructs men and women alike to establish relationships to images and to others of all kinds on less possessive grounds, and she works to enact the kind of viewing she has in mind in her poems. Rich vests her hope in women, turning the old gender dynamics on their heads without essentially altering them, asking *women* to use the power of looking and saying to expose patriarchal structures, and to use the knowledge so gained to remake their lives. In such ways, ekphrasis commented on and participated in the greatest shift in social relations in modern western history.

Chapters 4 and 5 seek to further open up our idea of the ekphrastic situation by showing how the relations between poet and audience and between poet and artist are often born of conversations, some created and performed in the structure of the poem, some actual exchanges with other commentators or with the artist. As I've indicated, ekphrasis is more dynamic, polyvocal and multiply responsive than the poet–work-of-art–audience triangle might suggest. Chapter 4, "Ekphrasis in conversation: Anne Sexton and W. D. Snodgrass on Van Gogh," explores Sexton's and Snodgrass's differing responses to Van Gogh's *The Starry Night* as part of the network of debate about the popular concatenation of artistic genius and suicide that attended the rise of Van Gogh's reputation and of confessional poetry. Chapter 5, "Ekphrasis in collaboration: Ted Hughes's and Leonard Baskin's *Cave Birds: An Alchemical Cave Drama*," explores the exchange between artist and poet in collaboration, an often hidden source of ekphrasis. In *Cave Birds* (1978), poet responded to artist who responded to poet who responded to artist, blending ekphrasis and illustration, calling those critical categories into question. The volume, I suggest, dramatizes its critique of western dichotomizing, and its proposed redress, in the play of word and image on the page.

Chapter 6, "Ekphrasis in the book: Rita Dove's African American museum" returns to the museum to read ekphrasis in its context in the poetic volume, in this instance Rita Dove's *Museum* (1983). In joining a tradition of the volume-as-museum that stretches back to the Greeks, Dove provocatively enters the contemporary debates about African American heritage shaping the collecting and display practices of the newly founded African American museums. Continuing to explore the issues raised in Chapter 3 on feminist ekphrasis, this chapter also opens the issue of race in ekphrasis, specifically the uses to which African American writers put the social dynamics of ekphrasis. It concludes by reading "Agosta the Winged Man and Rasha the Black Dove," on a painting by the German modernist Christian Schad, as a test of the implications of Dove's position as the creator of this transnational, transcultural volume-as-museum.

Along with canonical figures, I have chosen to discuss some poets less well known (Durcan), as well as those less often discussed than their contemporaries (Snodgrass and Sexton among the confessional poets), as one way of suggesting the deep field out of which the most interesting and best ekphrastic poems emerge. Often, ekphrasis seems to pose the challenge, exert the discipline of observation, offer the rhetorical situation that makes a good poet write a very fine poem, as it did for Sexton and Snodgrass. Part of my aim has been to broaden the emerging canon of twentieth-century ekphrasis, especially to modernists beyond Williams (Yeats and Moore) and to women poets (Moore, Rich, Sexton, Dove). I've tried to balance a need for the familiar and more canonical examples (Auden) with a need for an expanded roster of examples, just as I've tried to balance close readings of selected examples with a wide range of reference to other poems to suggest how the arguments I make might be extended. That every reader will have a list of writers they would like to have seen treated in detail I take as indicative of the prevalence and vitality of ekphrasis.

A plethora of possibilities also pertains to the aspects of ekphrasis on which I've focused. One might well write a book on photographic ekphrasis (in American poetry alone there is wealth enough, though I'd like to see Heaney's bog poems and Ted Hughes's poems on Fay Godwin's and Peter Keen's landscape photographs in there). Or on ekphrases of film (Adrienne Rich's on Leni Riefenstahl's *Olympiad* in Part 4 of "Waking in the Dark," or Barbara Guest's *Confetti Trees*, for example), which complicate in interesting ways the ekphrastic trope of stillness. Ekphrases of public monuments (Emma Lazarus's "The New Colossus" on the Statue of Liberty, Lowell's "For the Union Dead," Brooks's "Chicago Picasso" and "The Wall," Komunyakaa's "Facing It" on the Vietnam Memorial) raise issues I haven't addressed here, though I discuss Brooks's poems in Chapter 6 in a different context. Michael North's work on public sculpture and Kenneth Gross's on moving statues suggest how rich a field this is. Ekphrasis and mourning, a topic that threads continuously through the present study, deserves its own extended treatment.[99]

This book is meant to contribute to the growing body of evidence for a vital and energizing relation between word and image in twentieth-century literature. As we begin to reckon with the past century as a whole, a sustained and various engagement with the visual arts is coming to look like one of the distinguishing characteristics of its literature. It has helped define a vanguard, and it has enlivened, quickened, and expanded the possibilities of the main stream of poetry. We think of the avant-garde poets as border-crossers, and of their engagement with the visual and other arts as part of a self-consciously avant-garde practice. As David Lehman observes, the would-be avant-garde artist "could transmute his adversarial impulses into a struggle with artistic tradition or with the formal limitations of his medium."[100] Much important work has been written about avant-garde crossings of media, especially among the New York School, and their importance to broadening the horizons of poetry in the twentieth century. Marjorie Perloff's work is key in this regard. While the poets discussed in this book have all charted new directions, none, except perhaps Moore, could be considered part of an avant-garde. Yet all have been deeply involved with the visual arts. I would like this book to make visible their interactions with the visual arts, to stand with those of their avant-garde contemporaries.

I see the poetry discussed here as part of a much larger field of talk about images ranging from casual conversation about a film, or an image in an ad, or a photograph, to the most considered analysis of a work of art. We are always talking about pictures, it seems. If what Michael Baxandall has said is true – that "we explain pictures only in so far as we have considered them under some verbal description or specification"[101] – then ekphrasis, broadly considered, may be the paradigmatic act in a culture of images. I hope this book makes clear the richness and interest of poets' words about images, not least so that our own viewing might be enlivened by their talk.

1 | Private lives in public places: Yeats and Durcan in Dublin's galleries

Into warm regions of Romance I stared:
Sat down; produced my note-book, and prepared
To fabricate iambics: something rich,
Serene, perpetual; tuned to concert-pitch:
Carthage without the climax; autumn-gold;
Red sunrise on a crag-set castle ... Bold
With pursuance of the encharioted Sublime,
I set my brains to work till closing-time.

> (Siegfried Sassoon, "In the Turner Rooms (At the Tate Gallery)," 1926)[1]

I retreated to the cool of the Prado.
Goya's "Shootings of the Third of May"
Covered a wall – the thrown-up arms
And spasm of the rebel, the helmeted
And knapsacked military, the efficient
Rake of the fusillade. In the next room
His nightmares, grafted to the palace wall –
Dark cyclones, hosting, breaking; Saturn
Jewelled in the blood of his own children,
Gigantic Chaos turning his brute hips
Over the world. Also, that holmgang
Where two berserks club each other to death
For honour's sake, greaved in a bog, and sinking.

He painted with his fists and elbows, flourished
The stained cape of his heart as history charged.

> (Seamus Heaney, "Summer 1969," 1975)[2]

I remember a city
like this –
the static coral
of reflected brick
in its river.

> I envy these
> pinpointed citizens
> their complacency,
> their lack of any need
> to come and see
>
> a beloved republic
> raised and
> saved and
> scalded into
> something measurable.
>
> (Eavan Boland, "Canaletto
> in the National Gallery of
> Ireland," 1986)[3]

When the private galleries of Europe were opened in the eighteenth century and the idea of the public art museum was born, the poets were there visiting and arguing the merits of this new, powerful institution.[4] The grounds of the debates that animate current museum studies were set at that early moment in what poet John Hollander describes as "the complex social and institutional distinctions between a palace of art and the city around it."[5] For Goethe, writing at the opening of the Dresden Gallery in 1768, "the freshly-gilded frames, the well-waxed parquetry, the profound silence that reigned" distinguished the museum as a space cleared and ordered for contemplation.[6] William Hazlitt similarly greeted the founding of the National Gallery, London in 1824 as a place set aside from, and above, an increasingly frantic and hostile industrial city: "What signify the hubbub, the shifting scenery, the fantoccini figures, the folly, the idle fashions without, when compared with the solitude, the silence, the speaking looks, the unfading forms within?"[7] But some thirty years later, Goethe found himself troubled by the destruction that underwrote the drive to collect and display, particularly Napoleon's plundering of conquered countries for cultural booty to be reinstalled in the first national art museum, the Louvre.[8] Down through the twentieth century, the hegemonic and colonizing motives of much collecting for the museum, as well as the class status associated with it, have continued to trouble commentators, including Marianne Moore, as we'll see. In addition, for the moderns, the backward-looking focus of the museum, its mandate to preserve, began to feel like a drag on the forward propulsion of modernity so visible in the cities around the museums. "You can be a museum or you can be modern," Stein famously quipped.[9] Nevertheless, poets throughout the nineteenth and twentieth centuries continued to join the swelling ranks of a popular audience, delighted, disturbed, and above all compelled by the curious and powerful experience of museum-going. Paul Valéry captured the mix of feelings and attitudes when he wrote in his seminal 1923 essay, "The problem of museums," that they savor "of temple and drawing room, of cemetery and school." "Did I come," he asked, "for instruction, for my own beguilement, or simply as a duty and out of convention? Or is it perhaps some exercise peculiar to itself, this stroll I am taking, weirdly beset with beauties, distracted at every moment by masterpieces to the right or left compelling me to walk like a drunk man between counters?"[10]

When Sassoon drew his ironic self-portrait as ekphrastic poet, he pointed to the origin of the modern ekphrastic poem in the controversial and charged space of the public art museum, and in the poets' self-conscious and ambivalent attitudes toward it. As museums became the place people went to see art, museum-going became the cultural experience on which ekphrasis founded itself. The rise of ekphrasis as a prevalent poetic genre coincides with the rise of the public art museum.

Implicitly and explicitly, poets folded the experience of the museum into their poems: "Musée des Beaux Arts," "Christmas Night in the Elgin Marble Rooms," "The Municipal Gallery Re-visited," "Canaletto in the National Gallery of Ireland." As Sassoon's poem suggests and such examples as Wilbur's "A Dutch Courtyard" and Ashbery's "Self-Portrait in a Convex Mirror" confirm, the awareness of museum space that passed from Keats through such popular nineteenth-century ekphrases as Michael Field's series *Sight and Song* (1892), with its grand tour organization, each poem naming work and gallery, became in modern ekphrasis an acute self-consciousness about the site of viewing. The deictic gesture of ekphrasis acquired a spatial habitation in the museum: "This canvas yells the fury of the sea./ Across a quiet room;"[11] "Here at right of the entrance this bronze head."[12] Museum guards enter ekphrasis as those who live with art in daily life in a way the rest of us no longer do: "Here dozes one against the wall,/ Disposed upon a funeral chair."[13] Ekphrastic speakers stand as ordinary museum-goers, and look at pictures.

Ekphrasis in the museum is part of the story of the museum's influence on twentieth-century poetry as a whole, beginning to be told in recent work by Catherine Paul and Susan Rosenbaum.[14] The New York poets' involvement with the institutional art world is well-known. Frank O'Hara occupied various positions, including associate curator, at the Museum of Modern Art (1952–1966) where he organized important exhibitions. O'Hara, James Schuyler and John Ashbery were on the editorial staff of *Art*

News, in whose pages they and other poets tirelessly reviewed shows and explained the new American painting, which was, from the beginning, conceived for the space of the modern art museum.[15] Ashbery was also senior art critic for *Newsweek* from 1980 to 1985. But the New York School poets are not alone. Earlier in the century, William Butler Yeats led the battle to found Dublin's Municipal Gallery and served on the Board of Governors of the National Gallery of Ireland. Marianne Moore visited exhibitions, and wrote essays on artists, reviews of museum and gallery exhibitions, and entries for exhibition catalogues, setting the terms by which works of art in museums were viewed. Lawrence Ferlinghetti (who did his M.A. thesis at Columbia on Ruskin's criticism of Turner) covered the growing San Francisco art scene for *Art Digest*. In the 1980s museums began commissioning poets to curate exhibits and write the catalogue copy – as Seamus Heaney did in 1982 for the Ulster Museum (*A Personal Selection*).[16]

Museum space

When Goethe and Hazlitt described the museum as a secular-sacred refuge, away from "the hubbub, the shifting scenery, the fantoccini figures, the folly, the idle fashions," they were beginning to articulate what critic Carol Duncan calls the "liminal" nature of the art museum. Duncan borrows the term from anthropologist Victor Turner to mean a space "betwixt-and-between the normal, day-to-day cultural and social states and processes of getting and spending."[17] The art museum is liminal in the sense that it "enable[s] individuals to ... move beyond the psychic constraints of mundane existence, step out of time, and attain new, larger perspectives."[18] The comments by Goethe and Hazlitt show that such stepping out of time is often experienced and explained as religious or spiritual. Germain Bazin, curator of the Louvre (1951–1965), described the art museum as a "temple where Time seems suspended."[19] "This hallowed ground," Yeats called it. Architecturally, museums descend from temples as well as palaces. They contain objects elevated, often literally, for contemplation. In removing the work of art from its daily life and holding it up for special value, the art museum has sacralized the objects in its collection. Modernism, Brian O'Doherty argues, took the art museum as temple to its conclusion, as demonstrated by galleries for modern art:

A gallery is constructed along laws as rigorous as those for building a medieval church. The outside world must not come in, so windows are usually sealed off. Walls are painted white. The ceiling becomes the source of light. The wooden floor is polished so that you click along clinically, or carpeted so that you pad soundlessly, resting the feet while the eyes have at the wall ... In this context a standing ashtray becomes almost a sacred object ... Art exists in a kind of eternity of display, and though there is lots of "period" (late modern), there is no time. This eternity gives the gallery a limbolike status ...[20]

The transcendentalizing impulse of ekphrasis that the moderns inherited from the romantics was ratified and promoted by the modern museum, a sacred space for a secular age.

Yet there is among modern poets profound discomfort with this idea of a world of art set aside and venerated. When Williams observed in "History" (1917), "The steps to the Museum are high./ Worshippers pass in and out,"[21] he pointed to the social paradoxes of the museum that Pierre Bourdieu's 1969 study confirmed. Although born of democratic fervor and founded on the principle that a nation's cultural heritage belongs to all (the Louvre opened in 1793 in the midst of the French Revolution), it's the well-educated and better-off who mostly visit galleries.[22] Increasingly large numbers of people attend museums, but do they come from a broad enough social spectrum to be called "popular"? The height of the museum steps in modern ekphrasis becomes a focus for anxiety about the relation of art to its audience, and about its simultaneous institutionalization and marginalization. "Monet never knew/ he was painting his 'Lilies' for/ a lady from the Chicago Art Institute," as Ferlinghetti said.[23] Institutionalization meant visibility and the power of resources to advertise and so bring the work to the attention of a public. But it also meant a certain ghettoizing. If being collected by a museum meant the arrival of an artist or the validation of a style, it could also seem like entombment. As Stein knew, the museum derives from the mausoleum too.

As a threshold between worlds, the museum is a place of both/and: it is both secular *and* sacred, drawing room *and* temple. When worshippers pass into the museum, they bring the city with them. Intermingled with moments of quiet, sometimes exalted, contemplation, the business of daily life carries on inside, as it must – talking with friends, eating, buying souvenirs in the cafes, restaurants and gift shops the modern museum provides. Objects, originating in the world beyond the walls, sit uneasily in the museum. Works that once had a place in ordinary daily life as religious icons and pictures of people and places, now live apart in a land of art where they belong to narratives of artistic development, lines of influence or national schools. André Malraux commented that museums "have tended to estrange the works they bring together from their original functions and to transform even portraits into 'pictures' ": "What do we care who the *Man with the Helmet* or the *Man with the Glove* may have been in real life? For us, their names are Rembrandt and Titian."[24] And yet those objects are not entirely resocialized; they retain vestiges of their earlier lives. We *do*, I think, wonder who the man with the helmet might have been.

In the museum, cultures mix in provocative relation as works of different countries hang in neighboring rooms, and as visitors from various countries walk the galleries, looking through the lenses of their own cultures. Heaney, above, sees the Goyas in the Prado in terms distinctly Irish: "Also, that holmgang," he says pointing, "Where two berserks club each other to death/ For honour's sake, greaved in a bog, and sinking." In the museum, the living confront the dead, the present, the past. Especially important for the poets treated in this chapter, the museum is both a private and, in several senses, a public space. In a public building often given, like its contents, to "the public" by a private citizen, viewers are invited to meditate intensely and quietly, in the strained company of others. Words spoken to a companion are heard by those nearby, both private and public. It is this uneasy mixedness of experience, this in-betweenness, that makes the stroll through the modern art museum the "peculiar exercise" Valéry described.

Duncan argues that museums must be seen "neither as neutral sheltering spaces for objects nor primarily as products of architectural design ... [but as] a dramatic field."[25] As she and other museum critics have suggested, that field is defined by a script that directs and gives meaning to the experience of museum-going. The script includes the art, the architecture, and the very powerful words about the images and objects displayed: brochures on the museum and its collections; Acoustiguides; gallery talks; wall plaques, including titles, dates, artist, and so on; all informed by a curatorial staff of professional art historians. While I think the ritual played out on the dramatic field is more fluid, more open to accident, more susceptible to improvisation and individual response, and more actively creative than Duncan's ideological reading sees it, the general concept of the museum as a scripted space is provocative for thinking about ekphrasis. The museum may be distinguished from the city around it by its quiet, but it is filled with words that guide the experience of looking. The central drama of the ekphrastic situation – the writer engaging the work of art and representing it to an audience – is played over and over again in the museum. As Heffernan demonstrates in *Museum of Words*, the words with which museums frame experience inform modern ekphrasis. Titles, curatorial wall texts and other art-historical commentary enter the ekphrastic poem, shaping both its vision and its manner of speaking. Poets from Browning onwards have worked the persona of the gallery-guide. Even Williams' *Pictures from Brueghel* (1962), which has seemed to critics so deliberately uninterpretive, so much an attempt to say simply what the eye sees, draws, as Heffernan shows, on art-historical text.[26]

This chapter considers how the museum functions in ekphrastic poems and how those poems themselves become texts that guide the interpretation of works of art in the museum, and thereby participate directly in a burgeoning visual culture. Though I will have something to say about art-historical texts that inform ekphrasis, I am more concerned here with the experience of museum space and with ekphrasis as a way of negotiating the steps of the museum. Focusing on W. B. Yeats's "The Municipal Gallery Re-visited" (1937) and Paul Durcan's collection of ekphrases, *Crazy About Women* (1991), Chapter 1 considers two Irish poets, bracketing the century; both writing out of museums in Dublin; both working through the relations between the works in the gallery, themselves, and the public to which art and poetry speak. For the Irish Republic, liberated from British rule in1922, framing a cultural heritage through the art museum was an urgent matter of national identity. Yeats's and Durcan's poems speak out of art museums whose roles as preservers of the community's values were still being written, and by these poems.

I begin this book in the museum not only because it is where most modern ekphrasis begins, but because it seemed right to start an examination of how the dynamic structure of ekphrasis opens the subjective lyric into a social field with a discussion of the museum as a private–public space that situates physically the opening of private collections and the artistic visions they represent into a public realm. The mixing of private and public that characterizes the museum and the museum experience has particularly resonated through modern ekphrasis. Irving Feldman's ekphrastic sequence *All of Us Here* (1986), for example, is framed in recorded snippets of conversation – inconsequential, banal, profound, poignant – overheard in a gallery ("They say this show got some terrific reviews").[27] In the central poems, a series of meditations on George Segal's sculptures, the poet speaks in a "we" that hovers between a generalized lyric "I" speaking privately and a corporate identity speaking publicly: "So we come and stand here and look at them/ to make more answering life to answer us."[28] Part of the interest of museum space to modern poets has been that it itself dramatizes the complex interrelation of private and public that has been a preoccupation of the modern lyric. For the ekphrastic poet, the museum offers a place where subjective lyric vision can be grounded in the physical artifact and offered to a public. Increasingly, in the twentieth century, it was also a space where public events could be approached through the middle ground of the external artifact, and where the uttered response could be at once both private and public, as comments in a museum are.

Museum space is not unlike the space of the lyric itself, especially the lyric in a time of pressing public events that demand that the poet say something. This is perhaps one reason that the museum has such a striking presence in twentieth-century Irish poetry, as Boland and Heaney, above, and the two poets I take up in this chapter, Yeats and Durcan, suggest. If the museum offers refuge from the world outside, it does so in modern poetry only to return the poet to the world again. In the "cool" of the museum both Heaney and Boland confront the scalding violence of the world beyond its walls. The worshippers in Williams' "History" pass in, and out. In this sense the museum retains the etymological associations of its educational mission: to lead out.

Writing Irish history: The private–public space of Yeats's Municipal Gallery

The son, brother and father of painters, with Pater, Rossetti and Morris his acknowledged forefathers, Yeats stands at the head of the twentieth century's unprecedented ekphrastic production.[29] He used the genre to write some of the century's most important poems: "Leda and the Swan," "Sailing to Byzantium," "Lapis Lazuli," "Municipal Gallery Re-visited", as well as "Michael Robartes and the Dancer," "A Bronze Head," "On a Picture of a Black Centaur by Edmund Dulac," "Three Monuments," and Section III of "News for the Delphic Oracle." "Under Ben Bulben" and others contain what we might call ekphrastic gestures toward particular works of art. Yeats was attracted to ekphrasis early on as part of his campaign against "abstraction." The visual arts offered corrective to his youthful tendency toward abstraction. He was "content," he later recalled, only when "my abstractions had composed themselves into picture and dramatization."[30] His personal poetic program reflected his program for modern poetry in general. "A song should be," he advised in an early unpublished poem, "A painted and be-pictured argosy."[31] If Pater set one agenda for modern poetry to aspire to the condition of music, Pound expressed a counter-impulse for embodiment, for presence, for the thingness he and others thought the image possessed. Poetry was to be founded on the image – "that which presents an intellectual and emotional complex in an instant of time." The Imagist manifesto called for "direct treatment of the 'thing.'"[32] "No ideas/ but in things," urged William Carlos Williams.[33] "It could be argued," says the poet J. D. McClatchy, "that modern poetry was invented by the painters."[34] Yeats's desire for the concreteness of picture and dramatization is an early sign of the blatant envy expressed in the passage from O'Hara at the head of the "Introduction" to this book: "You do what I can only name."

Yeats's use of ekphrasis late in his career to write some of his great poems taps two other preoccupations of modern ekphrasis: the genre's ability to open into history, and its promise of eternal stillness. As for his acknowledged predecessor Keats, for the aging Yeats the work of art provided counter to the all-too-changing flesh, and offered a record of endurance to a civilization intent on destruction: "Consume my heart away; sick with desire/ And fastened to a dying animal/ It knows not what it is; and gather me/ Into the artifice of eternity," he pleaded to the static mosaic sages in "Sailing to Byzantium" (1927), a compendium of ekphrastic motives.[35] The tutelary function of ekphrasis runs strong here. The work of art teaches the poet to sing his way into eternity: "O sages standing in God's holy fire/ As in the gold mosaic of a wall,/ Come from the holy fire, perne in a gyre,/ And be the singing-masters of my soul."[36] In "Leda and the Swan," on a Hellenistic bas-relief in the British Museum, stillness yokes death and continuing life – "A sudden blow: the great wings beating still"[37] – suggesting that both can be had simultaneously. If the stillness of the work of art marks it as "out of nature," its presence gives access once again to this drama of the past. Creation of the past via images is the main work of "The Municipal Gallery Re-visited."

Three of Yeats's ekphrastic poems are set in galleries: "On a Picture of Mr. Nettleship's Picture at the Royal Hibernian Academy" (1886), "A Bronze Head" (1939) on a bust of Maud Gonne in the Municipal Gallery, and "The Municipal Gallery Re-visited" (1937); a fourth, "Michael Robartes and the Dancer" (1920), whose setting is unspecified (the couple could be in a gallery, or, living in the age of photographic reproduction, looking at a book), comically sends up the poet-as-docent Yeats plays in the other three. As a frequent gallery-goer from childhood, a governor of the National Gallery of Ireland (1924–1939), and vocal participant in the effort to found the Municipal Gallery, Dublin, Yeats well knew art museums, their practical underpinnings and their ideological foundations. He understood them as spaces of both national and personal memory, history and desire. Like Michael Robartes wooing the dancer, he had wooed Maud Gonne before a picture.[38]

The troubling, at times unattractive "Municipal Gallery Re-visited" fairly vibrates with the tensions of the museum, and with the uncertain position and motives of those who visit it. Written in 1937, it records Yeats's meeting in the Dublin Municipal Gallery with the figures and events of a past that is both his country's and his own. Like other poems set in museums, including "Musée des Beaux Arts" written the following year, "The Municipal Gallery Re-visited" stages its encounter with the pictures as a walk through the gallery.[39] The movement from title to first stanza replicates entry into the museum space; the poem's abrupt transitions mime the shifts of the gallery-goer's gaze as it lights on first one image, then another, then another, and response piles on response:[40]

Around me the images of thirty years;
An ambush; pilgrims at the water-side;
Casement upon trial, half hidden by the bars,
Guarded; Griffith staring in hysterical pride;
Kevin O'Higgins' countenance that wears
A gentle questioning look that cannot hide
A soul incapable of remorse or rest;
A revolutionary soldier kneeling to be blessed.[41]

Veering from descriptive statement to meditation, from the authoritative self-assurance of the connoisseur to the self-doubt of an aging man, from grand public gestures of high sentence to more private, less ruly responses, the poem demonstrates the dynamic nature of ekphrasis as the speaker tries to find his relation to the paintings he encounters. The liminality of museum space both calls up and exactly fits the speaker's own position as public living reminder: he is here poised between the living and the dead friends depicted in the pictures, suspended in the poem's present tense between the past and the future, the nation's and his own. He is not quite man, not yet image, or, rather, he is both image and man, living and dead, past and present. If not yet stilled into eternity, his knees are "mediaeval" and he speaks the final lines from beyond the grave.[42]

The paragonal strain of ekphrasis runs strong through this poem as the image's power to make the absent present ("And here's John Synge himself," Fig. 2)[43] provokes anxiety that such power may claim him permanently. Already, he sinks down under it. The threat of Shelley's "Medusa" turning the gallery-goer to stone echoes through the two poems' shared language ("lineaments," "trace," "face") and form (*ottava rima*). Yeats pushes back against the literally astonishing nature of art by exercising linguistic power. He orders the paintings in relation to himself ("Around me the images of thirty years"), claims them as, indeed, made by language (" 'This is not' I say/ 'The dead Ireland of my youth, but an Ireland/ The

Figure 2 John Butler Yeats, *John M. Synge* (1905).

poets have imagined, terrible and gay' ") and as his own ("Wherever I had looked I had looked upon/ My permanent or impermanent images").[44] He points up the representational limits of the image, ("But where is the brush that could show anything/ Of all that pride and that humility").[45] The poet's struggle to bring the still images under the control of living language shows in the poem's formal tensions. The images' verbless, frozen activity is posed – as the awkward carry-over of the catalogue from Stanza I to Stanza II dramatizes – against the poem's structure, its movement with the living speaker from one picture to the next.

Yet this is also a poem about friendship in which the power of images to literalize memory and bring the dead bodily into the realm of the living is celebrated. The gallery, Yeats said of the poem's originary experience, "restored [me] to many friends": "And here's John Synge himself."[46] Ekphrasis becomes here a place of meeting the past the images call up, a place of communion between present and past, viewer and artist, viewer and painted subject. It includes the audience, the "you" so explicitly called into the poem. The power of this poem derives from a sense that the speaker is negotiating the "dramatic field" of the museum both emotionally and spatially, a complex web of relations between word and image and world and memory, speaker and picture and audience and world.

Writing the script

While "The Municipal Gallery Re-visited" is a lyric of personal feeling, it is also a public poem. *Ottava rima* provided the form and ekphrasis the situation for turning the lyric to public use. The poem treads the uneasy intersection of identities between Yeats the ordinary citizen and museum-goer, and Yeats the poet, museum founder, and shaper of his country's cultural heritage. He is at once the viewer of the exhibition – he enters the museum and responds to what's there in very personal ways – and its curator – the selection of images, their arrangement and the narrative derived from them are all of his making, and he speaks, at moments, the public speech of curators ("Greatest since Rembrandt").[47] Most importantly, the poem responds to the idea of the museum as a public, political space to which, as Boland above suggests, people are driven by a compelling need to "see" what their nation is. In the museum, the "beloved republic" is "raised and/ saved and/ scalded into/ something measurable." What that republic might *be*, how the museum might answer the need to embody the nation outside its doors, is the central issue of this poem that configures that museum.

"The Municipal Gallery Re-visited" is Yeats's final foray into the debate over the founding of the gallery, a debate in which Yeats had committed the lyric to polemical use. The complex story may be summarized. In 1908, Hugh Lane, a connoisseur and highly successful art dealer, and nephew of Yeats's patron and great friend, Lady Gregory, opened the Municipal Gallery in Dublin in temporary quarters to display to the public his collection of fine European paintings. Lane promised to give his collection, at whose center were thirty-nine important French impressionist paintings, to Ireland if the Dublin Corporation would build a permanent museum to his specifications. The Dublin Corporation balked, sparking rancorous debate. From the start, the fight over the museum, symbolic as well as material, involved the ongoing struggle for independence from centuries of British rule. The participants recognized full well that museums serve as "preservers of the community's official cultural memory."[48] At stake were differing ideas of Irish national identity, defined both by the contents of that memory and by the building that would hold it.

A Europeanized dandy who spent most of his life abroad (a fact that nettled his opponents), Lane nevertheless understood his gift in national and democratizing terms: he argued for a central site for the museum so that all might visit it easily, and he claimed the museum was essential to founding "an Irish school of painting," for it meant that young painters would be exposed to the best of European contemporary art.[49] The museum might help loosen Ireland's parochialism. In 1913, despite (or perhaps in dismissal of) competing interest in the French pictures by the National Gallery, London, which promised to expand the Tate to house them, the Dublin Corporation finally refused to meet Lane's conditions. In letters to the editor and two poems published in *The Irish Times* – "To a Wealthy Man who promised a second Subscription to the Dublin Municipal Gallery if it were proved the People wanted Pictures" (January 11, 1913), and "September 1913" (September 8) – Yeats defended Lane's demands against what he saw as the short-sighted, Philistine reactions of the Dublin Corporation and the middle class that supported it.[50] "Romantic Ireland's dead and gone,/ It's with O'Leary in the grave," he bitterly observed of his opponents whom he sharply pictured as fumbling "in a greasy till" and adding "prayer to shivering prayer" in a display of narrow-minded materialism.[51]

When Lane died aboard the Lusitania in 1915, his will fanned the still-smoldering controversy, but dramatically altered its dynamic.[52] Leaving the bulk of the collection, including many fine Irish paintings, to Dublin, it gave the French impressionist pictures to London. An unwitnessed codicil, however, left them all to Ireland. England claimed the pictures as legally theirs. For the Irish, suddenly the French pictures became Ireland's right.[53] In 1926 the British government officially refused to return the paintings. When the Hugh Lane Municipal Gallery opened in permanent quarters seven years later in June, 1933 (in Charlemont House, many blocks from the central site on the Liffey bridge Lane had wanted), an empty room awaited Ireland's rightful legacy. While using the power of ekphrasis to invoke the presence of the images of his friends, in "The Municipal Gallery Re-visited" Yeats pointedly never once invokes it for the French pictures. Their absence stands in the poem like the empty room. It was not until 1959 that the parties reached a compromise: the pictures would rotate between London and Dublin, each city having half the collection at a given time.[54]

In 1937, four years after the gallery opened, Yeats re-entered the debate over the museum in "The Municipal Gallery Re-visited" by using ekphrasis to write the script by which the pictures that remained would be read. While all modern ekphrasis set in the museum to some degree writes a script, in "The Municipal Gallery Re-visited" Yeats explicitly takes on that task in the last stanza, instructing the young republic to read these paintings as the record of its history. Like Virgil's description of Aeneas' shield, "The Municipal Gallery Re-visited" is an ekphrasis that promotes the founding of the state. It marries that function to the ideological function of the art museum as the preserver of the nation's memory.

Participating in the process by which objects are resettled in the land of art in general, Yeats's poem raises up for veneration both the paintings and the story he has them tell: "come to this hallowed place/ Where my friends' portraits hang and look thereon;/ Ireland's history in their lineaments trace."[55] This is ekphrasis doing the museum's business of turning "portraits into 'pictures' "[56] and into national history. Whereas Aeneas' shield directly imaged the future, Yeats's gallery looks to the past as foundation for the future. His script for reading the gallery begins by establishing the lineage of the modern Irish state from the "romantic nationalism of Keating's 'Men of the West' ['An ambush'] and the Catholic devotional Ireland of Lavery's 'St. Patrick's Purgatory' ['pilgrims at the water-side']" to a heroic culmination in the defining moments of Easter, 1916 and the War of Independence and Civil War (represented by the images of Roger Casement [Fig. 3], Arthur Griffith and Kevin O'Higgins) to the (dangerous) growth of "clerical influence on the Free State" ("a revolutionary soldier kneeling to be blessed").[57] Rather than stop, however, before these pictures of events and portraits of statesmen and soldiers as one might expect a writer of a national history to do, Yeats moves on to cultural figures and friends (Robert Gregory, Hugh Lane: son and nephew of Lady Gregory) and settles on two who form the center of his history of national origins: the playwright and co-founder of the Abbey Theatre, Lady Gregory (Fig. 4); and the playwright, John Synge (Fig. 2). If "Easter 1916," written twenty-one years before, recognized and idealized the "terrible beauty" born of the giving of life for the nation, "The Municipal Gallery Re-visited" passes by the paintings that would solidify that history as the central one, to focus instead on the giving of "the implements of national culture" that Yeats believed central to the function of the art museum, and that he promoted in a 1924 speech before the senate of the young Irish Free State.[58] Although many of the works

Figure 3 Sir John Lavery, *The Court of Criminal Appeal* (1916).

named in the poem were given by Sir John Lavery in 1935,[59] Yeats dramatizes the giving by attributing it all to Hugh Lane. "Onlie begetter" suggests the intimate other side of public acts of collecting, displaying and giving. Behind the idea of the Municipal Gallery as a physical place lies the example of Lady Gregory's house at Coole Park, which she had opened up and given over to Yeats, Synge and other writers and artists of the Irish Renaissance. This kind of generous beneficence, repeated in Hugh Lane's gift, is the ideal Yeats's script promotes as both national history and foundation for the future Irish state. The core of Irish national identity, then, is not only preserved in, but embodied by, the museum.

The costs of going public

Critics since the late 1960s have faulted Yeats's vision of Irish history for depending on an idealized view of the Protestant Ascendancy as cultured, aristocratic, generous and wise, and thereby replicating the

Figure 4 Antonio Mancini, *Lady Augusta Gregory* (1908).

social and political structures of colonial rule as a foundation for the
new nation.[60] Looking back to a world of aristocratic patronage, his
critics argue, retarded moving forward into modern democracy. "The
Municipal Gallery Re-visited" seems clinching evidence for such
arguments. Yet Yeats understood, perhaps more clearly than his critics,
the way the future must be built on the legacy – no matter how
troubled – of the past, and, especially, the high personal cost to those
who attempt to define and secure that legacy for the country. The

poem ripples with doubts about what it means to act on the ideals he sets out, specifically about the high cost of a generosity that gives all to the public, and about the terrible loss the poem itself entails by turning his friends over to history.

If Yeats's Municipal Gallery is a kind of temple before whose icons the poet sinks down, it is also a mausoleum. He knows that in sacralizing the images of his friends to raise them into history, he moves them out of the circle of friendship and intimacy. As Lane and Lady Gregory gave over their private spaces and spheres to Ireland, so Yeats in this poem gives them over to posterity. Such giving enacts a kind of death, or double-death. The private is no longer held within the confines of the house, of the body, even, but is on display, to be used by others however they will. The price of public generosity may be an extinguishing vulnerability. Synge's judgment of Mancini's portrait ("Greatest since Rembrandt") cuts two ways: it praises painter and woman as it confirms that both have passed into Art and History, and are available to be judged. In this way the poem explores the Janus face of the museum as mausoleum: it entombs the dead and takes them out of the living stream, at the same time that it makes them available to animate memory and make the past present for those who come after.

The overwhelming sense of loss that Yeats feels in this place before these pictures – physical weakness, "despair" that the world will never have again the "selfsame excellence" of a Lady Gregory – registers what it means to turn over all: the richnesses of private lives lost, the sense of intimacy that animates relations to people erased, ignored. "The Municipal Gallery Re-visited" is a group elegy and also a self-elegy.[61] As Jahan Ramazani acutely observes, Yeats stages a "confrontation with the unthinkable otherness of death" as a "confrontation with the accessible otherness of the visual arts."[62] In facing the portraits of his friends and turning them into history, Yeats faces the moment of his own death when all would be released into the public realm and he would, as Auden said, become his admirers, and his enemies. In "You who would judge me," he measures his audience. Yeats's emphatic language of command to future visitors ("come," "look") is an index of his need to write, while he still can, the history that would keep him and his friends from the hands of their enemies, to secure a script that stresses precisely the dignity so vulnerable when the future treats the dead unkindly, or, worse, forgets.

The troublesome final lines of the poem attempt to write into Irish history the intimacy of friendship that Yeats knows will be lost when he gives over all and History claims him. He tries to preserve the private by writing it into the public:

You that would judge me do not judge alone
This book or that, come to this hallowed place
Where my friends' portraits hang and look thereon;
Ireland's history in their lineaments trace;
Think where man's glory most begins and ends
And say my glory was I had such friends.[63]

We might read these lines, as critics have, as striking the false note of a conventional public gesture. More sympathetically, we might understand their sententiousness as a sign of just how difficult it is to bridge private and public, to preserve the individual life in public, to speak publicly, and officially, of the intimate. The poem is full of Yeats's effort, unsteady and uncertain, to speak both privately and publicly as he negotiates the public–private space of the museum and his place in it.

The poem's general "you" raises the question of who or what, exactly, the "public" is. No less for the poem than for the public art museum at its inception, the "new collective in the face of which all future art will exist and agonize is 'the public,'" as Fisher suggests.[64] If, by 1937, Yeats had all but abandoned the "dream of my early manhood, that a modern nation can return to Unity of Culture" in which everyone participates, the museum keeps open the possibility of art for "the people." Yeats specifies one public he, Synge and Lady Gregory fostered by writing the "Dream of the noble and the beggarman." We may agree with Yeats's critics that he is stubbornly deluded in his persistent yoking of aristocrat and peasant, especially in this context of the museum where beggarmen seem especially scarce. Despite his hope and the promise of the Louvre,[65] the poor do not much visit galleries in the end, no matter where they're located.

What Yeats assiduously avoids in his poem is a vision of "the public" as middle-class, believing it to be materialistic, self-serving and hostile to the demands of art. Yeats's objection is not so far from Lawrence Ferlinghetti's analysis some forty years later, by which time the middle class had entered the museum in droves:

Monet never knew
            he was painting his "Lilies" for
      a lady from the Chicago Art Institute
         who went to France and filmed
               today's lilies
                  by the "Bridge at Giverny"[66]

The publishing history of "The Municipal Gallery Re-visited" reflects Yeats's uncertainty over the identity of the public for both poetry and art.[67] The poem did not appear in a newspaper like Yeats's other poems in the gallery controversy, but first made its way to that public obliquely and second-hand, in a news report on a speech Yeats gave on August 17, 1937 at the Banquet of the Irish Academy of Letters, in which he announced that he was working on the poem: "I think, though I cannot yet be sure, that a good poem is forming in my head."[68] Although the poem envisions its audience in broad terms ("you that would judge me"), it was, as reported, explicitly conceived as a thank-you note to a group of American patrons who had given him a grant, and was first published in *A Speech and Two Poems* in a limited edition of seventy copies printed by the Sign of the Three Candles and sent to the patrons.

In 1996, the Municipal Gallery mounted an exhibition of the pictures Yeats names in "The Municipal Gallery Re-visited," attaching his words to the walls, making images of *them*. Here is the ekphrastic poem realized as script, replacing the usual art-historical commentary. The only addition to the gallery of images Yeats curated is that of Yeats himself, painted by his father, now installed in the secular church he had helped build. The power of Yeats's poem is clear in this moving show. But there is also a nostalgic, backward-looking focus to the exhibition. It's not clear that anyone takes *what* Yeats says about Ireland seriously. Rather, he and his vision have passed into history, and are themselves in need of preservation as part of a more romantic Ireland, before the EC came, before the Celtic Tiger leaped into the twenty-first century. A slide packet with the poem can be purchased in the museum gift shop. The poem originally published in a limited edition now is publicly displayed and is doing the work of making the images it names and the story they tell known to a middle-class public.

Paul Durcan Hibernicizes the National Gallery of Ireland

Laughter demolishes fear and piety before an object, before a world, making of it an object of familiar contact (M. M. Bakhtin, *The Dialogic Imagination*)[69]

Some fifty-four years after Yeats sacralized his friends' portraits in the Municipal Gallery, the critically acclaimed Irish poet Paul Durcan wants none of it. "Sanctity! I have my doubts about sanctity!" declares

St. Galganus, the speaker in the opening poem of *Crazy About Women* (1991), a volume of poems on works in the National Gallery of Ireland.[70] Sending up the secular sacred in modern museums and poetry, Durcan mounts a lively protest against the decontextualizing of art and the resocializing script the museum would have us follow. If Yeats sacralizes the museum, Durcan desacralizes it. Confidently postcolonial in a way Yeats could not be, Durcan (though a descendant of Maud Gonne) has little use for national or art-historical pieties, except to poke fun at them. There is no embodied Ireland here with "lineaments" that might be "traced," only painted and sculpted figures from various times and places given new identities in Durcan's poems as ordinary contemporaries, going about their lively, gossipy, everyday lives. Durcan peoples the dramatic field of the museum with characters speaking variously and demotically out of their peculiar individual experiences, each playing out a particular personal drama. He has little programmatic interest in nationalism, or the ways a museum might support it. That the National Gallery is a colonial institution is not an explicit issue, although the way its international collection of art may be made Irish and may, occasionally, speak of the violence in Northern Ireland is.[71] Nor does Durcan have much use for the kind of public face museums create for the works they display. Museum-going is insistently personal business here. Tweaking religious and cultural decorum, defying those "regulations concerning behavior in and around the museum" first specified by the Louvre,[72] saying and doing what you're not supposed to ("Don't Touch!"), Durcan sets out with outrageous bad-boy wit to rewrite the script that guides our behavior in art museums and our responses to the works of art we see there.

By his own and others' accounts, Durcan has been obsessed with pictures from the time as a child when he accompanied his mother to painting classes given by artist Sheila Fitzgerald.[73] Since 1980 when he visited daily the R. B. Kitaj show at the National Gallery, London, he has, he says, "regarded painting and cinema . . . as essential to my practice as a writer. Picture-making is the air I breathe."[74] Ekphrasis has been a staple of Durcan's work, from "The Jewish Bride" and "The Pièta's Over" in *Berlin Wall Café* (1968) through two volumes of ekphrases in the 1990s including *Crazy About Women*.[75] For Durcan, ekphrasis has served neither as a way to still the moment, nor to celebrate the eternal, but as access to a world of feeling and situations through which he narrates the present, often with surreal comedy.

By and large, poets of the twentieth century, like those of the past, have addressed works of art with the high seriousness required by Art with a capital "A" and by museums that display it. But in the twentieth century, there have been exceptions, notable exceptions. Humor, sometimes ironic and wry, often broad (in the tradition of Robert Browning's ekphrases and dramatic monologues by painters and patrons), has become a modern ekphrastic mode deployed to unseat what Wilbur calls the "surprising strict propriety" of the work of art, and of the museum. Wilbur and others (including Lawrence Ferlinghetti and Billie Collins) have responded to the strictures of the museum's behavioral script by going outside of it, by acting up, by calling attention to the way the museum guides behavior, by talking about pictures in ways that violate the established proprieties, by turning humor and irony on the experience of museum-going, and in so doing, have disturbed, overturned, and rewritten the scripts that guide our responses. Museum guards – "The good gray guardians of art," as Wilbur calls them in "Museum Piece" (1950)[76] – feature prominently in these poems. For some, the museum's sacred objects are just so much furniture:

Here dozes one against the wall,
Disposed upon a funeral chair.
A Degas dancer pirouettes
Upon the parting of his hair.[77]

The body and its demands speak loudly, constantly pulling against transcendent experience. Casual, profane talk abounds.

Commissioned by the National Gallery of Ireland and published in 1991 to accompany an exhibition of the works on which Durcan wrote, *Crazy About Women* is not only an extended exercise in acting up in the museum, but also one of the best examples of the recent phenomenon of museum-sponsored ekphrasis. The Tate began the trend when in the mid 1980s it published two collections, *Voices in the Gallery* (1986), edited by Dannie and Joan Abse, and *With a Poet's Eye: A Tate Gallery Anthology* (1986), edited by Pat Adams. The success of these well-illustrated volumes of ekphrases, some collected, some commissioned, some prompted by a poetry competition, has inspired numerous descendants, including the fine *Transforming Vision: Writers on Art* (1994), edited by Edward Hirsch for the Art Institute of Chicago; two volumes by Durcan (for the National Gallery of Ireland and the National Gallery, London); and numerous collections from smaller institutions.[78] Offering poets beautifully printed books, access to a new market, and the advantages of institutional affiliation, museums have thus helped underwrite the great blossoming of ekphrasis in the last twenty years.

These books are both new inventions of the museums' PR departments – a kind of educational outreach – and part of a tradition of ekphrastic collections stretching back through Michael Field's *Sight and Song* (which Yeats reviewed in 1892) to the private and notional galleries of Marino's *La Galeria* (1620) and Philostratus' *Imagines* (third century CE). They extend the expansion of museum culture begun in the 1930s when the Museum of Modern Art began actively and explicitly inviting writers into the galleries by sponsoring various verbal–visual collaborations. Monroe Wheeler at MoMA not only organized the 1936 ground-breaking exhibition *Modern Painters and Sculptors as Illustrators*, but in 1946 began sponsoring collaborations between artists and poets on limited-edition books that included Marianne Moore's *Eight Poems* with drawings by Robert Andrew Parker (1962). In 1957, *Art News* began soliciting and publishing, with illustrations, poems on works of art by such poets as Williams, Randall Jarrell, Harold Rosenberg, Richard Eberhart, Hayden Carruth, Kenneth Koch and Louise Bogan.

Personalizing the museum

A moving record of Durcan's love affair with pictures, *Crazy About Women* is an extraordinary achievement – passionate, witty, brash. It is unusual among volumes published by museums both because it is single-authored, and because it is a sustained but affectionate critique of the hand that feeds it. Durcan was given free range to pick from the museum's collection in writing this volume; many of his choices are religious pictures or icons and portraits, those kinds of images most violently resocialized in the museum. Though he doubted whether that "selfsame excellence" would come around again, Yeats, in "The Municipal Gallery Re-visited," urged us to go back to learn the lessons past excellence might teach. In *Crazy*, Durcan pursues with glee the opposite claim, one that Robert Lowell had, to different effect, spun out in *History* (1973):

But we cannot go back to Charles V
barreled in armor, more gold fleece than king;
he haws on the gristle of a Flemish word,
his upper and lower Hapsburg jaws won't meet.
The sunset he tilts at is big Venetian stuff,
the true Charles, done by Titian, never lived.[79]

If we can't go back to Charles V, Durcan's poems argue, Charles V can come to us. So, with insistently colloquial language and brash prosopopoeia,

Durcan metaphorically drags images of all kinds out of the museum and down the steps into the stream of contemporary Irish life, reinvesting long-forgotten subjects with personality, returning them to ordinary use, removing them from the art-historical narrative the museum age has created, Hibernicizing the international collection of the National Gallery of Ireland. If Hugh Lane had wanted young Irish painters to have French pictures that they might learn to be more French, Durcan wants French pictures to be more Irish.

Playing comically on class assumptions implicit in our view of Art, museums and their proprieties, the poems speak in a language that pokes fun at the high-toned. So Delacroix's *Demosthenes on the Seashore* is an Irishman "attired/ In scarlet pajamas and buff dressing gown/ Striding out the seashore to the corner store/ To deliver his message to the grocer" and the speaker of "Kitchen Maid with the Supper at Emmaus" is "perched on the kitchen counter," eying Velazquez's kitchen maid, "fancying her."[80]

Some of the poems (like much of Durcan's non-ekphrastic work) are explicitly autobiographical, the statues and figures in paintings given names and made to play out scenes (often wildly fanciful) in the poet's tangled personal life. The narratives Durcan draws out of the paintings' and sculptures' frozen moments are resolutely personal. As a so-called "postconfessional" poet, Durcan tests the limits of just how personal you can be about and in a public place, and how public you can be about the personal. "Two years after Paul died," begins the female speaker of "The Knucklebone Player," conflating divorce and death,

I met Nuala cycling in the park ...
We fell to chatting about Paul:
What a cheerful, solitary fellow he was.
I asked her if there was anything of his
She would like as a souvenir,
Keepsake, relic.
After all – in the middle of all –
He had been her partner.
She whistled, nostalgically.

She said: I would like his knucklebones.
Both knucklebones?
Both knucklebones.[81]

On the one hand, this is the height of ekphrastic *paragone*: the poet radically drafting the works of art and their subjects to a contemporary, personal world. Such a move at once acknowledges that there is no return while resisting the estrangement Lowell takes as inevitable and the elegiac approach to pictures it implies. On the other hand, the sheer outrageousness of Durcan's prosopopoeia liberates him and the pictures from the conventional conflict. His words are so at odds with the proprieties of the pictures and the historical narratives we are accustomed to see in them, that the poems release the images back into their own historical time and place, as Durcan claims his own. As Eamon Grennan observes, Durcan "refused the sense of enclosure, wanted desperately to break down the sense of artifact as an exclusive space, a confinement, a Grecian Urn or a golden bird, wanted to make art in some way coterminous with life."[82] The argument – and there certainly is one in this volume – is less with the pictures than with prescribed ways of describing the pictures, with who gets to put words to pictures and what kind of words are permitted. Durcan will not follow Yeats and will not mime the curators who usually comment on works of art. For the most part, he will not be a James Fenton, John Hollander or Mark Strand, writers who speak comfortably in the language of museums.

The body and awareness of bodily functions most insistently undermine the sanctified propriety of the museum in this volume. Both Durcan and *his* gallery-goers are resolutely not the abstract "Eye" separated from the mundane body that Brian O'Doherty understands the modern gallery, and modern art, to demand.[83] Much to the good gray guardians' disgust, the gallery-goers here have few transcendent experiences, make too much noise and can't get the restaurant out of their heads. "Another thing that I do not understand," says the gallery attendant who sits beneath Jack Yeats's *Grief*:

Is people who make a racket with their footwear on the parquet.
It never fails to grate on my nerves.
What's in it for a body to wantonly introduce
Noise into a place of worship? [84]

These same viewers quickly "scamper off for their coleslaw./ Punters scoff a lot of coleslaw in the National Gallery of Ireland."[85] More self-consciously and brashly than the punters, Durcan himself ignores the "good taste" that is part and parcel of propriety. Here is his "Joseph Leeson" (Fig. 5):

I am a chap
Who dictates his best novels
Standing at the urinal.

Figure 5 Pompeo Girolamo Batoni, *Joseph Leeson* (1744).

Indeed, it ought to be clear from Batoni's portrait of me
(A beauty of a chap himself – Batoni)
That I am a chap of the first water.
In twenty-seven words:
The sort of chap who even while he waits

His turn to go the gents
In his mother's fur hat
Holds himself in
With verisimilitude, tact, ego.[86]

As the speaker of "Grief" says, "A man's own ordure/ Is the basis of culture."[87] Sex is on everyone's mind, gallery-goers and painted subjects alike, as Durcan plays up and plays with the sexual politics of ekphrasis, the male gallery-goer gazing on the female image, the poet having his will with the picture, all of the politically incorrect attitudes suggested by the volume's title. As Wilbur's frustration before the *Dutch Courtyard* attests, desire-creating distance is amplified, even created, in the museum with its estrangement of objects from quotidian use and separation of objects, one from the other, by space.

All are extravagantly sent up in Durcan's poems, obsessed with the touch of human hands. "I hold the Gospel in my left hand," says Bishop Robert Clayton, seated beside his wife Katherine, "Her thigh in my right hand."[88] Giving the rich metonymic possibilities of the ekphrastic situation wide range, Durcan doubles the abstracting, transcendentalizing power of the museum over that of the church, in a wry tweaking of both. Behind every pulpit is a bedroom. This bishop does Robert Browning's bishop one better:

This Xmas night
I having placed three pillows beneath her back
She will draw back her knees up past her cheeks
Until her knees recline upon her shoulders
So that I can douse her haunches with my tongue,
Install myself inside her,
Until we two are become as one divinity[89]

Lest we think that we as good gallery-goers, and perhaps church-goers, can stand back from such thoughts, Durcan often uses speakers who are themselves viewers, and we are forced to recognize our position in theirs as we speak their words. From a vantage point just outside the picture frame (like us and Durcan), the clerical speaker of "Bishop of Derry with His Granddaughter" views his bishop friend in a funhouse of viewers viewing viewers viewed that conflates art and young girls, money and sex, collecting and desiring:

And I know what he is thinking,
Alas I do. He is thinking –

For many is the occasion I myself
Have taken a small girl to the cinema
And been emancipated by those credulous eyes
Forever gazing upward into the silver screen . . .

One thing that re-assures me
When I am taking out small girls
Is the recollection that I never touch
My capital. I live always
On my income most of which I re-invest
In *objets d'art*. I have amassed so many *objets d'art*
I am obliged to amass much of it under my bed.[90]

If, in such poems, Durcan turns the "blameless fun" of looking at pictures
into the kicks of a fantasy peepshow and so forces us to play out an
exaggerated, comic version of the gendered dynamics of ekphrasis, in other
poems he turns the tables and uses prosopopoeia to "liberate" the
objectified female image. If prosopopoeia is a means by which words take
over images, it is also a way of giving those images their say. Durcan makes
the revolution of image against viewer comically explicit, as in "Bathers
Surprised":

Having been a bather in the foreground for many years
I would welcome leeway to tell my side of the story –
That I am not surprised at being surprised.[91]

Durcan is not willing to get too polemical about this; his speaking
women/pictures are not usually the outraged suppressed objects of male
desire, but women embroiled in complex social situations which they
negotiate with remarkable aplomb and a pragmatic attitude toward their
own sexuality and its uses. "Papa put me up for auction when I was
nineteen," says Katherina Knoblauch. "It was the happiest day of my life."[92]
"When I was a nineteen year old girl," says Saint Cecilia, "They tried to turn
me into a virgin/ But I held onto my innocence/ By becoming a mother/ Of
nineteen children."[93] Sometimes Durcan the feminist (or "womanist," as
Derek Mahon prefers)[94] seems as willing as any unreconstructed male to
pull out the female stereotypes. So, the speaker of "The Levite with His
Concubine" is the village gossip (Fig. 6):

After Paul Durcan left his wife
– Actually she left him but it is more *recherché* to say
That he left her –

Figure 6 Jan Victors, *The Levite with His Concubine at Gibeah* (*c.* 1650).

Would you believe it but he turned up at our villa
With a woman whom we had never heard of before,
Much less met. To *our* villa! The Kerrs of Dundalk![95]

As in so many of the ekphrases here, the ekphrastic situation Durcan
undermines by using prosopopoeia is reinscribed in the picture itself. In a
comic reversal of the usual gendered power dynamics of ekphrasis, Durcan
is posed as the central figure of the picture, himself the object of the gaze.
With that "windowframe around [her] neck" serving its conventional
metonymic function as a picture frame, Mrs. Kerr is the picture who talks
back. But from *her* position, the window frames *him* and she is the viewer
who dominates the poor, abject male image with her words. All of our
sympathy is with him. But, of course, Durcan is hoisting himself on
his own petard, suggesting that those who look on and give words to
what they see are as self-serving and parochial as Mrs. Kerr, calling
into question once more the "authority" of these poems as truth-telling
commentary.

Although most of the poems in *Crazy* are humorous and brash, postmodernly protean about the ethical implications of looking at and writing on pictures, there are a few notable exceptions that address the implications of the title with full seriousness. In a poem on Giovanni di Paolo's *Crucifixion*, the critique of the church/museum carried on in many of these poems is given a particularly dark twist that implicates all gallery-goers in the damage done when we look on an image pinned to the wall. There the male sufferer Christ is regendered female, a change that signals what inevitably happens when a religious icon (or any object) is stripped of its original set of meanings and "resettled" "in the land of art."[96] She is a young girl in a psychiatric unit, visited by her father/Father (who is also the poet, and, uncomfortably, us, the viewer of the picture):

I am a woman, Father,
In spite of the fact that I've got hairs on my upper lip . . .
Father, why have you dumped me?[97]

He sees her "Half-astride the sill,/ Pretty shrew in the badger's jaws."[98] In a biting parody of Christian abasement, Durcan has her say to her father:

I want to stretch out
On the gold-paved path
In a dream of velvet loneliness
With carparks all around me
From head to toe,
Under the gleaming hub of your right front wheel.[99]

Behind this scene of love forsaken lies the incest of word and image: "Open the window and take me in your arms./ Call me by that name/ You used first call me by, remember?/ 'My pretty shrew.'"[100]

In this self-indicting poem, the image, it seems, is victim and has little power, except, of course, that as a Christian icon it has governed much of western civilization for the past 2,000 years. The ironic, powerful powerlessness of the image is made clear in "A Portrait of the Artist's Wife/A Self-Portrait." William Leech speaks from his self-portrait to the portrait of his wife in Durcan's brutal mapping of his own marital pain onto another (Fig. 7):

My sweetest wife
Although pain is our sole portion
I do thee honour.

Figure 7 William Leech (1881–1968), *A Portrait of the Artist's Wife* (*c.* 1920).

I can no more disown you in your melancholy
Than I can disown you in your sleep.

But should your melancholy like sleep
Roam from your cheekbones, what then?
Should you disown melancholy
What then would become of fidelity?[101]

Here is the layered complexity of gendered relations in ekphrasis –
homage of word to image, but also of image to image, of painter to sitter,

of viewer to image. Here is the viewer/painter/poet, unable to disown his wife, not frozen by bald terror as the viewer of Shelley's "Medusa," but checked by the subtler imperatives of art and love – the painter needs his wife, as the viewer the painting. Durcan sees with indicting clarity that for the faithless and alcoholic speaker, an unsteady partner, "fidelity" – in marriage and painting – requires his wife's emotional subordination, her melancholy. He has no illusions, however, about who has final power over her emotional state and keeps her still for contemplation: she, the poem implies, could well gather the energy and walk away. Nor does he maintain illusions about what would happen should she throw off the established proprieties of their relationship and "disown" her melancholy. The painter retains the power to paint, husband to be faithless, poet to tell in words, gallery-goer to turn and wander off, but all depend upon the wife/image to remain. She, in a reversal of the common trope of the still image, can stay or not, as she will. There is power on all sides from the start, and it is interdependent.

For all the defiance of the museum's proprieties, there is no sense in *Crazy About Women* that objects ought, really, be taken out of museums and returned to everyday life. As the collaboration that produced the volume makes clear, museums are too useful and too deeply embedded in our cultural lives, and have themselves become places we love too much, for us to think of undoing them. Instead, Durcan is bent on extending the ways we are permitted – and permit ourselves – to think and feel about works of art. By insisting that the public be made personal, that the historical be made contemporary, the sacred profane, these poems return works of art to everyday familiarity. Our relationships in the museum, he suggests, need not be guided by the decorum established by its founders and perpetuated by docents and curators. We might do better, be more human, were we *not* to genuflect in the secular church, but to treat it like home.

It may well be that the phenomenon of gallery-commissioned ekphrasis marks a change in the way art museums do business, in how they conceive of themselves. In *The Museum in Transition*, Hilde Heine speculates that at the turn of the millennium art museums (among others) are beginning to "recast" their educational missions to deliver experiences rather than display objects. Increasingly, museums see their roles as stimulating inquiry, and understand their audiences to be diverse.[102] Poets, it seems, have a role to play in this reconceptualization. Certainly, *Crazy About Women* suggests that the museum wants to open up a different kind of approach to the work of art, one that might be more variously personal than one that stresses an art-historical narrative of influence and innovation and seeks to establish a single national identity. If Yeats was there helping to establish a script for a national art museum that would conserve and preserve, Durcan may well signal a new phase in the conception of what the museum does for a culture. The pressures to maintain the museum as a sacralized space where the rituals Carol Duncan traces are carefully guided are tenacious, as the paratexts of *Crazy About Women* attest. In their repeated assertions of the poems' personal nature and the museum's sponsorship of the project, the volume's "Acknowledgments" by the museum's director Raymond Keaveney suggest both a willingness to venture forth and some unease with what it feels like to hand control of the guiding words to someone who is not a museum professional.[103] The "Foreword" by the Assistant Director Brian P. Kennedy, who first proposed the project, stresses Durcan's ability to straddle the world of poems and the world of the museum: "In this book, Paul Durcan demonstrates that he is a radical, brilliant poet, and a traditional art curator."[104] And, indeed, Durcan has, as Kennedy points out, organized the book chronologically according to the dates of the works of art and titled his poems with the names of the works of art, "the titles favoured by scholars."[105] We are, Durcan's volume tells us, still in the museum even as he insists we be given the freedom to range imaginatively. In his own "Preface," he declares his independence from the museum's conventions as he agrees to work with it: "I accepted the invitation on the basis that the book would not be a coffee table book but a book as well-founded and inexorable as any other book of mine."[106] The gestures and counter-gestures in these opening words suggest how difficult it is to see the museum as a space for collaborative innovation. And yet, it can be, as the existence of *Crazy About Women* makes clear.

"Art is private relations – not public relations," says the speaker of "Portrait of a Man Aged Twenty-Eight."[107] *Crazy About Women* seems an extended proof of the assertion. But if "public relations" means the scripting of a national story, the kind of use to which Yeats put ekphrasis in "The Municipal Gallery Re-visited," then *Crazy* perhaps simply shifts the terms, replacing a concept of Irish identity as inherent in noble benefactors in the broadest sense with a concept of it as residing in ordinary, colloquial, work-a-day lives. It confirms, though in a different way than he envisioned, Yeats's claim about Hugh Lane's French paintings that foreign pictures feed the self-concept of a people. If "public relations" means advertising, audience-building, the fight for a slice of the public's leisure time, then *Crazy About Women* also refutes its own claim. Private relations are good for public relations, as the

confessional poets discovered. The book has been something of a minor
phenomenon commercially – it sold an astonishing 20,000 copies in its
first two months (October–December, 1991), catapulting the National
Gallery of Ireland to "the number-one position in the best-seller lists" on
November 2, and attracting some 40,000 people to the exhibition in that
same time.[108] In a reversal of colonial relations that would have pleased
Yeats, this success surely encouraged the National Gallery, London to
commission Durcan for a volume on its own collection that appeared in
1994, *Give Me Your Hand.*

It would be tempting to see in the socializing and resocializing of works
of art performed by Yeats and Durcan some template of literary history
from modernism to postmodernism, or at least some trajectory of
changing responses to the museum in ekphrasis. Certainly, difference is
marked, most especially in Durcan's de-sacralizing intent, but what is most
striking is the similarity of the issues that confronted the poets as they
entered the museum and wrote on works of art. And we must remember
that sixteen years before Yeats sought to fix a script for a national museum
in transcendent terms, Marianne Moore was visiting museums and, while
searching for art "lit with piercing glances into the life of things," was, like
Paul Durcan, writing poems that reintegrated art and daily life, for her in
some more domestic space:

WHEN I BUY PICTURES
Or what is closer to the truth,
when I look at that of which I may regard myself as the
            imaginary possessor,
I fix upon what would give me pleasure in my average mo-
            ments.[109]

And, while we may regard Durcan's multiple voices and upending of
convention as typically postmodern, Yeats himself had written (in two
voices) one of the finest send-ups of the sexual dynamics of ekphrasis in
the museum in "Michael Robartes and the Dancer" (1920), where the
lover–docent tries to woo the "new woman" by showing her pictures:

He. Opinion is not worth a rush;
In this altar-piece the knight,
Who grips his long spear so to push
That dragon through the fading light,
Loved the lady; and it's plain

The half-dead dragon was her thought,
That every morning rose again
And dug its claws and shrieked and fought.
Could the impossible come to pass
She would have time to turn her eyes,
Her lover thought, upon the glass
And on the instant would grow wise.

She. You mean they argued.
He.   Put it so;
But bear in mind your lover's wage
Is what your looking-glass can show,
And that he will turn green with rage
At all that is not pictured there.

She. May I not put myself to college?[110]

For both Yeats and Durcan, the ekphrastic situation is dynamic, the relations of self to work of art and both to their audiences develop within a given poem and vary across poems. We also see in both how those specific relations open into a broader field of relations: how poets have participated, through ekphrasis, in a culture of images, building it and critiquing it from inside one of its major institutions. When Gertrude Stein said, "You can be a museum or you can be modern,"[111] she was wrong, if what she meant was that museums are inevitably backward-looking and necessarily disengaged from the present. For Yeats, as for Durcan after him, and for Heaney and Boland in the passages quoted at the head of this chapter, to enter the museum, to engage in ekphrasis, is not to retreat from what it means to live and write in the twentieth century, but to encounter the past in vital relation to the present and the future. Going into the museum is a way of being modern.

> Portrait or nature morte or landscape (nature vivante) –
> Pencil and brush make all a still life, fixed...
>
> > (Michael Hamburger on Lucien Freud's portrait of Francis
> > Bacon, "A Painter Painted," 1986)[1]

> About suffering, about adoration, the old masters
> Disagree.
>
> > (Randall Jarrell, "The Old and New Masters," 1965)[2]

All ekphrasis could be said to begin necessarily in elegy, in the fact of difference between the living poet and the fixed image, always already a corpse. The long, explicit association between ekphrasis, death and mourning builds on this fact. From tomb inscriptions describing the monuments to which they are attached or giving voice to the depicted dead, to Shakespeare's "Rape of Lucrece," Wordsworth's "Peele Castle" and Keats's "Ode on a Grecian Urn," and continuing through the twentieth century in such works as Yeats's "The Municipal Gallery Re-visited," Robert Lowell's "For the Union Dead," Adrienne Rich's "Mourning Picture" and John Ashbery's "Self-Portrait in a Convex Mirror," elegiac ekphrasis finds grief in the gap between the living observer and the stilled dead, and consolation in the presence of the past the image embodies.[3] Like Yeats's, sometimes the loss mourned in such ekphrases is of specific people depicted as in life. Some, like Michael Hamburger's, above, ply the ekphrastic trope of stillness to affirm the power of art to make of the living body a corpse more eloquent and "true." Sometimes the loss mourned is of a broader past, as in many of Lowell's ekphrases. Nostalgia and urgent desire for connection to a past that seemed too rapidly receding drive some of the most powerful ekphrases of the twentieth century:

Today as the news from Selma and Saigon
poisons the air like fallout,
   I come again to see
the serene great picture that I love...

O light beheld as through refracting tears.
Here is the aura of that world
   each of us has lost.
Here is the shadow of its joy.

> (Robert Hayden, "Monet's
> 'Waterlilies,'" 1970)[4]

Yeats called the Municipal Gallery "hallowed ground"; the place to which Hayden "come[s] again" is the museum: both suggest how the museum has helped shape elegiac ekphrasis. In museums – many with architectural echoes of the mausoleum – the past is entombed, artists, their sitters and patrons preserved. Poets went, and go, to the museum, as to the grave, to mourn and re-collect lost worlds.

The power of Hayden's poem proceeds from the contrast between what's inside the museum and what's outside, and between two sets of images. Behind Monet's lilies as our lost Eden lie the unspoken photographs of the "news from Selma and Saigon" and of Hiroshima and Nagasaki that spring inevitably to the mind's eye: police attacking Civil Rights marchers on Bloody Sunday, 1965; the field execution of a Vietcong in 1968; the scarred victims of the atomic bomb. This poem points to ekphrasis that looks on images of dead and dying bodies less to mourn than to raise, self-reflexively, what it means to be a spectator to suffering and death. From Auden's famous meditation on suffering to Randall Jarrell's "The Old and New Masters," Seamus Heaney's bog poems, Larry Levis's exploration of Caravaggio's *David with the Head of Goliath*, Irving Feldman's "The Bystander at the Massacre" and poems by Ferlinghetti, Walcott, Feldman and others on the works of Goya, pictures have made present dead and dying bodies, and ekphrasis has provided the occasion for observing and representing their features. In the position of the ekphrastic observer, poets have found a correlative for the bystanding that M. L. Rosenthal called, in talking of Feldman, "a kind of modern fate."[5] So Seamus Heaney looks at the hauntingly beautiful photographs of the preserved bodies of Iron Age men and women exhumed from the peat bogs of Denmark and Ireland (the victims, it is thought, of ritual violence):

His lips are the ridge
and purse of a mussel,
his spine an eel arrested
under the glisten of mud.

The head lifts,
the chin is a visor

raised above the vent
of his slashed throat

that has tanned and toughened.
The cured wound
opens inwards to a dark
elderberry place.

Who will say "corpse"
to his vivid cast?
Who will say "body"
to his opaque repose?
               ("The Grauballe Man," 1975)[6]

Deploying conventional description as a means of knowledge, self-
conscious about the act of putting words to the image, Heaney uses
ekphrasis in an effort to know the particulars of the North's violence and
judge his implication as poet in it.

Such poems emerge in part from the century's unprecedented violence
and the need to address it, and in part from the simultaneous (and not
coincidental) distancing of death in much western culture, what Ernest
Becker termed "the denial of death."[7] As historian Philippe Ariès has
shown, attitudes toward death underwent a profound and rapid revolution
after World War I: the rituals of communal grieving (the closed shutters,
the lit candles, the tolling bell, the funeral procession) disappeared as death
was driven into secrecy in a society in which unalloyed happiness was
the goal. Death was deemed "dirty," the viewing of it shameful. Deathbed
farewells attended by family and friends, children and adults alike,
disappeared. The dead were whisked out of sight, their handling no longer
the province of family and friends but of a growing mortuary industry. The
viewing disappeared as a custom in England and, in the United States,
embalming made certain that the dead don't look dead.[8] Beginning in the
1930s, commonplace by the 1950s, dying was transferred from the home to
the hospital, "the only place where death is sure of escaping a visibility."[9] It
was not unusual for even the bereaved never to have seen a dead body.

Simultaneously, with the advent of photography, death came to be
mediated by images. Much of what we know of death and its occasions
comes from pictures. In the nineteenth century, the practice of photo-
graphing the dead (especially children) as mementos for the bereaved
became common; by the twentieth century, that practice had faded
(though not disappeared), and the photographed dead had become most

often victims of violence, unknown personally to those who looked at their images. From the Civil War and especially after 1885, when the halftone process made it possible for newspapers to print photographs, they and, later, film and TV, became increasingly important in bringing the death and suffering of distant wars back home.[10] Both a symptom of our status as bystanders and a way of getting at what is hidden or distant, such pictures have provoked debate about the cultural and moral effects of images: does looking at them create empathy and provoke ethical action, or does it create indifference by desensitizing us to the pain of others?

Susan Sontag, who has done the most to raise these issues, mostly about photography but also about other kinds of images, recalls her encounter with photographs of Bergen-Belsen and Dachau in a bookstore in Santa Monica when she was twelve. The pictures provoked the twin responses central to debates about the efficacy of looking at such images, profound empathy and a deadening of feeling:

One's first encounter with the photographic inventory of ultimate horror is a kind of revelation, the prototypically modern revelation: a negative epiphany ... Nothing I have seen – in photographs or in real life – ever cut me as sharply, deeply, instantaneously ... What good was served by seeing them? They were only photographs – of an event I had scarcely heard of and could do nothing to affect, of suffering I could hardly imagine and could do nothing to relieve. When I looked at those photographs, something broke. Some limit had been reached, and not only that of horror; I felt irrevocably grieved, wounded, but a part of my feelings started to tighten; something went dead; something is still crying.[11]

This is the modern condition of bystanding: helplessness combined with empathetic horror, a hardening of the heart, and an uncertainty about the good of looking.

In the relation of self to other, ekphrasis provided a structural situation for exploring the moral dimension of looking in general, and looking at depictions of the dying and dead in particular. Ferlinghetti, for example, hopes that looking at Goya will raise social consciousness: "In Goya's greatest scenes we seem to see/ the people of the world/ exactly at the moment when/ they first attained the title of/ 'suffering humanity' ... they are so bloody real/ it is as if they really still existed// And they do."[12] For U. A. Fanthorpe, Luke Fildes's *The Doctor*, which depicts a doctor absorbed in observing a dying child, is about attentive observation that creates empathy and honors the dying: "The painters knew./ Gainsborough eyed his lovely, delicate daughters/ And rich fat brewers: Turner his hectic skies./ They brooded on death by drowning (Ophelia, in real water) ... As if such absorbed attention were in itself/ A virtue. As it is."[13] The painter, the doctor and the viewer all look. For Irving Feldman, however, looking at Brueghel's *The Massacre of the Innocents* and the sculpture of George Segal suggests the impossibility of observation as a means of understanding: "For his is the spectator's essential doubtfulness,/ this feeling that among the sum of appearances/ something important doesn't appear, and may never."[14]

While photography played a major role in making the dilemma of onlooking an acute modern problem, ekphrastic poets also turned to painting and sculpture whose explicitly aesthetic nature throws into relief the relation of art to death. Shelley had worried about the effect of looking on "the agonies of anguish and of death" depicted in Leonardo's Medusa: "the melodious hue of beauty thrown/ Athwart the darkness and the glare of pain … turns the gazer's spirit into stone."[15] Such self-consciousness about the artist as aesthetician of death and the poet/viewer as spectator becomes in the twentieth century ethically charged. Speaking as the artist, deploying ekphrastic prosopopoeia, Edward Hirsch folds the poet over the painter in recording the cold distance of Monet painting his wife's portrait:

My wife Camille is sick and, perhaps, dying.
Yesterday – with a strange, fascinated horror – I watched
Myself watching the deep grays and yellow golds
Seeping into the hard planes of her face. We have
Never had enough to eat – never – and her lips
Were already turning blue, like a gasping fish.
Hear my words carefully:
I was only interested in the colors of her face!
                     ("Impressions: Monet," 1998)[16]

Heaney called himself "the artful voyeur,"[17] signaling what historians of death have noted: in the twentieth century "death had become as shameful and unmentionable as sex was in the Victorian era."[18] Death is private, looking on it voyeuristic. "The pornography of death," Geoffrey Gorer titled his important 1955 essay on modern attitudes toward it.[19]

In many ways, what twentieth-century ekphrastic poets have done is to activate ethical issues already inherent in the ekphrastic situation itself: in western society, looking at pictures has been a morally suspect activity, as many scholars have documented.[20] Pictures lie, they reveal only the (deceptive) surface of things, they offer (tempting) bodily forms, they focus our attention on the material (sinful) things of this world. Behind ekphrasis inevitably lurks the iconoclastic cultural assumption Barbara

Stafford has aptly summarized: "that pictures, their creators, and their beholders *essentially* lack integrity."[21]

On the other hand, looking at pictures has a long history in moral education. Pictures were often painted with frankly didactic purposes, and, as David Freedberg records, advice on the moral training of children through images goes back at least to the Middle Ages. Giovanni Dominici's *Rule for the Management of Family Care* (1403), for example, advised parents to hang "paintings in the house, of holy boys, or young virgins, in which your child when still in swaddling clothes may delight as being like himself, and may be seized upon by the like thing, with actions and signs attractive to infancy."[22] Paintings could provide models of good behavior and depict the consequences of bad. In a more general way, the conviction that looking at pictures would morally uplift the citizenry underlay the foundation of public art museums throughout the West. Carol Duncan observes of the early days of American art museums around 1900: "Educated Americans, like educated Europeans, incessantly evoked the improving power of art objects, whose display presumably could produce Anglo-Saxon moral and social values in beholders."[23] The presumption was that museum-goers would re-enter the world, their moral senses sharpened for action by what they had seen. To such explicitly moral uses of pictures can be added the long history of metaphorical "sight" as indicator of insight and knowledge, and modern scientific belief in sight in general, first articulated by Leonardo: careful observation will reveal the truths of the world. Not to see is not to understand; lack of understanding leads to factual and moral errors.

The most famous ekphrasis of the twentieth century probes the ethical issues of looking. To explore how ekphrasis has provided a means of opening such issues in relation to looking on death and suffering, I'd like to return to Auden's much discussed "Musée des Beaux Arts," a poem about the condition of bystanding. "Musée" is probably the modern ekphrasis most frequently treated *as* ekphrasis,[24] though the ethical complexities of its ekphrastic situation have not been. Significantly, "Musée" has prompted more direct responses from other poets – counter-ekphrases, comments in letters and essays – than any other modern ekphrasis, and all have involved the ethics of looking.[25] Auden's awareness of the ethical implications of observation were sharpened by his experience with documentary photography in the 1930s; the questions his poem raises have become most familiar in discussions of photography: what is the photographer/artist's responsibility to those he observes when observing and recording mean not intervening to help?

What is the ethical relation of the observer to such images? What do such images do to/for us?

The implications of the artifice of images in these questions are highlighted by Auden's decision to set his poem in the museum and to focus on paintings, in which the artist's manipulation is indisputable in ways it is not in photographs. Like Yeats's "The Municipal Gallery Re-visited" (1937), Auden's "Musée" (1938) was written in the midst of the Spanish Civil War when another world war loomed, and museum culture burgeoned: the Municipal Gallery had opened in 1933, the Museum of Modern Art in New York in 1929, and the National Gallery of Art in Washington was under construction, to open in 1941, two years after Auden's emigration to the USA. Looking on images of death in the museum might be seen as part of the privatizing of death that took place around World War I, the move to an indoor space away from the public realm in which death had become taboo. At the same time, the museum is also a public space. Ekphrasis on death in the museum both enacts the privatizing of death, and recoups death for the public. With its presumption of public display, the setting also importantly highlights the question of spectatorship. It activates the idea of looking as morally beneficial (the tutelary function of ekphrasis doubled over the educational mission of the museum) and the idea that looking is morally suspect (it involves fascinated looking safely detached from the realm of helping action). In choosing a genre and setting whose central act is looking as the means of exploring the ethical import of not looking, Auden raises – tentatively and with much contrary evidence – the possibility that art may offer a way of attending to death and suffering that can loosen the indifference to others the poem claims as a fact of life. Ekphrasis in the museum offered Auden a way to stage the essential challenge he believed he must take up to "suffer dully" with his fellow humans.[26]

"Musée des Beaux Arts"

Auden wrote few ekphrases on works of art: "The Shield of Achilles," a notional ekphrasis that returns to the origins of the genre, is the only other major example. But putting words to images for his experiments in the 1930s in documentary photography and film constituted a varied ekphrastic practice, and one that opened the ethical questions of making and viewing images. During 1935 and 1936 Auden worked for six months for the General Post Office Film Unit, the brainchild of documentary film maker John Grierson who, as Marsha Bryant explains in her seminal study of Auden's work in documentary, "introduced the word 'documentary' to British culture and founded what would become the largest center of documentary production in the thirties."[27] Auden contributed poetic narration to the most famous GPO film, *Night Mail* (1936), and collaborated on five others.[28] The poem "Madrigal," written for *Coal Face* (1935) and addressed to a "lurcher-loving collier" it depicts, appears in *Another Time* (1940) with "Musée."[29] In the late 1930s, Auden himself took up documentary photography, which resulted in two collaborative phototexts, *Letters from Iceland* (1937) with Louis MacNeice, and *Journey to a War* (1939), composed with Christopher Isherwood in the midst of the Sino-Japanese War in 1938 shortly before he wrote "Musée." Both contain Auden's photographs of the poor and down-trodden; the second also contains photographs of the displaced, the wounded and the dead. Lines from Auden's poems and prose (and those of others) serve as ekphrastic captions for and commentaries on his own photographs,[30] as in "The student of prose and conduct" from *Letters from Iceland*, with its caption from "Journey to Iceland."[31] In *Journey to a War*, ambivalent, provocative captions, such as "The innocent" and "The guilty," frame photographic meaning. *Journey to a War* also contains the ekphrastic sonnet "The Sphinx," a descendant of Shelley's "Ozymandias," which introduces the theme of artistic representation of suffering that was to become central to "Musée." The Sphinx's "huge hurt face accuses,/ And pardons nothing … 'Am I to suffer always?'" it asks. "Yes."[32] Some of the films and the phototexts sought to advance a social agenda, signaling Auden's hope for the efficacy of the imagetext.

Written in Brussels in December, 1938, some eighteen months after Auden's disillusioning service in Spain, shortly after his return from the Sino-Japanese war, on the eve of war in Europe and a month before his emigration to New York, "Musée des Beaux Arts" is an exploration of the marginalization of suffering and death by a society reluctant to attend to what happens elsewhere and to someone else. "Musée" can be seen as a self-probing response to Orwell's accusations that same month in *The Adelphi* that "Spain 1937," Auden's long poem on the Spanish Civil War, glossed over the murders committed by the Valencia government: "Mr. Auden can write about 'the acceptance of guilt for the necessary murder' because he has never committed a murder, perhaps never had one of his friends murdered, possibly never even seen a murdered man's corpse."[33] Later he added, "Mr. Auden's brand of amoralism is only possible if you are the kind of person who is always somewhere else when the trigger is pulled."[34] Auden had, in fact, seen the dead and injured, and photographed them for *Journey to a War*, but the ethical questions Orwell raised troubled him. That the distance of death and its denial were on his mind is clear from *Another Time*, the collection that gathered poems written largely from 1937 to 1939, including "Musée des Beaux Arts," "Spain 1937," the elegies for Yeats, Freud and Ernst Toller, and "September 1, 1939." The speaker of "September 1" sits "in one of the dives/ On Fifty-Second Street/ Uncertain and afraid" while "Waves of anger and fear/ Circulate over the bright/ And darkened lands of the earth": "The unmentionable odour of death/ Offends the September night."[35] The volume bears the pressures of Auden's desire to "save civilization" through art, and his growing sense of how limited were its abilities to do so.[36]

The bystanders in Brueghel's painting: Looking and not looking, good looking and bad looking

Like Yeats's "Municipal Gallery," Auden's poem is staged as a walk through the gallery; the space between title and first stanza marks the entry.[37] Setting the poem in the museum, Auden assumes the museum's power as repository of cultural authority that Yeats had struggled to establish and Durcan to unsettle. Activating the didactic strain of ekphrasis, donning, like Yeats, the role of docent, he takes up directly and very specifically the general claim of museums to educate:

About suffering they were never wrong,
The Old Masters: how well they understood
Its human position; how it takes place
While someone else is eating or opening a window or just walking
     dully along.[38]

Ekphrasis, the museum, and the authority of both to interpret the image are deployed to make a point. The walk through the gallery is no casual affair, but highly structured according to the logic of argument: in the first stanza the speaker surveys Brueghel's *The Census at Bethlehem* and a copy of *The Massacre of the Innocents*[39] in the Brussels Musée to support the sweeping generalization, before settling on his prime evidence in the second, Brueghel's *Landscape with the Fall of Icarus* (Fig. 8). Here the

Figure 8 Pieter Brueghel the Elder (*c.* 1525–1569), *Landscape with the Fall of Icarus* (*c.* 1558).

presence of the ekphrastic object matters less for its ability to make the past present than as empirical fact:

> In Brueghel's *Icarus*, for instance: how everything turns away
> Quite leisurely from the disaster.[40]

Following the narrative impulse of ekphrasis, Auden sees in Brueghel's painting the story of bystanders who look on disaster and turn away.

   Despite the assurance of the statement that the Old Masters were "never wrong," this view of Brueghel is very much open to question: some art historians believe the painting illustrates Folly, in keeping with Brueghel's other early work depicting proverbs.[41] Succeeding poets disagreed vigorously on various grounds. For William Carlos Williams in *Pictures from Brueghel* (1960), the picture does not depict people turning away. The ploughman is absorbed in the vibrant springtime business of generating new life ("the whole pageantry// of the year was/ awake tingling/ near// the edge of the sea/ concerned/ with itself"), and simply doesn't see the disaster: "off the coast/ there was// a splash quite unnoticed."[42] Writing in 1948 to Robert Lowell, Elizabeth Bishop thought the bystanders *would* look:

> What I really object to in Auden's "Musée des Beaux Arts" isn't the attitude about suffering – you're probably right about that – it's that I think it's just plain

inaccurate in the last part. The ploughman & the people on the boat will rush to see the falling boy any minute, they always do, though maybe not to help.[43]

For her, the painting depicts the moment before, not after, looking. And when the bystanders do look, they will gawk. Randall Jarrell in "The New and Old Masters" (1965) quoted at the head of this chapter, decided that "About suffering, about adoration, the old masters/ Disagree."[44] He observed that in Georges de la Tour's *St. Sebastian Mourned by St. Irene* everyone looks: "All the eyes . . . are fixed on the shaft/ Set in his chest like a column . . . They watch, they are, the one thing in the world."[45]

In Williams's poem, as Mary Ann Caws observes, "no morality attaches to the scene."[46] For Auden, Bishop and Jarrell, it does. Bishop's view of looking on disaster as voyeurism that excites no empathy, and no helping hand, throws into relief the fact that for Auden and Jarrell, however they might disagree about whether bystanders look or look away, looking has a positive moral force. What Jarrell sees – a looking that creates an empathy so strong the observers identify with, "they are," the suffering Sebastian – is what's fundamentally missing for Auden and what he calls on the wisdom of Old Masters to help us accommodate: human disinterest in the pain of others. It would be good, Auden assumes, if people did look at and feel for others who suffer, but, he argues, the demands of dull, ordinary life exert claims that are just too great, and that's simply how it is.

"Musée" belongs to the noticeable strand in twentieth-century Anglo-American ekphrasis of self-reflexive poems, including Jarrell's, on pictures containing onlookers to suffering. Sometimes such poems themselves turn away from the suffering (of Christ, for example) to focus on a depicted bystander (as in Earle Birney's "El Greco: Espolio"), sometimes they are interested in the different reactions of the depicted bystanders, as in Jonathan Price's "Experiment with an Air Pump by Joseph Wright 'of Derby'" and U. A. Fanthorpe's "The Doctor." A distrust of the heroic aspects of suffering, perhaps a discomfort with looking on it, and an attendant affinity for the minor characters who look (or don't) and suffer in smaller, more approachable ways may draw the eye of twentieth-century ekphrastic poets to bystanders who are at the margins of pictures. Certainly ekphrastic bystander poems derive from a general sense of the shared position of the bystander: the onlookers in pictures both express a common plight (we are all bystanders to the suffering of others) and mirror in their looking the poet who looks at the picture.

The bystanders in the museum: Looking at pictures of bystanders looking

In its authoritative tone and its institutional setting, "Musée" might seem to support Orwell's general line of argument that Auden is disconnected from his subject. "Indifference" is how one critic characterizes Auden's tone.[47] Irving Feldman, who has repeatedly used ekphrasis to address the greatest horror of the century, put the case uncompromisingly:

Schoolmaster Auden gave them full marks,
"the Old Masters," for having understood
"about suffering" its "human position."
The view from Mt. Lectern was clear. They were,
he noted, "*never wrong.*"
                    One is pleased to see
things put in place, grateful for instruction
                    ("Just Another Smack," 1983)[48]

Failure to apprehend the abundant, awful life of suffering unelevated by legend is what the poem's didactic universalizing signifies to Feldman. To put Feldman's case in terms of the ekphrastic situation, the gap between self and other (poet and painting) signifies a distance that condemns Auden even as he thinks he stands outside the painting's moral loop commenting on the indifference of its onlookers.

Yet, *Another Time* shows how painfully aware Auden is of the poet's need to sympathize fully, of its difficulty, and of his uneven success in doing so. In the poem that immediately precedes "Musée," Auden says the novelist must, if he is "to achieve his lightest wish ... struggle out of his boyish gift and learn/ How to be plain and awkward," how to be ordinarily human. He must be

                    subject to
Vulgar complaints like love, among the Just

Be just, among the Filthy filthy too,
And in his own weak person, if he can,
Must suffer dully all the wrongs of Man.[49]

Ekphrasis in the museum gave Auden a genre and a situation that stage the essential challenge to "suffer dully" with his fellow humans. The relation of poet/speaker and ekphrastic object tests the ability of the viewer to empathize with an other. João Ferreira Duarte has suggested that Icarus' fall from his aerial perspective represents Auden's own verdict on the distanced position of his early poems, a condemnation of what Duarte, nicely for our purposes, calls Auden's "katascopic vision": "a look downwards by someone who can see better and further away because he occupies a superior place in both senses of the term."[50] "Musée," as ekphrasis, itself perpetuates, in part, that katascopic vision: looking at another as other is built into the situation, and Auden's authoritative voice emphasizes the otherness of the ekphrastic object. Simultaneously, however, Auden seeks an alternative in ekphrasis' opportunity to establish relation across distance. The poem stages both looking and not looking, indifference and empathy: the uneven achievement of the poet's desire for an empathetic relation to others.

As an ekphrasis of bystanders looking at bystanders, "Musée" poses the question of whether those in the picture who turn away are like the museum-goers, including the poet:

> the ploughman may
> Have heard the splash, the forsaken cry,
> But for him it was not an important failure; the sun shone
> As it had to on the white legs disappearing into the green
> Water; and the expensive delicate ship that must have seen
> Something amazing, a boy falling out of the sky,
> Had somewhere to get to and sailed calmly on.[51]

The poem's record of the museum experience may suggest a similarly detached and distractable spectatorship. The first stanza's string of details (some accurate, some not), from *The Census at Bethlehem* and *Massacre of the Innocents*, could mime how gallery-goers wander among pictures, pausing for a moment, not getting it all, moving on: "The balloon pops, the attention/ Turns dully away," as Ashbery laconically observes in "Self-Portrait in a Convex Mirror."[52] Both describe the predominant way of moving among images, recognized by museums and counted into their design of exhibitions. Gallery-goers spend, on average, 7.3 to 15 seconds before a picture.[53] "Dreariness, boredom, admiration, the fine weather I left outside, my pricks of conscience, and a dreadful sense of how many great artists there are, all walk along with me," wrote Valéry.[54] We might add to this the evidence of Michael Riffaterre's reading of Auden's poem: he associates "musée" and "beaux arts" with the adjectives used to describe the ship, "expensive delicate."[55] The ship's ultimate indifference to the "amazing" sight works as a figure for the visitor's movement through the gallery.

One might also read evasion in the speaker's choice of pictures on which to settle. Just touching down on *The Massacre of the Innocents*, a scene showing the most horrific suffering and bystanders of all kinds, the speaker turns finally to *Landscape with the Fall of Icarus*, not a particularly good example of how the Old Masters regard suffering; there is little apparent suffering in it. Auden had been looking at the Rubens in the Musées Royaux[56] and could have chosen, say, the violent *Martyrdom of Saint Livinius*, but does not. And what are we to do with the fact that the poem doesn't mention the dead body in the shadows to the left in Brueghel's painting, the top of its head just showing? If Auden's poor eyesight permitted him to see the corpse, he further enacts what he observes in the painting, a willful disregard for death (a move which also indicates a moral dimension to ekphrasis' necessary selectivity). Whereas Auden's documentary photographs give the literal lie to Orwell's accusation that he had not looked sufficiently on death, Auden seems here to demonstrate, self-indictingly, its truth.[57]

All of this suggests that his conduct of the ekphrastic relation bears out the poem's central argument. And yet, there is the painful long drag of the poem's fourth line, "While someone else is eating or opening a window or just walking dully along," that expresses empathy for the weight and pull of the dull lives that keep people from attending to others. Here, for a moment, the docent feels *for* those depicted in *Census* and *Massacre*. More important to the central ethical question of the poem, there is in the last phrase, "and sailed calmly on," a connection to the drowning Icarus whose hope passes by so obliviously. Here is feeling for the isolation of suffering.[58]

The very fact that ekphrasis requires looking, however distractable, opens the possibility that the museum-goers offer counter-evidence for the inevitability of inattention. One goes to a museum precisely to look, and the poem dramatizes the process of the eye casting around a roomful of pictures, then settling on one for sustained attention. While the bystanders depicted in the picture may be turning away from "the white legs disappearing into the green/ Water," *Auden* looks at them and his ekphrastic description makes us look. The ability of the documentary I/eye to point out what is ordinarily not seen is one of the aspects of documentary that drew Auden to it and that shows in such photographs as "What the tourist doesn't see" from *Journey to Iceland*. What the documentary photographer can do for a scene, Auden here does for Brueghel's image. Using the power of language in ekphrasis to select and order, Auden rearranges the scene to make central the suffering and death the painter has relegated to the margin. From its start, the poem's second stanza is organized in relation to "the disaster" – the event from which everything turns – and to which Auden directs our attention. The poem expresses a submerged hope that poetry *could* make something happen – it makes us look – a hope in conversation with his famous claim later in the volume in the elegy for Yeats, written shortly after "Musée": "For poetry makes nothing happen."[59]

Artist and poet as bystanders

As a means of looking on suffering and death, looking at a painting, even of the most horrific suffering and death, hardly seems a substitute for looking on real bodies. Art aestheticizes death, and the very act of representation requires an objectification that may work against empathy and preclude intervening action to help. In a 1991 ekphrastic response to Auden's poem, Dannie Abse broaches these issues explicitly. Speaking in the voice of Icarus, he condemns Brueghel with playful seriousness:

Lest I leave no trace
but a few scattered feathers on the water
show me your face, sailor,
look up, fisherman,
look this way, shepherd,
turn around, ploughman.
Raise the alarm! Launch a boat!

My luck. I'm seen
only by a jackass of an artist
interested in composition, in the green
tinge of the sea, in the aesthetics
of disaster – not in me.

I drown, bubble by bubble,
(Help! Save me!)
while he stands ruthlessly
before the canvas, busy busy,
intent on becoming an Old Master.
             ("Brueghel in Naples," 1989)[60]

Like Monet in Edward Hirsch's poem quoted above, Brueghel in Abse's view stood in the position Susan Sontag ascribes to the photographer: "The person who intervenes cannot record; the person who is recording cannot intervene."[61] By its nature, ekphrasis is twice removed from the scene of action; in it, death is doubly aestheticized and action impossible. As Mary Ann Caws points out, Auden's poem trains the reader's eyes "on the aesthetics of the picture: green sea and white legs, ploughing borders and a splendid ship."[62] As a self-reflexive genre, ekphrasis inevitably raises the question of the poet's ethical relation to what he depicts as well.

Auden meets this question with the poem's formal properties, and, paradoxically, with the decision to set the poem in the museum. Although "Musée" is neatly structured as an argument, it itself – with its uneven lines, its colloquial diction, its distorting of the sonnet – works against the aestheticizing to which he points in the painting and to which his own formal facility, he knew, made him liable. The poem self-consciously avoids what the painting does: make the central action subsidiary to the aesthetic. In the museum, Auden escapes the morally charged position of the photographer or of Abse's Brueghel, a position he had explored in *Journey to a War* and found untenable, as his deliberately self-commenting, unpolished photo-graphs of the war's victims demonstrate.[63] In ekphrasis in the museum, looking hurts no one. Looking at pictures may be, finally, the most harmless way of viewing suffering and death. Indeed, it may be efficacious. The hope of the museum is to send viewers back into the world with moral vision sharpened for action, a hope, as other ekphrases attest, it is naive to view as naive. Fleeing demands to respond to the violence of Northern Ireland, for example, Seamus Heaney, in the ekphrastic "Summer 1969," retreats into the Prado, only to confront there Goya's depictions of atrocity, and to discover, unexpectedly, instruction in how to meet it: "He painted with his fists and elbows, flourished/ The stained cape of his heart as history charged."[64]

As Heaney's poem implies, looking at pictures is also a psychologically and emotionally *possible* way of looking on death. Terence Diggory has observed that for Williams, pictures offered a way to "approach the enormity of WW II without being overwhelmed."[65] Like Heaney and Williams, in the museum Auden grapples with the violence outside its doors. Susan Sontag puts the challenges of such looking clearly in a poetic commentary on Goya's *Disasters of War* in the Chicago Art Institute:

How to look at, how to read, the unbearable?
   The problem is how not to avert one's glance. How not to
give way to the impulse to stop looking.

The problem is despair. For it is not simply that this
happened: Zaragoza, Chinchón, Madrid (1808–13). It *is* happening:
Vucovar, Mostar, Srebrenica, Stupni Do, Sarajevo (1991–).[66]

For Sontag, pictures might press the distant and unbearable upon us, and
thus be a means of knowledge and possibly empathy, if only we can
manage to look steadily enough. The disciplined looking ekphrasis
requires and the distance available in it may make it possible to look on
suffering and not succumb to despair. Again, Auden's poem dramatizes
partial success: it turns away from the most demanding pictures, but
chooses one in which he can look at, and consider, suffering.

Another Time is commonly taken to mark the transition from early to late
Auden, from, in Edward Mendelson's characterization, vatic poetry (of lyric,
personal vision that legislates, unacknowledged) to civil poetry, an inquiry
into "truths he could share with his audience."[67] "Musée des Beaux Arts" is
the pivotal poem.[68] If Mendelson is right that the fundamental change had
to do with the poet's relation to his audience and subject, then the museum,
rather than being implicated in the world of dying vatic modernism as
Mendelson suggests,[69] may have seemed to Auden to offer a way forward
through the hope of a public common ground, a place where anyone could
see the Old Masters and speech might be founded in experience of a shared
object. Surely he chose Brueghel for the exemplary old master, as Williams
would later, because Brueghel could be seen as a painter of the people in
both senses. And perhaps he truncated the museum's official name – Musées
Royaux des Beaux Arts – to de-emphasize its royal, private provenance in
favor of its more democratic function. That the museum, in the end, did not
provide the kind of entrée into the common world he needed is clear; he
never set his speaker in a gallery again.[70] He needed an artistic performance
and a spectatorial setting more playful, less weighty – a tumbler in a traveling
show, for example.[71] But, for a moment in 1938, ekphrasis and the museum
offered him a charged set of relationships between viewer, viewed and
audience whose complex ethical ambivalences suited his restless moral
probing of what it meant to look on suffering and death. In terms of
ekphrasis as a twentieth-century poetic genre, "Musée des Beaux Arts"
highlights the centrality of ethical considerations to the ekphrastic situation,
and became the chief example. Marianne Moore, as we'll see in the next
chapter, had already taken up ekphrasis to practice and address how we treat
others, and that would remain important to ekphrasis throughout the
century from Moore to Heaney.

3 | Women looking: The feminist ekphrasis of Marianne Moore and Adrienne Rich

Citing the long history in western discourse identifying time and language as male, and space and picture as female, W. J. T. Mitchell justly observed in his influential essay "Ekphrasis and the other" that "the treatment of the ekphrastic image as female other is commonplace" in canonical ekphrasis.[1] From Keats's rounded urn, that "still unravish'd bride of quietness,"[2] through Rossetti's enthroned brides and William Carlos Williams' "Portrait of a Lady," practitioners of ekphrasis have worked the trope of the active male poet gazing on the silent, passive, female image, and having his verbal way with her. Mitchell further suggested that "ekphrastic poetry as a verbal conjuring up of the female image has overtones ... of pornographic writing and masturbatory fantasy," often compounded by guilt and fear that the female image may turn dangerous, rise up and silence him, as Shelley's Medusa threatens, or worse.[3] That ekphrasis is gendered has itself now become a commonplace in the criticism, indeed so commonplace that ekphrasis often appears inevitably gendered, and in the way Mitchell describes. But, said Mitchell in summing up, "all this would look quite different, of course, if my emphasis had been on ekphrastic poetry by women."[4]

This chapter returns to Mitchell's comment to take it up, at least in part. *Would* the dynamics of ekphrasis look quite different were we to consider ekphrasis by women? If it would, *how* would it differ? Do women even write ekphrasis? If ekphrasis works in the gendered ways Mitchell describes – and I think it surely has – then one would expect it to be inhospitable ground for women, especially in the twentieth century when women are presumably more sensitized to such dynamics and might be expected to be more wary of entering into them. Certainly modern feminist literary criticism and art history have pointed out the powerful association between looking and the exercise of specifically male power. Luce Irigaray's argument that western ocularcentrism perpetuates a phallocentric culture makes looking suspect activity, especially for a woman.[5] And yet, when one reconsiders the history of ekphrasis, it's clear women have practiced it all along from the Greeks through Joanna Baillie to Christina Rossetti, Elizabeth Barrett Browning and Michael Field, and *especially* in the twentieth century: Marianne Moore, Mina Loy, Elizabeth Bishop, Adrienne Rich, Sylvia Plath, Anne Sexton, Roseanna Warren, Jorie Graham, Rita Dove, Eavan Boland, Maya Angelou, among others.[6] Have these women simply assented to the options Laura Mulvey famously set out for female spectators: to "take the place of the male or to accept the position of male-created seductive passivity"?[7]

As a way of beginning to sketch out a place for women in the tradition of ekphrasis, I'd like to turn to that strain of modern ekphrasis by women that recognizes the power of a sexually charged, male tradition of looking, takes it on, and challenges its gendered dynamics. We can call this "feminist ekphrasis." In the 1980s, while feminist film critics debated the dynamics of female spectatorship, art historian Griselda Pollock entertained the "possibility that texts made by women can produce different positions within this sexual politics of looking."[8] Feminist ekphrasis recognizes that a woman's place as viewer is established within, beside, or in the face of a male-dominated culture, but that the patterns of power and value implicit in a tradition of male artists and viewers can be exposed, used, resisted and rewritten. This is not to say that male ekphrasis might not also be shown to be shot through with its own resistances and rewritings of the power dynamics Mitchell describes (as it is in Williams, for example), or that women practitioners of the genre don't also participate in those dynamics (something Moore understood, as we'll see), but that the strand of ekphrasis I'm calling feminist works specifically in self-conscious conversation with the idea of a mastering male gazer and a feminized art object. Such feminist ekphrasis might include Joanna Baillie's "Lines to a Teapot" as domestic counterpart to Keats's urn,[9] and would certainly describe Moore's and Rich's meditations on the tapestries I'll discuss below, as well as such a public poem born of the early twentieth-century women's rights movement as Edna St. Vincent Millay's "To Inez Mulholland," "read," as the subtitle tells us, "November eighteenth, 1923, at the unveiling of a statue of three leaders in the cause of Equal Rights for Women."[10] Not surprisingly, many feminist ekphrases take as object portraits and nudes of women, and thereby explicitly address the issue of female objectification.[11] One might trace this line from Christina Rossetti's sonnet "In an Artist's Studio" (1856), a protest against the idealizing objectification of the female sitter (using her brother's favorite form for his own poems on his pictures of idealized women) through such poems as Lisel Mueller's 1967 "A Nude by Edward Hopper" to Carol Duffy's "Standing Female Nude" (1985). Feminist ekphrasis can and has been written by men – Irving Feldman's "*Portrait de Femme*" (1965), on one of Picasso's portraits of Dora Maar, might be considered an example – but it has tended to be written by women who have found in ekphrasis, especially in the twentieth century, a rich field for charting, exploring and asserting different relationships between self and other.

I choose Moore and Rich for this foray into women looking because they are among the twentieth century's most important poets and used ekphrasis to write some of their finest poems, though Rich has not been thought of before as an ekphrastic poet and Moore's ekphrastic innovations have not been considered as such. The differences in their ideas about negotiating gender barriers yielded dramatically different ekphrastic practices that, together, suggest the various ways the genre has been transformed under the pressure of feminist awareness. My aim, then, is to re-read Moore and Rich in terms of ekphrasis in order to read them into the history of ekphrasis and thereby complicate our understanding of how gender works in the dynamics of ekphrasis. As ekphrasis played a role in the museum's work of forming national identity, so it played a role in reimagining gender relations in the twentieth century.

Marianne Moore's ethical ekphrasis

"Almost every poem Moore wrote involved a picture or art object at some stage of composition," notes Bonnie Costello.[12] Herself an avid sketcher who had thought of becoming an artist, Moore loved museums at a time when New York City's great art galleries were being founded: the Metropolitan had opened in 1880, seven years before her birth; MoMA would open in 1929; the Whitney in 1930. The last two were founded by women, signaling the entry of female collectors into what had been, until then, exclusively male territory. The dynamics of looking, and the pleasures and problems it presents to those who would say what they see, are at the very core of Marianne Moore's practice as a poet. When she wrote on a basilisk or a glacier, Moore practiced a kind of submerged ekphrasis, often working off of photographs of her subjects. Her explicit ekphrases, such as "No Swan So Fine," "Nine Nectarines," and "An Egyptian Pulled Glass Bottle in the Shape of a Fish," raise to the surface of the poem the issues and a mode of inquiry always implicit.

The kind of looking Moore set herself to practice engaged both the long tradition of sight as the avenue to truth and the positive moral value that implied. Looking carefully, steadily, particularly was, for Moore, a way of practicing justice. Moral scrupulosity required disciplined observation. It was no easy matter. As she says in a line in "England" that itself stretches one's capacity for attention as it continues and continues across the page: "To have misapprehended the matter is to have confessed that one has not looked far enough."[13] Moore never believed with theorists back to Lessing that the visual image, unlike the written word, could be perceived instantaneously.

Moore well understood that intense observation had its dark aspect. "The desire to see good things is in itself good when not degraded by inquisitiveness or predatoriness," she observed.[14] "Predatory," "inquisitive," "voracious," "rapacious" are the terms she used repeatedly to describe the viewing practices she sought to resist. She knew the relation of viewer to viewed could be one of power and the desire to dominate, and she understood that desire to be coded male. She also knew that women, too, could be predatory, inquisitive, and voracious, and that men were not so inevitably. Cristanne Miller's nuanced analysis of Moore's feminism is suggestive here. Moore's poetry, she argues,

is implicitly ... feminist in its manipulation of received truths about identity and authority and yet ... is more apt to strive for a non-gendered or multiply gendered positioning than for ... the kind of simple oppositionality (us/them, female/male, black/white) that characterizes much openly political poetry."[15]

The implications for thinking about Moore's use of ekphrasis are clear: Moore's poetic seeks to subvert the oppositions inscribed in the very ekphrastic situation itself as the poet encounters the "semiotic other" of the visual sign.[16] Or, rather, Moore seeks to confound and unseat the dynamics by which otherness is met as opposition, by which word engages image as inevitably "rival" and "alien."[17] Ekphrasis could be understood as "a literary mode that turns on the antagonism – the commonly gendered antagonism – between verbal and visual representation,"[18] but it need not be. As a genre that encourages the play of many kinds of difference figured in that between word and image (quick/still, living/dead, mortal/eternal, present/past, mind/body, for example), ekphrasis was various and capacious enough for Moore's inquiring, perspicacious imagination. At the same time, its strain of gendered *paragone* kept active in her poetic field the model of looking that her own work sought to revise. Though working largely independently and in different ways, Gertrude Stein and H. D. were engaged in a similar reimagining of sight (in part through ekphrasis),[19] suggesting that Moore belongs to a wider effort by modernist women poets to change the perceived gender dynamics of seeing and saying.[20]

A product of early twentieth-century American feminism – bred in eastern women's colleges, steeped in a belief in the gender-neutrality of the professions, and dedicated to showing that women could do what men could – Moore came of age at a time when women were making headway in what might be called the "viewing professions," among them the sciences, anthropology and art history.[21] Developing an ability to observe objectively and precisely was associated with advancing the cause of women's rights. Moore took courses in biology and studied writing at Bryn Mawr with the remarkable pioneering art historian Georgiana King, a friend of Gertrude and Leo Stein, who taught her students to "speak to the picture" and hung pages of Alfred Stieglitz's *Camera Work* around her room.[22] Moore visited Stieglitz's New York gallery, 291, in 1915 and saw the "straight photography" he and Paul Strand were pioneering as a means of breaking the bonds of artistic possessiveness. The importance they assigned to the selection of subject, rather than manipulation of the negative, carried over into Moore's ekphrastic practice, as we'll see. The major strategies of Moore's feminist ekphrasis can be indicated by two poems, both on tapestries, that bracket her career: "Sea Unicorns and Land Unicorns" from *Observations* (1924), and "Charity Overcoming Envy" from *Tell Me, Tell Me: Granite, Steel and Other Topics* (1966).

Observation

Observations (1924), Moore's first authorized volume, and full of ekphrases, initiates her life-long exploration of non-predatory looking. "Sea Unicorns and Land Unicorns" is a notional ekphrasis whose details are gathered from a number of artifacts, including the famous fifteenth-century tapestries at the Cluny Museum (Fig. 9) and The Cloisters (Fig. 10), and paintings of the Virgin Mary.[23] In this poem Moore describes the depiction of a fabulous world where sea unicorns and land unicorns are twinned in "strange fraternity" and "unanimity" with those "by nature much opposed . . . their respective lions." So described, her subject echoes the conventional ekphrastic situation in which she finds herself in writing this poem – word and image, poet and artist, "by nature much opposed" – but she refuses to accept that *paragone* is their necessary relation, imagining instead the possibility of reciprocal exchange:

You have remarked this fourfold combination of strange
    animals,
upon embroideries,
enwrought with "polished garlands" of agreeing indiffer-
    ence – . . .
This is a strange fraternity – these sea lions and land lions,

Figure 9 "Smell", from *The Lady and the Unicorn* tapestry series, the motto of which is *A mom seul désir*. Woven in Brussels, after Parisian designs, for Jean le Viste, burgher of Paris (1480–1490).

land unicorns and sea unicorns:
the lion civilly rampant,
tame and concessive like the long-tailed bear of Ecuador –
the lion standing up against this screen of woven air
which is the forest:

Figure 10 *The Hunt of the Unicorn: The Unicorn at Bay* (1495–1505).

the unicorn also, on its hind legs in reciprocity.[24]

Explicitly in the poem Moore uses this fourfold combination to counter, wittily and cannily, the rapacity that characterized Europe's discovery of the New World by the explorers and "cartographers of 1539" who brought pictures and pieces of these strange animals home. For Moore, colonial hegemony, collection, and visual appropriation expressed the same need to possess. As Costello observes, the oppositions of sea and land unicorns and of unicorns and their accompanying lions "represent an ideal of dynamic reciprocity held out for the beholder."[25] They constitute a model by which Moore would instruct the conduct of our relations to others of all kinds – a model of exploration, of observation, and of ekphrasis.

The gendered underpinnings of Moore's instruction are highlighted by
the poem's resolving image of the unicorn, who is "impossible to take
alive," and the virgin, who alone can tame him, depicted in many
medieval and early modern representations, which Moore gathers here in
a notional tapestry. Unlike the dogs and the male hunters in The Cloisters
tapestries (Fig. 10), Moore's virgin is "inoffensive like itself – /
as curiously wild and gentle." The unicorn "approaches eagerly;/ until
engrossed by what appears of this strange enemy,/ upon the map, 'upon
her lap,'/ its 'mild wild head doth lie.' "[26] The sexual charge of this final
image reimagines the gendered dynamic between human and nature
already hinted at earlier in the poem when the rapacious "voyager"
despoils the sea unicorn to obtain its horn "to give Queen Elizabeth."[27]
In representing "an ideal of dynamic reciprocity held out for the
beholder," the final image of the virgin and unicorn rewrites those
relations between beholder and beheld so often described in terms of sex
and rape: (male) viewer and (female) viewed, word and image, poet and
artist, artist and subject. "We need," Moore said in 1929, quoting a
passage from *The New Image* by Claude Bragdon, " 'the feminine ideal . . .
the compassional' not 'the forceful.' "[28] Her virgin becomes the ideal type
of the observer–explorer, implicitly instructing Moore's own ekphrastic
looking.[29]

Despite the liberating possibilities that the reversal of gendered
ekphrastic dynamics and the poem's final, attractive image hold up for
us, the word Moore does not shy away from is "tame": the unicorn can be
"tamed only by a lady inoffensive like itself." It raises one of the thorniest
problems for her: how to avoid what she understood could be the
arrogance of the civilized eye, no matter how inoffensive it tries to be.
How was it possible to look upon anything without following "human
nature['s]" impulse "to stand in the middle of a thing," as she put the case
thirty pages earlier in *Observations* in "A Grave."[30] In "Sea Unicorns and
Land Unicorns," Moore sounds the alarm for women as well as for men:
the will to conquer and possess characterizes not only the men who
ravage the new world, but the poem's other virgin, Queen Elizabeth, who
paid "a hundred thousand pounds" for the horn of the sea unicorn to put
on display at Windsor with works of art and other curiosities plundered
from the New World. In embodying an ideal of open, wild, curious,
respectful regard for the other, the virgin suggests an alternative way of
exercising power in the world. Yet in taming the unicorn and bringing it
into her civilized realm, she remains importantly related to Queen
Elizabeth. Moore thus opens up the central ethical problem ekphrasis

raises for her: to look and to record one's looking is inevitably to set the scene in relation to oneself. "Tell Me, Tell Me," Moore says in the late poem of that title, "where might there be a refuge for me/ from egocentricity."[31]

"Sea Unicorns and Land Unicorns" itself suggests strategies for mitigating the egocentric and acquisitive. If ekphrasis conventionally masters the image by establishing a particular view of it, Moore multiplies points of view, unfixing authority. By incorporating quotations – from Spenser, Violet Wilson's 1922 book on Queen Elizabeth's maids, J. A. Symonds, an anonymous medieval poem and Charles Cotton – Moore diffuses the central power of the ekphrastic viewer, dispersing it across history and gender as well as across descriptive languages.[32] Moore also does not stand and stare at one thing too long. Though she may return again and again to an object, she looks obliquely, favors the fleeting glance rather than the fixed gaze, the gallery rather than the single work of art. Her ekphrases are rarely based on one picture. "An Egyptian Pulled Glass Bottle," for example, derives not only from a bottle from Tell El-Amarna, but from two sculptures by Icelandic artist Einer Jonsson.[33] Such refusal to be pinned down to one object, such eclectic and plural looking, is a poetic version of her own practice as a museum-goer. Her friend Monroe Wheeler, director of exhibitions at MoMA, recalls her wayward, subversive approach to looking at pictures: "She was always darting about from one thing to another, making her own discoveries. We would go to see a certain exhibition, but she would always find something else she liked better."[34] In "Sea Unicorns and Land Unicorns," images of one tapestry blend into those of another; a quick look at Leonardo's *St. Jerome* interrupts a description of a tapestry's pack of dogs; "an old celestial map," a painting of the Virgin Mary, and an image from a tapestry appear in quick succession. Such radical intertextuality is both the height of ekphrastic *paragone* – the word rearranging the image at will, disrespecting its boundaries – and its opposite – an effort to respect integrity by not trying to possess the whole, by not saying "here it is."

Selection of object also mattered. Moore's ekphrastic objects most often come from museums; they are emblems of the possessive urge. But she liked objects that didn't settle comfortably into their place in museums; she liked, especially, those that might not be considered "art," or that come trailing evidence of domestic use: Chinese plates, a glass bottle, a pair of candlesticks, a patch-box, a carriage from Sweden, a six-foot painted wooden organ in the shape of a tiger devouring a man, tapestries, embroideries. No respecter of hierarchies and well aware of the feminist implications, Moore participated in the challenge to high art's claims mounted by the growing interest in "naive" art and in craft promoted by the artists she encountered at 291, MoMA and the Whitney. As she said in "When I Buy Pictures," she wanted "what would give me pleasure in my average moments," objects that evade possession by being made specifically for use, by being so much already to hand that they condition the power of possession: "the old thing, the mediaeval decorated hat-box ... a square of parquetry; the literal biography perhaps."[35] These objects stand in line with Joanna Baillie's teapot; Gertrude Stein's "Things" in *Tender Buttons*; and Eavan Boland's mug, porcelain doll and Irish silver; except that Moore would not claim such a resolutely domestic space for them. Hanging in museums, the tapestries on which Moore writes evoke domestic craft and use, while reminding Moore of the strength of the desire to possess and display that brought them to that place.[36]

Silence

Late in her life, Moore would return to writing on a tapestry, and again would choose one featuring a central, instructive female. Based on a Franco-Flemish tapestry in the Burrell Collection at the Glasgow Art Gallery and Museum (Fig. 11), which Moore knew from a postcard, "Charity Overcoming Envy" (1963) continues Moore's strategy of multiplying points of view via quotations from various sources, but it proposes an even more radical response to the dilemma of the observing "I" than "Sea Unicorns and Land Unicorns."[37]

From the start of the poem she refuses to speak for/of the tapestry with the kind of authority the ekphrastic tradition grants her. With the poem's title and subtitle naming the work, the date, the country of origin and the collection like a good museum label, the speaker seems about to take up the role of ekphrastic docent that poets like Yeats and Auden had so effortlessly assumed to instruct us about the Old Masters or how to read the "lineaments" of portraits. But Moore immediately deflects that authority by asking our leave to speak, then offering to tell us not anything about the history of art or about the fineness of the artifact, or even about the human lessons depicted, but a homey "story": "Have you time for a story/ (depicted in tapestry)?"[38] The presumptions of museum culture are fondly, firmly tweaked.

The story she gives us – what *she* sees in the tapestry – is neither the conventional story of virtue defeating vice, nor the story offered by the inscription on the tapestry itself, which might be translated as: "The grief

Figure 11 *Charity Overcoming Envy*, tapestry (late fifteenth century).

of the envious soul born of a goat is near. His joying is from evil things like a dog. But the elephant does not know this and Charity beats down this evil."[39] Instead, Moore parodies the gendered ekphrastic situation itself: the tapestry she sees is a scene of looking and saying, a scene of ekphrasis. Envy personifies that major motive of ekphrastic *paragone*: the perception that the image does it better than the word, has more signifying power, indeed is worth a thousand words. Envy "looks up at the elephant" on which Charity rides, and, like the ekphrastic poet, he talks, and talks, cajoling, calling for pity, trying to wheedle and beg in a bid to master the situation, or at least save his skin:

> He is saying, "O Charity, pity me, Deity!
> O pitiless Destiny,
>   what will become of me,
> maimed by Charity – *Caritas* – sword unsheathed
> over me yet? Blood stains my cheek. I am hurt."
> In chest armor over chain mail, a steel shirt
> to the knee, he repeats, "I am hurt."[40]

Like Moore the ekphrastic poet, who calls on other texts, he calls to his aid the word *Caritas* displayed on the tapestry, thus pointing up the text Moore's counters. The poem is thoroughly self-reflexive as Moore presents a parody of herself via Envy, and works to retrain the possessive impulses of her word-making.

Charity, as conventional female object of the gaze, is silent. She says nothing. But, of course, it is the silent female who has the power; she, not Envy, holds the phallic sword. This is the revenge of the image, what Mitchell suggests the male viewer fears. And yet, in Moore's story, though Charity holds the sword and occupies the superior position, she neither acts nor speaks. Moore might have used two of the most prevalent devices of ekphrasis to give this silent female image the power of action and speech – prosopopoeia to envoice her, and narrative to liberate her from the frozen, pregnant moment. Instead, Moore turns the supposed liability of the silent, "passive" female image into a strength. While composing the poem, Moore recorded in a notebook: "Charity has a problem – how to preserve itself and to learn patience, the ... mastery is from within."[41] That is Moore's problem, too. Moore recognizes that for Charity to act and speak would be for her simply to invert the power dynamic of Envy's desire to possess and dominate. Mastery is certainly required ("The problem is mastered" in the end, we're told), but not the mastery of either male Envy or female Charity over the other. The mastery must be over the impulse to master. Female Charity must stay her hand. Restraint in speech (and action) is here a sign of patience, and of expertise, that other sense of mastery.[42] For Moore, Charity's still silence is the sign of actively chosen restraint, not of constraint placed upon her, and certainly not of anything inherent in her nature as female.

The situation Moore sees depicted in the tapestry echoes one of Moore's own ekphrastic strategies used here and elsewhere in her poetry. She had difficulty finishing the poem. She recorded one ending in her diary, but a month later wrote that she "had a problem with the poem and [would] not try to solve it":[43] "the Gordian knot need not be cut."[44] Silence, Moore concluded, could be a telling option in response to the image. The gendered dynamics of ekphrasis that depends on a conventionally male word responding to a female image, language filling silence with speech, need not be played out to the end. Moore need not take on the mantle of Alexander the Great come to claim Asia by untangling the knot. Like Charity who does not lower her sword on Envy, but with her other hand holds his hand (the knot at the center of the image), Moore can simply leave potential as potential. The silence of Moore's Charity and Moore's silence about Charity are as powerful as the talk.

"The deepest feeling always shows itself in silence," she recorded her father saying in the early poem "Silence": "not in silence, but restraint."[45] Moore's poems in general exist someplace between the assertive language of Envy and the silence of Charity. They are, perhaps, best represented by the elephant who bears Charity. Of unspecified gender, s/he negotiates between Charity and Envy in Moore's account: "The elephant, at no time borne down by self-pity,/ convinces the victim/ that Destiny is not devising a plot."[46] Moore uses the prerogative of ekphrasis to turn a seemingly disinterested elephant (it looks, expressionless, away from the scene between Charity and Envy) into an active participant. Like the elephant who features in other poems as a self-image of natural dignity and restraint, unifying self and other,[47] Moore here represents one party to another, using a combination of speech (she narrates the elephant's actions) and silence (but gives the elephant no direct words to speak, and will not speak herself about the story's knot), precisely so that word and image might both have their space, the Gordian knot left intact.

For Moore, egocentricity could never be eradicated without eradicating the self; speech must always organize the world around the speaking subject. But there were ways of indicating a desire to let the other be, and to enact that as far as possible. Declining a single speaking subject of ekphrasis in contest with an image that it seeks to possess for poetic use through such strategies as description and narrative, Moore's feminist ekphrasis multiplies the speaking subject and its objects, chooses objects less challenging to the desire to possess, and recognizes silence not as defeat by the image but as an option of response to the image. Reciprocity, as far as it is possible to enact in language, is the ideal she holds up for the relation between viewer and viewed, an ideal her ekphrastic poems enabled her to both talk about and test.

Adrienne Rich's ekphrastic power

Across the divide of the 1950s, it was difficult for the second wave of American feminism to see in Marianne Moore much to suggest a way forward, or even a fruitful way back. In search of a female literary tradition that might guide and sustain her, Adrienne Rich famously recorded her bitter disappointment: "I discovered that the woman poet most admired at the time (by men) was Marianne Moore, who was maidenly, elegant, intellectual, discreet."[48] Impersonality and reticence hardly seemed the marks of a feminist; indeed, they seemed, historically, to have played right into the oppressors' hands. While Moore was deciding that "the Gordian knot need not be cut," Tillie Olson was writing the series of essays that would become *Silences*. Amidst her specters of "mute inglorious Miltons," Moore's restraint looked like a chance thrown away.[49] Rich, Plath, Sexton and others spoke out in their poems in ways that would have been unthinkable to Moore. And they did so in ekphrases, using the opportunities the ekphrastic situation offered by rewriting its strategies to explore issues of female identity in unapologetically performative, self-mirroring and self-revealing ways.

Re-vision

Like Moore, Rich understood sight as a ground for rewriting "the received truths about identity and authority,"[50] but Rich attacked them by renouncing the optimistic, failed assumption of gender equality in favor of outspoken accusations of inequality and deliberate efforts to wrest from the male gaze the power inscribed in the gendered workings of ekphrasis. Notably, Rich couched her feminist program in terms of sight, most famously as "re-vision" in "When We Dead Awaken: Writing as Re-vision" (1971), which, with *Diving into the Wreck* (1973), set Rich at the center of the American feminist movement. In the foreword to *On Lies, Secrets, and Silence* (1979) in which "When We Dead Awaken" was collected, Rich called upon women "to look afresh at, and then to describe for ourselves, the frescoes of the Ice Age, the nudes of 'high art,' the Minoan seals and figurines," along with "the moon-landscape embossed with the booted print of a male foot, the microscopic virus, the scarred and tortured body of the planet Earth."[51] "The old masters, the old sources,/ haven't a clue what we're about,/ shivering here in the half-dark 'sixties," she had declared in 1969, in a retort to the authoritative voice of the most famous ekphrasis of the twentieth century.[52]

Working in some of Moore's scientific terms but rejecting what seemed distanced observational techniques, Rich argued for engaged, active reanalysis of what women see, and she urged women to recover what had been overlooked by the male viewers of the past. Rich's aim was not so much to revolutionize the dynamics of looking, as Moore did, but to train the eye to select and understand what it saw differently. Her viewing is more actively analytical than Moore's, and more driven by a desire to effect specific social and political change. In her ekphrases, Rich aims to put power into the hands of viewing women.

From her first volume, *A Change of World* (1951), through *Fox* (2001), ekphrasis served for Rich to further feminist aims by founding metaphorical re-vision in concrete acts of literal seeing. In what follows, I look at ekphrases from Rich's first four volumes, through *Necessities of Life* (1966), which chart the period during which American feminism was beginning to redefine its ground and Rich was learning how "to write directly and overtly as a woman."[53] Rich published *A Change of World* some twelve years before Betty Friedan's *The Feminine Mystique* (1963) galvanized the movement, but already in it, as the title suggests, are the rumblings of change. The poems display what Susan Van Dyne calls "the particular strengths of a frequently ambivalent poetic stance," which spoke of the painful struggle of coming to feminist consciousness.[54] Some of them, among her best poems, are ekphrases. They make clear that "the main concerns of the later mature work" are not just "adumbrated" in this early work, as critics have argued,[55] but are already being explored in complex, nuanced ways, and often more movingly than in the later programmatic poems on which her reputation as a feminist poet rests.

Women's history/women as historians

In her search for foremothers, Rich helped pioneer the feminist movement's crucial recovery of the effaced history of women. Her poems are full of the lives of exemplary women, many of them artists, brought out of the back rooms of history: Paula Becker, Clara Westhoff, Emily Carr, Mary Jane Colter and others. By 1979 when Elaine Showalter called on literary critics to "focus . . . on the newly visible world of female culture" uncovered by a decade of work by feminist historians, anthropologists, psychologists and sociologists,[56] Rich had already grasped the importance of seeing women not as isolated heroic individuals, but as part of a female subculture that might be constituted as a women's tradition.

Figure 12 "Harold swears fealty to William, Duke of Normandy," detail from the Bayeux Tapestry (eleventh century).

Figure 13 "Here King Harold is killed, " episode 57 from the Bayeux Tapestry (eleventh century).

In the poems, Rich first turned to art as historical evidence of women's lives, and to ekphrasis as mode of historical re-vision. "Mathilde in Normandy," on the Bayeux Tapestry (Figs. 12, 13), is her first foray into writing women's history.[57] Using ekphrasis to gain access to the past, Rich links herself to the modern male ekphrastic practice of such poets as Yeats and Lowell, but where they see a male line connecting the present, however uncertainly, to the past of Byzantine sages and Colonel Shaw, she would recover a female line. With "Design in Living Colors" and the much anthologized "Aunt Jennifer's Tigers," "Mathilde in Normandy" forms a trio of feminist ekphrases in *A Change of World* that puts stitched and woven images to feminist ends.

Opening "Mathilde in Normandy" by conventionally detailing the image, Rich suggests the powers of ekphrastic description as a tool of feminist historiography: naming and describing anew, she makes women's past accomplishments, previously unremarked by history, present and available as example. The poem builds on the legend that, while their men sought "harsher hunting on the opposite coast," William the Conqueror's wife Queen Mathilde and her ladies embroidered the tapestry depicting William's invasion of England and his defeat of King Harold.[58] It is a monumental achievement: a continuous narrative worked in colored wool on unbleached linen 231 feet long and 19.5 inches wide. Displayed in the Bishop of Bayeux's palace (now a museum) since shortly after the French Revolution, the tapestry may originally have adorned a church where William's subjects, both literate and illiterate, read on it his great deeds. Like *Charity Overcoming Envy*, this tapestry itself is a verbal/visual field with embroidered labels describing and dating the events depicted: for example, "Here King Edward addresses his faithful ones," "Harold swears fealty to William, Duke of Normandy" and "Here King Harold is killed."[59] Like Moore's "story," Rich's opening description might be considered a responding re-vision of those labels:

From the archaic ships the green and red
Invaders woven in their colored hosts
Descend to conquer. Here is the threaded headland,
The warp and woof of a tideless beach, the flight,
Recounted by slow shuttles, of swift arrows,
And the outlandish attitudes of death
In the stitched soldiery.[60]

By constantly reminding us that we look at a crafted artifact, Rich raises to consciousness the fact that history is made rather than simply reported, and that it is made, here, by women. Choosing as ekphrastic object a tapestry that still serves as an historical document enables Rich to assert not just the lasting achievement of the women's fine needlework, but their roles as important historians, a role she simultaneously takes on herself in writing the poem.

While the static stillness of the work of art conspires with its literal silence to code it as ideally feminine in so much ekphrasis, Rich taps the ekphrastic trope of art's endurance (the other sense of "still") to proclaim the durability of female accomplishment. "That this," Rich says, using ekphrastic deictics, pointing to the tapestry,

> should prove
> More than the personal episode, more than all
> The little lives sketched on the teeming loom
> Was then withheld from you; self-conscious history
> That writes deliberate footnotes to its action
> Was not of your young epoch.[61]

While the men are dead and gone, the women's work lives on. Such enduring accomplishment is set implicitly against the fleeting and invisible domestic work of women in postwar America, prescribed by a conception of "female life," as Rich described it, "with its attention to small chores, errands, work that others constantly undo, small children's constant needs."[62]

At the same time, Rich uses the ekphrastic occasion to point out that the power and importance of that accomplishment were "withheld" from the women. She puts to historical use what would become one of the crucial insights of Kate Millett's *Sexual Politics* (1970): that patriarchy's denigration of women's worth is so pervasive, women internalize it as natural.[63] Mathilde and the court ladies did not even think to write "self-conscious history" or "deliberate footnotes." Constrained by patriarchal culture, they never considered recording or figuring themselves in history: they could not write "history charged with meaning," as Rich would come to define it.[64] Following the recuperative program she later prescribed "for reading between the lines, watching closely for symbolic arrangements, decoding difficult and complex messages left for us by women of the past,"[65] Rich spins the narrative out beyond what's visible on the tapestry, as so much ekphrasis does, to bring to light the story the women could not tell themselves, the story of the challenge they faced and overcame in their work:

> Say what you will, anxiety there too
> Played havoc with the skein, and the knots came

When fingers' occupation and mind's attention
Grew too divergent[66]

Capturing the tension of anxiety in the echoing vowels and internal
rhymes, Rich here makes an early contribution to an important part of
feminist historical revision, rewriting the history of wars to tell the stories
of the women who stayed at home. Her words correct what she sees as the
limitations of the image to tell the whole story.

Between the lines of the tapestry Rich also reads a tradition of female
community:

> For a pastime
> The patient handiwork of long-sleeved ladies
> Was esteemed proper . . .
> Yours was a time when women sat at home
> To the pleasing minor airs of lute and hautbois,
> While the bright sun on the expensive threads
> Glowed in the long windless afternoons.[67]

While irony registers and resists the prescriptions that enforced such
community and such reduced expectations, the warm direct address and the
natural imagery suggest a utopian co-operative sisterhood, stretching across
time, that was to become a central feature of American feminists' efforts in
the 1970s to challenge competitive individualism. Whether Rich appre-
hended in 1951 the exclusiveness of her vision, as she later would under the
pressure of international politics, multiculturalism and growing class
consciousness, is uncertain – "expensive threads" suggests she has an inkling
– but Rich's commitment to a constantly evolving vision of sisterhood is
displayed in her immediate correction of the nostalgic, utopian vision of
Mathilde and the women: "anxiety there too/ Played havoc," as it did with
Rich's more self-conscious contemporary sisters.

Connoisseur of perfection

Amidst the dislocating turbulence of personal and social change, pictures
often offered Rich an image of the peace she knew could not be hers.
"That fragmentary world is mended here," she says of the tapestry in
"Design in Living Colors," "And in this air a clearer sunlight plays."[68] In
her ekphrastic interactions with those pictures Rich plays out, in some of
her most moving passages, the internal struggle between a deeply felt

need for time, tranquility and the beauty associated with them, and the necessity for change that would steal tranquility and undermine conventional beauty. In "Pictures by Vuillard" from her second volume, *The Diamond Cutters* (1955), the depicted scenes again make present women's past, here understood as a collective female memory:

Now we remember all: the wild pear-tree,
The broken ribbons of the green-and-gold
Portfolio, with sketches from an old
Algerian campaign; the placid three
Women at coffee by the window, fates
Of nothing ominous, waiting for the ring
Of the postman's bell; we harbor everything –
The cores of fruit left on the luncheon plates.
We are led back where we have never been,
Midday where nothing's tragic, all's delayed
As it should have been for us as well – that shade
Of summer always, Neuilly dappled green![69]

Feminism must reject precisely what Rich sees in Vuillard – blank afternoons with nothing to do but wait, women made placid, stripped even of the role as fates they once occupied – but Rich nevertheless yearns for the beauty of eternal summer, the wild pear tree, the peace of women together in their waiting. This composite ekphrasis names no specific images, but one might think of *Breakfast Near the Window* or *The Thread* (Fig. 14). If, as David Kalstone observes, Rich differs from Lowell in being "no longer elegiac about history,"[70] she is so willfully, with knowledge of its great temptation for the present. The tensions of the poem suggest the pull of elegy and her determined setting aside of it. In bitter Yeatsean language, she forcefully wrenches the viewer/reader out of the pleasant, stable ordinariness Vuillard offers to face the present conditions:

But we, the destined readers of Stendhal,
In monstrous change such consolations find
As restless mockery sets before the mind
To deal with what must anger and appall.[71]

Nowhere is the lost Eden of old gendered power relations and old images of women more longingly evoked or regretfully set aside, nor Rich's talent for conveying in heart-breaking language her own response to pictures, than

Figure 14 Edouard Vuillard (1868–1940), *The Thread* (1893). Oil on canvas, $16\frac{3}{8} \times 13\frac{1}{8}$ in (41.6 × 33.3 cm).

in "Love in the Museum" (also from *The Diamond Cutters*), her ekphrastic exploration of sexual desire born of the gaze. In "Love in the Museum" Rich rewrites the ekphrastic situation, anticipating the debate in feminist art history and film theory about how women find pleasure in looking at images of women. This is a poem of complex, shifting gender identities and relations in which Rich seems to reckon every which way with the pleasures of desire sustained by posing and framing the beloved, with the possibilities of eternal beauty that past images of women promised, and to say good-bye to them.

Figure 15 Jan Vermeer (1632–1675), *The Milkmaid* (1658–1660).

Written soon after her marriage, before the birth of the first of her three sons, years before Rich began to write frankly of lesbian sexuality in *Twenty-One Love Poems* (1976), "Love in a Museum" achingly re-enacts the male objectification of the female. "Now will you stand for me, in this cool light,/ Infanta reared in ancient etiquette," Rich begins, posing the beloved in a series of attitudes and dress that mirror famous types of paintings: "a Louis' mistress, by Boucher" or "in a bodice by Vermeer" (Fig. 15).[72] The speaker is not specifically gendered. If we read it as male (as in Rich's many other male-persona poems), Rich plays a feminist riff on Keats's Grecian Urn (evoked explicitly in the ekphrastic "Antinoüs: The Diaries" in her next volume). Rather than the accumulating fear of unfulfilled desire Keats's "never, never" records even as he celebrates its eternity, this speaker fears the moment *can't* be fixed. He staves off fulfillment, defers, pleading lest perfection slip away,

> let me be
> Always the connoisseur of your perfection.
> Stay where the spaces of the gallery
> Flow calm between your pose and my inspection,
> Lest one imperfect gesture make demands
> As troubling as the touch of human hands.[73]

We might think of Rich here, in viewing through a man, as performing what Laura Mulvey calls transvestitism, identifying by necessity with the masculine spectator for whom images of women are made.[74] But rather than acceding to the conditions of such spectatorship, the poem suggests that the tradition of stilling the woman in art, sustaining the desire for the child-bride ("Infanta"), mistress, ("Louis' mistress") and domestic muse ("Vermeer") is a fantasy. "Always" cannot be. Art is a temporary stay against time and the demands of human hands. Truth and beauty are fictions. The speaker has his pleasure only with the consent of the beloved he poses ("will you stand," "let me think," "let me be"). Rich thus unsettlingly conditions gendered ekphrasis: the male viewer can tell the female image what to do, but his urgency suggests he knows his commands have uncertain authority. That women will not stay on the walls, at least not for long, is the feminist hope held in the balance with the poem's genuine regret that such images cannot be timeless and immutable.

If the speaker is female, we might read "Love in the Museum" as a lesbian love poem. Rich tries on the gaze as an agent of female sexual desire, savoring its pleasures, feeling its tenuousness, before admitting and acknowledging the touch that will destroy. Rich's frequent appeals to the hands of her beloved in her poems about women evoke Irigaray's claim that the sense of true female desire is touch, the greater humanity and intimacy of which stands in stark contrast to the distancing idealizing of the male gaze.[75] But "Love in the Museum" suggests an even more complicated and conflicted view of female sexual desire. It contains some of the loveliest ekphrastic description in twentieth-century poetry:

> Or let me think I pause beside a door
> And see you in a bodice by Vermeer,
> Where light falls quartered on the polished floor
> And rims the line of water tilting clear
> Out of an earthen pitcher as you pour.[76]

The poem's first line, "Will you stand for me ..." opens up the question of representation by signifying identity as well as objectification: will these images represent, "stand for," the poet/speaker? The line's implicit question, never brought to fruition by a question mark, seems to take up Rich's later charge in "The Images" (1976–1978) that we are so seduced by the beauty of art, particularly "beaten gold worm-worn Pietàs," that "we continually fail to ask are they true for us."[77] Rich does ask here, if not so baldly, and the answer is equivocal, pitting desire against truth: we want them to be true, but we know they are not.

Raising the issue of representation, "stand for" makes clear the extent to which a female persona undermines the dynamics of gendered ekphrasis: the beloved image is less recognizable in terms of "the other" than the self. A woman looks at a woman. Ekphrasis becomes a way of exploring issues of female identity, of what will stand for women, and what women will and will not stand for. The ekphrastic dynamic represents not only the play of difference, but also the play of similarity, disturbing the very terms of antagonistic dualism on which Rich believes patriarchal culture is founded.

The poem also suggests complex ambivalence about its site, the museum, so important to Moore and so rarely present in Rich's poems. The setting indicates the larger, institutional, cultural implications of acknowledging the touch of human hands as having, inevitably, greater claim on our attention than the pleasures of looking. The speaker wants the perfection that the gallery promises in its choice and display of works, but knows full well that the "Don't Touch" signs cannot be obeyed. In the end, museums rank high on the list of patriarchal institutions, unchanged in their basic male-oriented structures of power and display despite the influential role women founders had played in Moore's day and the differences they had made. In "The Images" Rich would angrily dismiss "the white expensive walls/ of collectors" on which "we are dis-membered."[78]

When we dead awaken

If "Love in the Museum" is Rich's most radical rewriting of the dynamics of gendered ekphrasis for feminist ends, "Mourning Picture" is her most dramatic appropriation of those dynamics for the same ends.[79] It demonstrates her fundamental conviction – which Moore never had – that human relations fixed in art, indeed history itself, can be altered by

Figure 16 Edwin Romanzo Elmer (1850–1923), *Mourning Picture* (1890). Oil on canvas, $27\frac{15}{16} \times 36$ in (70.9613 × 91.44 cm).

being re-narrated. While in "Love in the Museum" Rich tried on the role of observing artist, in "Mourning Picture" she speaks from the other side, for/as the image, deploying prosopopoeia as a tool of political liberation. It would become a standard technique in feminist ekphrasis of the second half of the century as a way of envoicing women silenced in an image.

Rich rejected Moore's scrupulous refusal to speak for another, and she did so on equally ethical grounds. What was for Moore a reluctance to dominate, was for Rich an abnegation of art's responsibility to speak for those who couldn't/wouldn't speak for themselves. The woman poet, said Rich, "is endowed to speak for those who do not have the gift of language, or to see for those who – for whatever reasons – are less conscious of what they are living through."[80] The ekphrastic trope of the still, dead, frozen image provided the perfect figure for the silenced victims of patriarchy, some of whom Rich would work to awaken through the regenerative power of her language.

"Mourning Picture"'s prosopopoeia arises from feminism's insight that patriarchy works with the co-operation of those it oppresses, an insight already suggested by the tenuous obedience of the posed in "Love in the Museum." Published in *Necessities of Life* (1966) the same year the National Organization for Women was founded, "Mourning Picture," on Edwin Romanzo Elmer's painting of himself, his wife and his dead daughter, Effie (in the Smith College Art Museum, Fig. 16), reconfigures the terms on which images, even images already made, appear. "In the poem, it is the dead girl who speaks," the headnote tells us.[81] Doubly silenced by the picture and by death, she rises up, one of the dead awakening to feminist consciousness, and not only speaks, but does so to claim her own role in the making of her image. She refuses to be complicit in the view of her and of death the painting depicts.

In the poem, Effie observes her grieving parents across the space that occupies the center of the painting and signifies the gap between death and life, a position that replicates Rich's (and our) own position, gazing on the work of art:

They have carried the mahogany chair and the cane rocker
out under the lilac bush,
and my father and mother darkly sit there, in black clothes.
Our clapboard house stands fast on its hill,
my doll lies in her wicker pram
gazing at western Massachusetts.[82]

Baldly asserting the pastness of this image, dismissing the picture's presence, Effie declares "This was our world," then goes on to claim her ability to re-make that world and to rival her father: "I could remake each shaft of grass," she says. Indeed, the second verse-paragraph suggests she *is* the maker of the scene she/we see; the dream of her life as it was "condenses" in an ekphrastic description:

Under the dull green of the lilacs, out in the light
carving each spoke of the pram, the turned porch-pillars,
under high early-summer clouds,
I am Effie, visible and invisible,
remembering and remembered.[83]

As the memory ("remembered") that inspired her father and as the "remembering" re-creator of these word-images of her gone world, she is doubly the maker of this image.

The assertion of female creativity is reinforced by Effie's description of how her mother responds to grief:

Mute and rigid with loss my mother
will ride the train to Baptist Corner,
the silk-spool will run bare.
I tell you, the thread that bound us lies
faint as a web in the dew.[84]

If the picture already provides evidence of how the father responds (by painting a picture), Rich recovers the elided story of Effie's mother by using the conventional narrativizing impulse of ekphrasis.

Denying the very foundation of her father's memorial, Effie tells the truth the living do not wish to hear: that the silk thread of memory is faint as a web, that the spool will run bare. This is a devastating truth for any dead child to tell her grieving parents. Brutal though it may be, it points the way of Rich's feminist future. As a truth told by the living (Rich) to/for the dead (depicted in the picture) and to us, it is the painful hope of those who need past ways of being to "run bare." In the end, "Mourning Picture" rejects Elmer's elegiac relation to the past. A family drama like many mid-century poems by women, it is an anti-elegy that refuses to mourn the loss of a family founded on the gender relations implied in the picture. The daughter will not, the voice asserts, die off like the mother, nor will she tell the lie about memory that her father's memorial embodies: "Should I make you, world, again ... and leave *this* out?" she asks. Fully awakened, she declares her old life past: "I am Effie, you were my dream."[85]

Unlike other feminist poets such as Eavan Boland, Rich was never interested in developing the arts of the domestic sphere as an arena for feminist ekphrasis. But like Moore, whose tapestries are recalled by Rich's metaphor of thread and spool, Rich participates in efforts to stop what she called "the dismissal of the traditional work of women as nonwork, of our art as mere 'decoration' or 'craft' or 'scribbling.'"[86] Mourning pictures were popular nineteenth-century forms of memorial, sometimes painted, often worked in embroidery.[87] The poem's image of memory as a silk thread may evoke the embroidered mourning picture, worked most often by women. Thus, the invisible ghost of such a memorial (what the mother might have made, running out her spool of silk thread) seems to lie behind the father's painted, visible memorial. Unlike the Bayeux Tapestry, it is irrecoverable, truly lost, if it was ever there, a further comment on history's effacement of women.

In "Transcendental Etude" (1975) Rich imagined a woman who

> quietly walked away
> from the argument and jargon in a room
> and sitting down in the kitchen, began turning in her lap
> bits of yarn, calico and velvet scraps . . .
> pulling the tenets of a life together
> with no mere will to mastery [88]

The vision of quiet, separate work is almost Marianne Moore's (though Moore never retired to the kitchen and would cast an ironic eye on such idealization); but in actual poetic practice, Rich often *does* display the "will to mastery" that she and Moore would agree must be repudiated. Even in "Love in the Museum," the relationship described between artist and model, viewer and viewed, lover and beloved depends on a dominant figure who gives directions. Rich said, "Poetry is above all a concentration of the *power* of language, which is the power of our ultimate relationship to everything in the universe."[89] Though she turned frequently to works of art in her poems, running beneath them is a wariness of images in both high and popular culture, a suspicion that they seduce, that they tell lies that must be brought within bounds by the power of language. Her suspicion stands, as it often has in the history of ekphrasis, side by side with despair that language will not suffice as counter, and an occasional longing for the seemingly pure presence of the silent image: "from time to time I envy/ the pure annunciations to the eye// the *visio beatifica*."[90]

Rich's uses of ekphrasis for feminist ends is finally a less radical exercise of the genre than Moore's, but a more politically effective one. With irony and indirection, Moore instructs men and women alike to establish relationships to images and to others of all kinds on less possessive grounds, and she works to enact the kind of viewing she has in mind in her poems, always keeping before her her own liability to the faults she would rid in others. To look and to speak is *already* to possess, she knows. Her view is flexible, self-conscious, never comfortable in fixed positions, and slippery in ways that make it of questionable use for political purpose. Rich vests her hope in women, turning the old gender dynamics on their heads without essentially altering them, asking *women* to use the power of looking and saying to expose patriarchal structures, and to use the knowledge so gained to remake their lives. Ekphrasis suited Rich's needs precisely because it could stage the exercise of power. Though Moore hoped little and Rich much for the social efficacy of poetry, Moore understood what Rich would assume: that ekphrasis offers a means of re-vision.

The feminist ekphrasis of Rich and Moore makes clear that the workings of canonical ekphrasis would look different were women practitioners written into the account. At the least the history of ekphrasis encompasses more than a century of poems that subvert, rewrite and use for feminist ends the idea of a mastering gaze and a feminized work of art. One might go on from Rich and Moore to consider how modern feminist ekphrasis would look were Elizabeth Bishop's quiet, attentive looking and describing seen in relation to them; or one might trace a line from Joanna Baillie's ekphrasis of domestic objects through Eavan Boland's. And what happens when Jorie Graham is figured in, or the experimental poetics of, say, Cole Swensen, or ekphrasis arising from collaboration between women poets (Katherine Bradley and Edith Cooper writing as Michael Field, for example) or between women poets and artists (Barbara Guest with a number of artists, C. D. Wright's recent work with photographer Deborah Luster)?

Were we to expand the field beyond feminist ekphrasis and undertake a full-scale history of women's ekphrasis, we might find traditions of looking that variously participate in and establish themselves beside and in exchange with those coded male. Such a reconstruction could test out Paul Fry's suggestion that women writers often strain against the trope of the indifferent self-absorption of painting so characteristic of much ekphrasis.[91] It might open to view the home as an ekphrastic arena, as influential in shaping the genre as has been the art museum for the past 200 years. (The home was, after all, where art was displayed before the founding of public art museums in the eighteenth century.) A refigured history might well find that the trope of the female looking in ekphrasis is present and strong, and that to imply, as some feminist critics have, that women who inhabit the position of viewer are "naive," is to underestimate the complexity and range of experiences to which art speaks and that looking involves.

A rethinking of the gendered dynamics of ekphrasis would also need to follow through the implications of Rich's "Love in a Museum": what would happen to our understanding were we to consider the many poems in which women look at women and men look at men? The play among difference, identity and desire in such poems as Ashbery's "Self-Portrait in a Convex Mirror" and James Merrill's "The Charioteer of Delphi" complicate significantly the nature of otherness at the heart of ekphrasis.

4 | Ekphrasis in conversation: Anne Sexton and W. D. Snodgrass on Van Gogh

What is it Braque
would have us see in this
piled-up table-top of his?

> (Charles Tomlinson,
> "The Miracle of the Bottle
> and the Fishes," 1986)[1]

The idea that paintings might denote friendship gets partial confirmation from an odd source, Mihaly Csikszentmihalyi and Eugene Rochberg-Halton's study *The Meaning of Things*, a sociological survey of people's feelings about their possessions. The authors find that what matters about "sofa paintings" is not their style, their subject, or even their value, but their function in starting conversations: their role as matchmakers or as signs of offered friendship. (James Elkins, *On Pictures and the Words that Fail Them*, 1998)[2]

The rhetorical structure of ekphrasis implies a listening/viewing audience, someone to whom the speaker addresses his/her remarks about a painting or sculpture. By its very nature, ekphrasis compels an outward turn to the world in which the poet speaks, the audience listens and sees, and the work of art means. Arguing that ekphrastic poetry and prose renovated literature in the late nineteenth century, Richard Stein observes:

The reference to a second art gives a new and important role to the reader-spectator, who shares the writer's contemplation of an external artifact ... In Ruskin, Pater, and even Rossetti, the reader is far more aware of the necessity for an audience: the introduction of an artifact outside the text helps to define the relationship between writer and reader; the reader is not merely invited but required to measure his response against the second work of art and thus participate in the meaning of the prose or verse.[3]

Awareness of the ever shrinking audience for poetry in the twentieth century charged this turn to the reader, further encouraged by the proliferation of high-quality reproductions whose widespread use and distribution in the popular media created a large pool of images readily available for audiences to consult. Mitchell places the poet

in a middle position between the object described or addressed and a listening subject who ... will be made to 'see' the object through the medium of the poet's voice ... The 'working through' of ekphrasis and the other, then, is more like a triangular relationship than a binary one; its social structure cannot be grasped fully as a phenomenological encounter of subject and object, but must be pictured as a *ménage à trois* in which the relations of self and other, text and image, are triply inscribed.[4]

Whether the audience is conceived as also looking at the work of art (Stein) or as "seeing" it only through the ekphrastic description (Mitchell), the necessary pressure of the audience is an important feature of ekphrasis' social structure. "Observe," "see," "look" are basic imperatives of the genre. In speaking, the poet responds not just to the artist who has "spoken" in the work of art, but to an audience.

In Stein's and Mitchell's formulations of ekphrastic representation, the listening subject is not envisioned as her/himself speaking. Yet many ekphrases display a high degree of awareness that the audience may well be reacting, engaging the poet's observations and judgments even as the poet speaks. Internalized in ekphrasis in various rhetorical nods to the audience (as in Tomlinson's question above) and in the structure of ekphrastic poems that explicitly stage a conversation over the work of art, the presence of an audience opens the possibility of a lyric in which the model of conversation with the audience replaces that of private meditation overheard by the audience. The relation of audience to poet is understood to be a two-way path. From Philostratus' responses to his pupil,[5] to Lovelace's "To My Worthy Friend Mr. Peter Lilly," to Yeats's dialogue poem "Michael Robartes and the Dancer," to William Carlos Williams' "Portrait of a Lady," to Richard Howard's "Giovanni da Fiesole on the Sublime, or Fra Angelico's 'Last Judgment'" and James Merrill's extraordinary "The Charioteer of Delphi" (in some of which questions from the audience shape the ekphrastic response), works of art, like Csikszentmihalyi and Rochberg-Halton's sofa paintings, occasion conversation.

In the poems just mentioned, the poet projects the audience's response, but sometimes the listening subject may, in actuality, speak or have already spoken. In its low-level form, this is a variety of allusion, an extension of the point that ekphrasis in the museum age draws on, could be said to be in conversation with, other writers on the same picture. It is what Moore makes explicit in "Charity Overcoming Envy," with its conversational opening gambit and its quotations from an article on the tapestry:

Have you time for a story
    (depicted in tapestry)?
    Charity riding an elephant,
on a "mosaic of flowers," faces Envy,
the flowers "bunched together, not rooted."[6]

The conversation here is multi-layered: the speaker talks to an audience in a way that presumes a response ("Have you time for a story …?"); by repeating Wells's ekphrastic commentary, she responds to it; and by making his words available to the audience, she opens an avenue between the audience and him. Later in this poem, prosopopoeia adds another voice to the conversation when the figure of Envy also speaks. There develops a polyphony of voices. The history of ekphrasis and that of the modern and postmodern polyvocal poem are significantly intertwined. In Ashbery's "Self-Portrait in a Convex Mirror" (1975), quotations give us Vasari's voice (and later Sydney Freedberg's) directly and in the present tense, and then the speaker's, extrapolating from, responding to, their talk of Francesco Parmigianino's painting:

              Vasari says, "Francesco one day set himself
To take his own portrait, looking at himself for that purpose
In a convex mirror …
                    … he set himself
With great art to copy all that he saw in the glass,"
Chiefly his reflection, of which the portrait
Is the reflection once removed.[7]

The possibilities for exchange opened by works of art make all the more chilling the dark underside of conversational ekphrasis – when the audience/listener is clearly present and his/her response silenced. Browning's "My Last Duchess" (1842), of course, is the most striking example, with its authoritative duke using the power of his position and of words to interpret images to convey his expectations of his future wife's behavior that broach no objection. Heffernan takes Browning's Duke to be the "prototype of the modern museum director," with implications for the way curators seek to dominate images with words and, we might add, the way museums' authoritative statements can inhibit conversations along non-prescribed lines.[8] Focusing on the poet/speaker–image side of the representational triangle, his point is that the Duchess' image speaks nevertheless. Heffernan takes this poem as paradigmatic of the paragonal nature of ekphrasis in the museum.[9] (We'll return to the poet–picture dynamic in the next chapter.) Seen within a context of conversational ekphrasis, Browning's "My Last Duchess" dramatizes the importance of the listening subject, the emissary who delivers a message we will never hear. The effort to silence that audience suggests how readily s/he might talk back, or say the "wrong" thing in conversation with someone else. Yeats's "Michael Robartes and the Dancer" comically plays out the attempt of the authoritative guide to silence the auditor, demonstrating an acute modern awareness of the issue – and just how difficult it is to avoid a discussion. When readers of Auden's "Musée des Beaux Arts," like Irving Feldman, object to "Schoolmaster Auden,"[10] they are protesting their own silencing by the poem's tone, and rebelling against it by writing responses. The assumption is that there can be more than one way of understanding a work of art; that ekphrasis begins, or continues, a conversation with the listener(s); and that it is a violation to try to close it. Once the ekphrastic conversation is opened, Feldman and Yeats's dancer attest, it will be joined.

As the example of Feldman and many others on Auden and Brueghel suggests, in the most pronounced form of conversational ekphrasis, other poets listen and talk back in poems on the same work of art that respond to each other as they respond to the work. Names are named, the contours of the conversation are clear, we know who spoke when and said what to whom. At least fifteen poets responded to Auden responding to Brueghel. Perhaps the most formalized such conversation in the twentieth century took up Jean-François Millet's *The Man with the Hoe.* A platform statement of sorts for the nascent labor movement, Edwin Markham's 1899 poem "The Man with the Hoe," probably the most popular American ekphrasis of the twentieth century and maybe the most popular poem, roused such sentiment with its universalizing of the picture's downtrodden field hand as the exploited worker that a competition was devised by one of the exploiters, the Southern Pacific Railroad, for the best poem countering Markham's interpretation.[11] The purse of $750 was won by John Vance Cheney, for whom Millet's field hand represented nature's noble child.[12] Gertrude Stein later weighed in, insisting that Millet's man is after all, a painting, that the hoe is not a hoe but a picture of a hoe:

But I still know exactly how the picture of the Man with a Hoe looked. I know exactly how it looked although having now lived a great deal in the french country I see the farmers constantly hoeing with just that kind of a hoe ... But I still do know Millet's Man with a Hoe, because it was an oil painting. And my brother said it was a hell of a hoe but what it was was an oil painting. Millet's pictures did have something that made one say these things.[13]

Stein depicts the conversational network: she, Markham and her brother all talking about one of the most well-known images of the early twentieth century, with Stein turning the conversation to the issues of representation that concerned her and the circle of modernist painters she supported, and that ekphrasis so often raises.

Markham's poem was published in Randolph Hearst's *San Francisco Examiner*, initially distributed to tens of thousands of customers, and both poem and image were reproduced again and again throughout the century. Overnight, Markham, an Oakland school principal, became famous. Hearst made him literary editor of the *Examiner*. As the phenomenon of "The Man with a Hoe" suggests, in the age of museums and mechanical reproduction, ekphrasis opens the possibility of speaking to a broad audience. Markham's poem appealed not just because it tapped growing popular dissatisfaction with labor practices, but because the accompanying picture imaged the plight, as any newspaper picture can. Ekphrasis has been able to take advantage of the culture's increasing attention to images and their easy distribution. If ekphrasis in the museum seems to speak to those who visit art museums, Markham's poem reminds us that there is nothing inherent in ekphrasis itself that limits its appeal in an age when reproduced images reach all. And it reminds us that not all exhibits in which ekphrasis functions are in art museums. The newspaper itself is a kind of exhibitionary space, and there are other kinds of museums. One thinks of Emma Lazarus' poem, inscribed on a bronze plaque attached to the base of the Statue of Liberty.[14]

Markham's poem made an already controversial picture famous and few ekphrases have done that, but many poets across the century have written on images already present in the culture, thus joining conversations already underway, and contributing to the pictorial turn. One thinks again of the many poems on Brueghel's paintings (some also concerned with work); of those on the impressionists; of those on the *Mona Lisa* (including Edith Wharton's and Walter Pater's prose passage, which Yeats lineated and called the first modern poem), and of those on Van Gogh, to which I'll turn shortly. Even when the response of one poet to the other is not explicit or direct, we might read ekphrases on a single artist or work of art together as conversations among poets working out their relation to images of cultural or social significance, creating or helping to create a conversation with their audiences.

In all cases of poets responding to the same work of art we have a more pointed version of what is true to some extent for all ekphrasis – that it not only represents the work of art for an audience, but represents the work of art in response to another or other representations of the work of art, and so carries on at least three conversations – with the reader/hearer, with other writers and with the painter/painting. Ekphrasis here is part of a representational network, and representation is better seen as an exchange. The lines of exchange may be so frequently drawn as poets look and read and then look again and themselves write, and readers read and look, and read another poem and look again and read again, that the network may come to be better described as a representational field.

This chapter and the next explore two examples of ekphrasis participating in and resulting from conversation to suggest the dynamic and interactive nature of the ekphrastic situation. This chapter will take up the way ekphrasis figures in the work of the confessional poets of the 1960s, focusing in particular on how Van Gogh's well-known *The Starry Night* became for two of those poets, Anne Sexton and W. D. Snodgrass, a touchstone for their developing and differing attitudes toward the self-destruction that became one of confessionalism's distinguishing marks in the popular and critical imagination. Both wrote poems on the painting in conversation with each other.

The next chapter will turn from the relation between poet and audience to that between poet and artist by addressing a more radical form of ekphrastic conversation, collaboration. I take as my central text Leonard Baskin and Ted Hughes's collaborative production, *Cave Birds: An Alchemical Cave Drama*, whose narrative deals with the dichotomizing tendency in western culture. It is both about the word–image opposition and itself an exploration of ways to move beyond it.

Anne Sexton's "The Starry Night"

Written in May, 1960, published in *The Nation* (September 2, 1961), collected in her second volume *All My Pretty Ones* (1962), and much anthologized since, Anne Sexton's "The Starry Night" on Van Gogh's famous painting (Fig. 17) builds on the long tradition of ekphrases on death. Rejecting Auden's meditative distance, it records with startling directness and economy the sensational death wish that came to be associated with the confessional poets in the critical and popular imagination of the 1960s and 1970s.

Figure 17 Vincent Van Gogh (1853–1890). *The Starry Night* (1889). Oil on canvas, $29 \times 36\frac{1}{4}$ in (73.66×92.08 cm).

Beginning *in medias res* with no setting of the ekphrastic situation ("The town does not exist"), the poem's three short stanzas compress observation and interpretation to convey the urgency of the speaker's discovery.[15] Looking at this famous painting's night sky she finds an image of death as she wants it, sensuous and glorious: "This is how/ I want to die."[16] The common deictic "this" and "that" as the speaker gestures, pointing out features of the painting to her audience, and the repetition of the refrain closing the first two stanzas suggest the immediacy, the conventional presence, of the image, and the speaker's obsessive desire to be taken into it. Death is figured as both embodiment (she wishes to be consumed by the "great dragon" of the painting's nebula) and transcendence ("with no flag,/ no belly,/ no cry"). Death will be violent ("sucked," "split"), but painless ("no cry") and will leave no sign remaining ("no flag").[17] Like many of her late nineteenth-century predecessors in ekphrasis, Sexton conflates the image as present, embodied and female with the image as eternal and transcendent. Except in the wish to specify the manner of her death, there is no indication here of the methodical, mundane, matter-of-fact preparations for death so characteristic of the suicide, and which Sexton knew so well by this point in her life. In place of the messy ordinariness of self-destruction, we have the Romantic belief in the transcendence of the image married to a concatenation of genius, early death and suicide as a "dramatic gesture."[18] Untroubled here by the ethical questions that haunted Auden, Sexton renders death sensational and beautiful.

When Sexton wrote "The Starry Night," W. D. Snodgrass' *Heart's Needle* and Robert Lowell's *Life Studies* – the founding volumes of what M. L. Rosenthal first called in his review of *Life Studies* "confessional poetry" – had just been published (1959). So far, no one had died, but many had had nervous breakdowns and some had tried to commit suicide. The ekphrastic conversation between Sexton and Snodgrass anticipates the debates that evolved as poets and critics began to define confessionalism in relation to personal psychological extremity, so I'd like to recall briefly the early history and reception of that movement. Shortly before 1960, reacting against the elegantly formal poetry of the "tranquilized Fifties" (Lowell's phrase), the new generation were beginning to find ways of writing about their personal experiences in verse. "Why not say what really happened," Elizabeth Hardwick famously advised her husband as he struggled with what would become *Life Studies*.[19] "I hold back nothing," said Anne Sexton: alienation, failures of all kinds, operations, menstruation, madness and, of course, suicide became fit and frequent subjects.[20] What distinguished the new way of writing about the self from "the continuing power of the Romantic tradition," thought Rosenthal in 1967, was "the strongly confessional, literally self-exposing vulnerability characteristic of the [poetic] statement."[21] He identified the "one distinctly modern quality in literature" as "the centrifugal spin toward suicide."[22] "In modesty of death I join my father/ who dared so long agone leave me," said Berryman's Henry in the *Dream Songs*, charting the centrifugal spin from the private horror of the suicide of Berryman's father to Henry's exposed torment.[23] The "Extremists," A. Alvarez called them in *The Savage God* (1971), that widely read and influential book historicizing suicide and establishing the powerful popular association of literary genius and self-destruction, especially in the twentieth century. More recently Sexton has been marginalized to the extremes of the confessional circle, but in much critical opinion from the 1960s through the 1980s, she was understood to be at its center, "the reigning high-priestess of the confessional school."[24]

Risk, poetic and personal, attended the enterprise of confessional poetry, the critics agreed from early on. Alvarez most extensively and persuasively described what was "involved" for the confessional poet:

an artistic intelligence working at full pitch to produce not settled classical harmonies but the tentative, flowing, continually improvised balance of life itself. But because such a balance is always precarious, work of this kind entails a good deal of risk. And because the artist is committed to truths of his inner life often to the point of acute discomfort, it becomes riskier still.[25]

Robert Phillips commented a couple of years later:

For the poet who does not dabble in confession, but is committed to it, such psychological self-probings and public exposures have their risks. Sylvia Plath, Randall Jarrell, and John Berryman took their lives. It also cannot be accidental that all, or nearly all, the great confessional poets of the 1950s and 1960s have at one time or other suffered mental breakdowns . . . '*We poets in our youth begin in sadness;/ thereof in the end come despondency and madness,*' Lowell attributes to Delmore Schwartz.[26]

Madness fed creativity; rather than exorcizing ghosts, creative activity raised them and put them on display; suicide offered a way out for the psyche thus forced to live and relive its own horrors. Suicide for Sylvia Plath, says Alvarez, "was an attempt to get herself out of a desperate corner which her own poetry had boxed her into."[27] Suffering stimulated her imagination: "the worse things got and the more directly she wrote about them, the more fertile her imagination became."[28] Continuing to mine that source was personally intolerable; not doing so would close the creative gates. "The passion for destruction is also a creative passion," he quotes Michael Bakunin.[29] "We are using our skins for wallpaper and we cannot win," said Berryman.[30]

Despite Rosenthal's own discomfort with his term "confessional" and its vigorous rejection by many of the poets to whom it was applied, it stuck, as did the correlative link between creativity and self-destruction.[31] Some at the time protested the romanticizing of suicide, including Denise Levertov in her famous 1974 memorial essay on Anne Sexton, "Light Up the Cave": "we who are alive must make clear, as she could not, the distinction between creativity and self-destruction. The tendency to confuse the two has claimed too many victims . . . self-destructiveness is a handicap to the life of art, not the reverse."[32] But three years after its publication Alvarez's analysis was already too powerful, she recognized, the public too "greedy," the critics too "ghoulish" and "irresponsible."[33] Although Alvarez himself concluded that no art "is worth the terrible cost," he had, in Levertov's terms, perpetuated "the myth that confounds a love affair with death with a love affair with art."[34]

For Sexton and many others, that myth was culturally well established and vitally present in the popular figure of Vincent Van Gogh, the prototypical "mad genius" and "paradigm of the 'modern artist'" that Griselda Pollock documents in her 1980 analysis of the construction of Van Gogh's reputation.[35] Helping to lay the general cultural groundwork for Alvarez's and others' understanding of the confessional poets, art historians and popular commentators beginning soon after Van Gogh's death in 1890 had developed the link between Van Gogh's mental illness and artistic genius, sometimes positing a causal relation. Pollock observes,

All aspects of VG's life story and the stylistic features of the work culminating in VG's self-mutilation and suicide has [*sic*] provided material to be reworked into a complex but familiar image of the madness of the artist – "sensitive, tormented, yet incredibly brilliant" . . . The condition of art as akin to madness, as a socially disruptive force or a personally dangerous one is remade as *the* condition of the artist's creativity . . . So in the case of VG, unspecified illness becomes doubly secured as artistic madness. It is treated not only as a facet of his artistness but *a confirmation of it* . . . In some interpretations, this madness is presumed to be the cause of his creativity.[36]

In "The Starry Night," Sexton's image of death gains power from the familiarity of this understanding of Van Gogh and of the image itself, already present for her many readers, both literally in thousands of reproductions, and mentally as a common image of the day. This audience could readily take up their role in the ekphrastic triangle; they knew what the picture looked like.[37] By 1960, Van Gogh had been established for some thirty years as "*the* well-known and popular artist," and the growth of his popularity continued unabated. "No other Western European painter," Pollock comments, "is so universally familiar. More reproductions are sold of his work than any other artist of any country, school or period."[38] Subject of the best-selling novel by Irving Stone, *Lust for Life* (1935), and of the 1956 film based on it starring Kirk Douglas and released a few years before Sexton's poem, Van Gogh drew block-buster crowds to exhibitions around the world, including one in Tokyo in 1958.[39] His images hung in dentists' offices, living rooms and college dormitories. Of them, *The Starry Night*, in the Museum of Modern Art in New York, was the most "widely reproduced."[40] In 1970, when asked who her favorite painter was, Sexton self-consciously acknowledged that it had become a cliché to admire Van Gogh, answering, "I suppose Van Gogh, although that's sentimental to say."[41] In 1958 the growth of Van Gogh's reputation in English-speaking countries was fed by the publication in English of the three-volume *Complete Letters* (crowded with sketches, themselves imagetexts), which made absolutely clear what the previously published selections of letters had suggested: Van Gogh was a writer of power, as well as a painter.[42] The relationship between the letters and the paintings became central to art-historical inquiry; A. M. Hammacher's influential essay, "Van Gogh and the words" (1970) can be seen as anticipating, or perhaps helping to initiate, theoretical debates over the use of language and linguistic models in relation to images that in the 1980s prompted the "new" art history.[43] Hammacher's consideration of poets and novelists as significant contributors to the body of words about Van Gogh reminds us again that ekphrastic poetry belongs to art criticism and art history as well as to literature, and that poets and novelists have played a part in the production of artists' reputations. By the 1960s when Sexton and Snodgrass added their words, Rilke, Antonin Artaud and Henry Miller, in addition to Irving Stone, had already written on Van Gogh; René Char, Robert Fagles, Paul Durcan, Derek Mahon and others would follow.[44] Van Gogh's first real critic was the symbolist poet Albert Aurier who began his famous essay on "a terrible and maddened genius" in the *Mercure de France* (January, 1890) with an ecstatic pastiche of Baudelaire's *Rêve parisien*.[45]

That Van Gogh could write well helped draw the poets to him. In 1959 W. H. Auden reviewed the letters and two years later edited a selection of them, *Van Gogh: A Self-Portrait*. In 1960, Snodgrass "began studying" not only Van Gogh's paintings but "the great collection of his letters which was just then becoming available in English."[46] Sexton knew the biographical material and perhaps some of the letters: "This is how I want to die" is her rendition of Van Gogh's last words, reported in a letter from his brother Theo, translated in the *Complete Letters* as the more wistful "I wish I could pass away like this."[47] In their Dutch original (*Zóó heen kan gaan*), these words also close Snodgrass's "VAN GOGH: 'The Starry Night.' "[48]

For Sexton and Snodgrass, the self-reflexive nature of ekphrasis could be used to test the implications of the popular understanding of artistic genius: painting can mirror not only the emotional states of the poets who view them, but concepts and modes of creative practice. Sexton and Snodgrass test those modes in response to a Van Gogh painting, in response to ideas about Van Gogh in the culture, and in response to each other.

Although the drama of Sexton's poem depends on an impression that the speaker apprehends the image directly, her understanding of it is, in fact, well mediated, steeped not only in biography, but in museum culture. The poem's principle elements and some of its language derive from Meyer

Schapiro's 1950 *Vincent Van Gogh*, as does the connection between the painting and the passage from the letters Sexton uses as her epigraph.[49] As Pollock suggests, Schapiro's reading of Van Gogh is a more sophisticated version of the popular vision, and this is certainly true of his view of *The Starry Night* as "the exaltation of his desire for a mystical union and release."[50] Working on a model of the relation between art and personal life that would become commonplace among critics of confessional poetry, Schapiro explains that when, "after a period of crisis and religious hallucinations," Van Gogh "returns to this theme" of the starry night that he had painted before,

> the pressure of feeling, with its hidden tendencies and content, forces the bounds of the visible and determines the fantastic projections, the great coiling spiral nebula, the eleven magnified stars, and the incredible orange moon ... The whole owes its immediacy and power to the impulsive, torrential flow of brush-strokes, the release of feeling along great paths.[51]

Turbulent, personal emotion, the result of psychological crises that cannot be contained, bursts forth in an art that presses the limits. In Schapiro, Sexton also found the clearly attractive psychoanalytic interpretation of the moon as "a possible unconscious reminiscence of the apocalyptic theme [from Revelation 12] of the woman in pain of birth ... whose newborn child is threatened by the dragon":[52]

> Even the moon bulges in its orange irons
> to push children, like a god, from its eye.
> The old unseen serpent swallows up the stars.
> Oh starry starry night! This is how
> I want to die:

> into that rushing beast of the night,
> sucked up by that great dragon ...[53]

For Auden, Van Gogh mattered because of his "absolute self-honesty and nobility."[54] It was not that Van Gogh adhered to what Auden recognized was the nineteenth-century "myth of the Artist" ("He dresses and lives like a tramp, he expects to be supported by others, he works at his painting like a fiend, he goes mad") – like Levertov, Auden dismisses that – but that Van Gogh's self-awareness distinguishes him and makes him a useful predecessor: "He knows he is neurotic and difficult but he does not regard this as a sign of superiority, but as an illness."[55] For Auden, Van Gogh's humility in the face of his illness is what's instructive; for Sexton it is the supposition that he turned the drives of illness into art.[56]

Sexton's "The Starry Night" is a case in which the demands of writing on a painting sharpen the poet to her best work. "Brief, perfect," Rosenthal rightly called this poem.[57] Full of dramatic gestures – the ecstatic refrain, the dramatic use of line, the direct syntax and vivid images, and that final stanza, shorter by one line than the other two, the lines themselves becoming briefer, squeezing down into nothingness – the poem nevertheless manages to avoid the melodramatic. It keeps its audience at some distance, performing the speaker's encounter with the picture. But the dramatic deictic "this" suggests a keen awareness of audience and its reaction to the rush of her outpouring and the unambiguousness of her desire to die.

"The Starry Night" asserts the individual's power to make life and death, to will what is and what isn't. Individual power, regardless of the claims of others, is all. Ekphrasis provides the structure within which the power of language and the power of the image, and hence the power of their makers, can both be flexed and proved. The power that interests Sexton here is the ultimate power – to destroy and create. Indeed, those two are inextricable in Sexton's twin deployment of the image as conventionally still, silent and implicitly "dead" (the town) and its ekphrastic animation as "alive," birthing, swallowing, rushing, sucking (the sky). The poem depends on Sexton's interpretation of the painting's structural division between town and sky. Making explicit the selective vision necessarily characteristic of all ekphrasis, Sexton opens with one of the boldest exercises of verbal power in the history of ekphrasis: "The town does not exist."[58] In recklessly denying what so clearly occupies the lower third of the painting, she establishes herself and her words as in control. What she means by "The town does not exist" becomes apparent three lines later in what critics have noted is a contradiction of the opening statement, but which is more accurately a clarification: "The town is silent." Unlike Moore, Sexton finds no virtue in silence. Identifying silence and non-existence, she talks her way through Van Gogh's painting, affirming thereby her own vitality. That identification, of course, has personal, biographical force for Sexton: it was her therapist who first urged her to write as a way of stimulating and affirming the life she found suppressed in her existence as suburban wife and mother. For Sexton, Van Gogh's silent, inanimate town is associated with the dulling effects of conventional domesticity, and means little in comparison to the vibrant, animated sky with which she contrasts it. Though she famously takes up the domestic in other poems, here Sexton eradicates it in a gesture of self-liberation.

In this poem, the power to use language is the power to choose one kind of death (the sky) over another (the town). There is shock value here in violating the taboo against expressing the desire to die. Whether or not Alvarez is right about a link between artistic creativity and self-destruction, he is surely right that in the midst of the ubiquitous, senseless death of the twentieth century, the need to have the power to choose the time and method of one's own death becomes more comprehensible. In this light, suicide can become an affirming exercise of power. There is a long distance between expressing a desire to die in a particular way and making that death happen, but speaking the desire and naming the death place self-destruction in the field of possibilities.

Despite the poem's display of language's power to edit the image, the haunting vividness of the death wish here depends on the fact that it is manifest outside the speaking self, that it *is* an image. To be able to point to the manner of one's death gives it a solidity and a presence at odds with the modern sense of death as unpredictable, unspecifiable and disembodied. Death for us has no conventional shape or form; it does not come with sickle and hourglass; it is an event, and it is as much internal as external. To be able to *show* it to someone else, to objectify it, as the speaker here does, verifies it and makes it knowable. The power of this poem would be very different were death named only in words. As shocking as the directness of Sexton's wish is ("This is how/ I want to die"), the poem makes us feel the exhilaration of being able to *see*, not just say, the manner of one's death.

Indeed, seeing is a central motif of the poem's middle stanza. What Sexton sees in Van Gogh's sky is death as a vibrant, living thing, couched partly in terms of the power of vision. Van Gogh's sky, suggests Sexton, twins life and death, linking creativity and destruction. The moon, uncontainable, bulging in "irons," births the stars: it "push[es] children, like a god, from its eye."[59] The eye, then, is the source of creation. The nebula, fabulous and powerful as any biblical snake, "the old unseen serpent," immediately consumes the just-begotten stars. By whom the serpent might be "unseen" has been a matter of critical discussion. Surely not by us; we see it clearly in the picture, as does Sexton. It must be unseen by its victims, the stars, and that may be the point: unlike those stars whom death overcomes unawares, Sexton *sees* hers and can take its measure: "that rushing beast," "that great dragon."[60] It is satisfyingly big and primitive.

This is all to assume that the speaker of "The Starry Night" is the confessional "I" of most of the other poems in *All My Pretty Ones*, not exactly Anne Sexton, but a persona who speaks directly of facts and feelings closely associated with the poet. But the unacknowledged quotation from Van Gogh ("This is how/ I want to die") suggests that we might also read the poem as a continuation of the voice of the poem's epigraph:

That does not keep me from having a terrible need of – shall I say the word – religion. Then I go out at night to paint the stars. (Vincent Van Gogh in a letter to his brother). [61]

Spoken by Van Gogh, this is the kind of ekphrasis that envoices the artist, like Browning's "Fra Lippo Lippi" or Edward Hirsch's "Monet: Impressions."[62] In speaking as and through Van Gogh, Sexton creates a connection between them at once closer and more distant. On the one hand, the death wish is not hers, and the poem becomes an explanation of the sources of Van Gogh's suicide: he rejects the life of the town, declares its non-existence, and opts for the life-and-death intensity of the sky. His suicide is understood as a tragic act, closely bound up with his painting and his need of religion. On the other hand, when Sexton takes on the voice of Van Gogh she suggests one of the prime motives for ekphrasis in the twentieth century – the perception of commonality among artists marginalized by modern society, the desire to be with, perhaps for a while to *be*, a fellow artist whose life and work fall similarly outside the "normal" life of the town. There is also surely the thrill of stepping into the shoes of an artist whose life was so precarious and yet whose work emerged into world-wide fame and appreciation. That Sexton identified with Van Gogh is clear: six years later in May, 1966, she sent a reproduction of "a picture that Van Gogh painted in the nut house" (possibly *The Starry Night*)[63] to the young poet, psychiatric patient and would-be lover, Philip Legler, explaining, "It's lovely. It writhes. It makes me want to stand out there with him taking my sleeping pills. Or maybe delay them for an hour or two and converse with him or be silent with him, whichever he felt like."[64] Van Gogh also appears in Sexton's late poem "The Fury of Flowers and Worms," again as the victim of self-destruction, which, the speaker satirically fantasizes, might have been prevented if only someone had given him flowers: "If someone had brought them/ to van Gogh's room daily/ his ear would have stayed on."[65]

Like Yeats, whom she took as her model in this regard, Sexton carefully arranged the poems in her volumes. "It was our practice over the years," said her friend Maxine Kumin, "to sit quietly with each other on the occasion of the arranging of a book, sorting through groups of poems, trying out a variety of formats, voting on which poems to save and which to discard."[66] In *All My Pretty Ones*, "The Starry Night" comes sixth, four poems after the title poem, itself an ekphrasis. It immediately follows the sonnet "To a Friend whose Work Has Come to Triumph," which, playing off of Yeats's poem to Lady Gregory, "To a Friend whose Work has come to Nothing" (one of the series of poems written around

the controversy over Hugh Lane's pictures and the founding of the
Municipal Gallery), takes up the myth of Icarus and Daedalus whose
immediate source, speculates biographer Diane Middlebrook, "may have
been" Auden's "much-anthologized" "Musée des Beaux Arts."[67] In its
place in the book, "The Starry Night" is embedded in the common
conversation of literary allusion and response. In "To a Friend whose
Work ...," the Icarus figure as poet "Feel[s] the fire at his neck ...
glances up and is caught, wondrously tunneling/ into that hot eye. Who
cares that he fell back to the sea?/ See him acclaiming the sun and come
plunging down/ while his sensible daddy goes straight into town."[68] As a
view from Icarus' side, the poem responds with deliberate indifference to
Auden's concern for suffering: for Sexton, the "flawless moment over the
lawn/ of the labyrinth," the effortless feeling of flying with the birds, the
momentary sense of escape and freedom are well worth the risk and pain:
"Who cares that he fell back to the sea?"[69] He acclaims the sun as he falls.
Poetry is ample recompense for the self-destruction of the flight, the
poem tells us. "To a Friend" shares imagery with "The Starry Night" in
its depiction of the sky as "hot" and the sun/moon as an eye into which
or out of which the poet or stars are propelled. It also contains "The
Starry Night"'s ruling dichotomy between the town, with its "sensible"
daddies, and the heated, ungovernable, catastrophic creativity of the sky.

The friend to whom Sexton wrote was W. D. Snodgrass. His first book,
Heart's Needle, about the loss of his daughter through divorce, had
recently been published and would win the Pulitzer Prize a few months
later. Sexton sent her poem to him on February 1, 1960,[70] shortly before
The Hudson Review, which had regularly been accepting her own poems,
published William Carlos Williams' "Pictures from Brueghel" containing
his famous response to Brueghel's *Icarus*, immediately followed by four
poems by Snodgrass.[71] Snodgrass' experiments with highly personal
subject matter contained by formal structure had taught Lowell, who had
read them in manuscript and periodicals, how to proceed with *Life
Studies*. Though Snodgrass gets little credit in our accounts of literary
history, he "invented" confessional poetry, as Lowell claimed: "He did
these things before I did, though he's younger than I am and had been
my student."[72] In 1958, the year Sexton published her first tentative
effort as a poet, she had read Snodgrass' title poem "Heart's Needle" in
the influential anthology *New Poets of England and America*, and it
opened her sense of what she might do in a poem. "[I]t was De
Snodgrass," says Middlebrook, "who helped her find an authentic first-
person voice ... Snodgrass catalyzed in her ... the talent for making

poetry the vehicle of autobiography, of self-analysis."[73] Later that year, Sexton won a scholarship to the Antioch Writers' Conference to study with Snodgrass. They "hit it off at once," beginning a friendship that was to be important to them both for the next several years. In addition to reading her poems and offering advice (especially on "The Double Image," as the letters show), Snodgrass became her entrée into the heady world of the talented young poets then on the rise. Through him, she gained access to Robert Lowell's writing seminar at Boston University in September, 1958 where she met, among others, Sylvia Plath. From the end of August, 1958 through mid 1959, Sexton was writing to Snodgrass several times a month. By the time she was at work on "The Starry Night" in May of 1960, the correspondence was less frequent but still intense. "The life of poetry is saving me (I hope) as some things are as bad as I've ever known," she wrote that same month in a letter congratulating him on the Pulitzer and asking him to write a promotional blurb for *To Bedlam and Part Way Back*, which had just been published.[74]

In 1960, Snodgrass was already at work on a series of poems on pictures that would take him a number of years to complete. Sometime in 1957 or 1958, he had been offered a tempting commission by the glossy quarterly magazine, *Portfolio and ARTNews Annual*. Struggling with a painful dry spell following *Heart's Needle*, he decided to take it up to see what it might produce. As he explains in his retrospective essay "Poems About Paintings" (1975):

Some years ago, a prominent art magazine suggested that I should write a poem based on a painting or sculpture; they promised in return to pay me well, print my poem handsomely, and offer it to a large, distinguished audience. Noble aims those seemed to me. Being young and innocent, I scarcely imagined all three promises could be false. And by the time I had wakened to the bloody facts, I could only thank the editors for taking advantage of me; I had never been seduced to better purpose.[75]

The result was "MATISSE: 'The Red Studio,'" published in *ARTNews Annual* in 1960,[76] and four additional poems: "VUILLARD: 'The Mother and Sister of the Artist'"; "MANET: 'The Execution of the Emperor Maximilian'"; "MONET: 'Les Nympheas'"; and "VAN GOGH: 'The Starry Night.'" All five were collected together as a group in his second volume, *After Experience* (1968).[77]

In the process of generating the poems, Snodgrass immersed himself in the works: "I looked at hundreds of pictures, read dozens of books."[78] All except the Manet are in the Museum of Modern Art in New York, which he visited.[79] Planning a reading trip to Boston, he wrote to Sexton on January 26, 1961, displaying the depth of his researches and the intensity of his looking:

I'm working on a poem about Manet's painting of "The Execution of Emperor Maximilian" – there's a version of it in the Boston Museum and I want to go in there and see it on one of these jaunts. It's not the best version of it – that's in Mannheim, though (do you suppose I could get a lecture engagement in Mannheim?). If you're familiar with the painting, the difference is that in the Mannheim version, the wall he's being shot against has a bunch of thoroughly bored-looking peasants looking over it – where it's only plants in the Boston version.[80]

As in Auden's "Musée," the issue of spectatorship emerges as central in "MANET: 'The Execution of the Emperor Maximilian.'" For "VAN GOGH: 'The Starry Night,'" Snodgrass "began studying other Van Gogh paintings all across the country" in addition to reading the letters from which the poem quotes extensively.[81] His own titles bear the influence of his museum-going: they look remarkably like museum wall plaques. Like Sexton's Van Gogh poem, Snodgrass' is born of museum culture, which tells also in the quotations and in the poem's rhetorical structure: an observer/speaker points and explains to his companion/audience.

As early as 1958 Sexton and Snodgrass were in communication about this series of poems on pictures, which recurs occasionally in their correspondence. In September, 1958, Snodgrass sent his Matisse poem to Sexton: "I'm beginning to do a little writing again," he wrote, "Here's a recent one about a painting by Matisse."[82] Nine months later (June 23, 1959), he wrote to Sexton, "My own writing has been lousy ... I've been working on a Van Gogh poem which is giving me fits and NOTHING comes of it. Oh well."[83] There is no evidence that Snodgrass' mention of his own Van Gogh poem inspired Sexton to hers, completed some eleven months later (May, 1960), though she was at the time very much still under his influence. Sexton's poem appeared in *The Nation* in September, 1961 and was collected in *All My Pretty Ones* the following year. Snodgrass's poem, on the other hand, was years in the finishing. (He was, he frequently wrote her, "green" with envy at the flood of poems coming from her during these years.)[84] By the time "VAN GOGH: 'The Starry Night'" appeared in *After Experience* (1968), he and Sexton had grown apart. It is unclear exactly when Snodgrass first read Sexton's poem, but it is certainly a poem he came to know.[85]

Snodgrass's "VAN GOGH: 'The Starry Night' "

A more nuanced and less tightly focused reading of the painting than Sexton's, Snodgrass' "VAN GOGH: 'The Starry Night' " probes the limits of the life lived, and the work created, by the kind of artist Sexton projected in her poem to him and in her own "The Starry Night." The poem depends, like Sexton's, on the contrast between sky and town, and understands that contrast in similar terms – the "still" and "calm" versus the "shock and dazzle." But as if in direct contradiction of Sexton's opening line, Snodgrass begins with a declaration of the town's enduring existence:

> Only the little
>   town
> remains   beyond
>   all shock and dazzle
> only this little
>   still
>   stands calm.[86]

The poem takes off from the dual implications of "beyond": only the little town (in its pedestrian ordinariness) is unable to comprehend the shock and dazzle; or, only the town remains when the shock and dazzle have burned themselves out. For Snodgrass, all depends on how we understand the town. The reverberations of that Keatsian "still" allow Snodgrass to hold open simultaneously the possibilities that the town's still silence signifies both the stultifying routine of daily life, as in Sexton's poem, *and* its continually life-giving generative powers. The conventions of ekphrasis encourage the play of ambiguity here.

The autobiographical "I" of *Heart's Needle* and poems earlier in *After Experience* is little in evidence here. This is a polyvocal poem, involving at least two voices: that of a speaker observing the painting, pointing things out, authoritative, and that of Van Gogh, represented in italicized fragments of his letters dispersed throughout the poem.[87] In addition, the observer speaks in two styles: block-shaped verse paragraphs dedicated to the town with its geometrically regular "angled roofs" and "stepped gables," and visually broken stanzas in fragmented syntax dedicated to the scattered stars and sky.[88] There are two additional stanzas, each representing some stylistic middle ground, one on what's "Behind" the town (the mountains) and one on what's "Before" it (the tree).[89] Already Snodgrass's poem pays more careful attention to the complexities of Van Gogh's composition. The mode of the poem is conversational: voices alternating, voices breaking in on other voices.

Row on row, the gray frame cottages, sheds
And small barns of an old Dutch town. Brownish-red
Houses with stepped gables and with high stoops,
With white or yellow doors. Plane over plane,
The angled roofs, receding, old as memory ...

Overhead: suns; stars; blind
           tracers bursting; pustules;
      swamp mouths of old violence
                      Metaphysics
cannot hold   the dizzying heavens'
    shock   *chaos in a goblet*
      outspattering:
   eleven fixed stars; one sunburst
moon. Mid-sky, mid-spasm,
      the spiral galaxy
tumbling in trails of vapor like the high
    gods on Garganos[90]

If Sexton's poem both glories in the power of the word to eradicate the image, and depends on the image for its vivid effect, Snodgrass' works with neither extreme. The form of the poem itself could be said to constitute a conversation with Van Gogh's paintings, responding "in kind" to the different visual properties of the painting's town and sky, using the graphicality of the poem to create common ground between word and image. All five poems on pictures were born in literal conversation. "The Starry Night" and "The Red Studio" derived from discussion among Snodgrass and his two students in a short-lived adult education class, "Mother and Sister of the Artist" from a comment Josephine Herbst made to him about the painting and from the comments he sought from a child in the care of some friends.[91] All the pictures were topics in Snodgrass's exchanges with his analyst to such an extent that he later wondered whether the ideas in the poems were his or his psychiatrist's: "I may well have claimed insights here which would be more properly credited to Dr. Sanford Izner."[92]

    In 1960, when he was working on these poems, Snodgrass made "a wild guess": that the "next direction" in American poetry would be "exploring deeply" the "problems of moral limit, of relativism, of meaninglessness."[93]

Fifteen years later he commented, "On the whole, I think that the most vital poems of the last ten or fifteen years have borne out this prediction. I did not at all suspect, however, that the method they would use to investigate an ethical and psychological space would be the polyvoiced poem."[94] For Snodgrass, the social structure of ekphrasis encouraged the use of multiple perspectives as a means of opening out the subjectivity of the personal lyric to explore the "ethical and psychological space" of town and sky, the artist and society. The poem begins with the viewer–speaker and Van Gogh agreeing, like Sexton, about the stifling limitations of the town. The first section describes the rigidly geometrical town and the village chapel (of Van Gogh's home town where his father was a minister) at the painting's "still dead-center ... where there shines/ No light"; Van Gogh adds, "*There is something about Father/ narrow-minded, icy-cold, like iron.*"[95] The sky, by contrast, is the scene of violent creativity, "fusing/ destroying/ burning to be whole." "*L'Art/ pour L'Art ... L'Energie pour L'Energie,*" declares Van Gogh. The observer looks more closely as his attention turns back to the town: "the ordered lives," he concludes, are "Like climbers huddled to a rock ledge, pigs/ Snuffling their trough, rooting at their dam," confirming their precarious non-humanity, their pathetic clinging together.[96] But then as he looks more closely still at the "Lanes beneath the eaves-troughs and the dark/ Shrubs," he suddenly conceives them as a place where "a bird might sing,"[97] though there is no bird in the painting. That imaginative leap, so characteristic of ekphrasis, to what's *not* in the picture, allows him to define the limits of the painter's vision and hence of our own, both literally and metaphorically. The poem turns as the speaker turns to address a "you" who is both us, the speaker's companion, and Van Gogh:

Down those dark lanes you cannot see
A lantern moving or a shadow sway,
No dog howls, and your ear will never know
The footfall of some prowler, some lover's tread,
Some wanderer, long gone ...
                    who cannot return.[98]

Like Keats imagining the emptied town, the speaker here imagines what goes on behind "those windows you can never see":

   You always wonder who is waking there
Sitting up late over a pipe, sitting, holding
   Some pious, worn book between worn hands,
Who sits up late together talking, talking

The night away, planning the garden for
Next year ...
    Who may have gotten out of bed to calm
Their children fitfully sleeping, each
        In his own bed, one by one another ...
                            But nothing moves
In those dark streets which you can never see,
    No one is walking or will ever walk there
Now, and you will never know[99]

This is the poem's central revelation: that Van Gogh and those who take his vision as theirs will never know such scenes of hard-won warmth, of human satisfaction, of renewal, of domestic fecundity. Like Auden, Snodgrass recognizes Van Gogh's self-awareness and humility. Rather than making an all-out argument for the glories of the sky as Sexton had done, Snodgrass' Van Gogh anticipates the speaker's revelation with a poignant expression of what he has longed for and never had, and of his own attempts at domestic life:

> *Sometimes, just as waves break*
>   *on sullen, hopeless cliffs ...*
>   *I feel a storm of*
>   *desire to embrace something*

This is no neat call for a return of the artist to the satisfactions of biological productivity and domestic stability, for Snodgra ss immediately offers up Van Gogh's counter-argument:

>   *Painting*
>   *and much screwing are not*
>   *compatible, man ...*
>   *becomes ambitious as soon as he*
> *becomes impotent*[100]

The unambiguous, epigrammatic quality of these statements and the violent colloquialness of "screwing" suggest the effort to push back doubt and regret. It is worth noting that in both Sexton's and Snodgrass' poems, the impulse of ekphrasis toward narrative shows with particular clarity: they are writing on a landscape with no human figures, yet both have made human dramas out of what traces of human life are there – the roofs, the lighted windows, the painting itself.

Like Sexton, Snodgrass picks up Van Gogh's last words. They are the final words of his poem and he gives them in their original Dutch: *Zóó heen kan gaan.* The deictic "this," however, refers not to the sky as in Sexton's poem, but to the town.

Still, though, the little town, how peacefully
It lies under the watchful eyes of that
Fierce heaven ...

And still so calm
and still
so still

Zóó heen kan gaan.[101]

For Snodgrass, Van Gogh's manic, violent creativity forever shuts him off from communal, domestic life. In a note he translates Van Gogh's last words: " 'This is the way to go,' 'I'd like to die like this,' or 'I want to go home.' "[102]

It can't be claimed that Snodgrass has proleptically heeded Griselda Pollock's call to move beyond the biographical model that has so dominated Van Gogh criticism. He works well within it. But his poem raises the dangers of identifying creativity with madness and exposes the limitations of the lonely artist even as the myth of the mad genius was being written into the reception of confessional poetry. Snodgrass may not have foreseen the dangers of madness and early death in the path of confessional poets, but the Van Gogh poem indicates that he was at least taking stock of the image of the poet Sexton's poem projected onto him. By taking on the voices of both the observer of the painting who comes to recognize the painter's limitations and the painter who creates inside of them, he moves away from the authority of Sexton's "This is how/ I want to die" to something more exploratory, more qualified, less certain of the glories of Icarus "wondrously tunneling/ into that hot eye." If Van Gogh inspired Sexton to a powerfully unambiguous expression of feeling, he inspired Snodgrass to a probing exploration of what it might mean for the artist to understand himself as staking his life for art. Sexton's poem grabs hold of and plays out the stance of the outsider: no art can come from inside a regulated social order. Snodgrass' leaves open the possibility that the stability and order of "those dark streets," which Van Gogh will never know, may prove important, even necessary, to a life of art, and that the life of the poet may require resistance to the allure of spectacular death.

Ekphrasis and confessional poetry

The fact that Sexton and Snodgrass participated in an ekphrastic conversation with each other and with the cultural commentary on Van Gogh suggests a confessional poetry that is less the overheard expression of the isolated self than it has often seemed. The widespread use of ekphrasis among the confessional poets – Lowell, Berryman, Plath, as well as Sexton and Snodgrass – adds evidence for what critics have recently begun to argue: that confessional poetry was deeply engaged in the social, cultural and political life of cold-war America.[103] It also suggests that confessional poetry could be polyvocal and self-consciously performative.

Ekphrasis has been understood in Snodgrass's career as a way *out* of confessionalism and its attendant danger of solipsism,[104] and a similar narrative might be devised for Lowell, from *Life Studies* (1959) via the ekphrastic title poem of *For the Union Dead* (1964) to *History* (1973) with its many ekphrases. "By requiring some measure of personal detachment on the part of the poet," explained Paul Gaston, writing on a painting could provide for Snodgrass "considerable safety from both preciosity and psychological crisis."[105] But Sexton's and Plath's careers cannot be understood in those terms. Indeed, Plath's early ekphrases helped her gain access to her own experience,[106] and Sexton's ekphrases, including the Van Gogh poem, were similarly a means of her confessionalism. Rather than understanding the confessionals in terms of a progression out of extreme lyric subjectivity, which poets either did (Snodgrass, Lowell) or did not (Sexton, Plath) make, we might better think of the problems of lyric subjectivity as a central challenge of confessionalism that ekphrasis offered a way of addressing. The social structure of ekphrasis mitigated the danger of solipsism by requiring a response to an other, and by including an audience in the act of observation and interpretation.

For the confessionals, ekphrasis opened individual consciousness into history. Both Snodgrass' and Sexton's poems enter into history through Van Gogh's painting and carry historical material, most especially words from Van Gogh himself. If we take Sexton's poem to be spoken by the painter, it becomes an exercise in historical prosopopoeia. Ekphrasis offered Lowell not only contact with history, but, in the work of art's specificity and limitation, a method for dealing with "the choking superfluity of human event," as Helen Vendler points out in reference to "For the Union Dead."[107] It located and stabilized the past, if only briefly, and, in the physically present object, offered a purchase on the insubstantiality of the past that challenged Lowell's efforts to "live in history."[108]

For Lowell, as for Sexton and Snodgrass in the Van Gogh poems and for other confessional poets, the work of art located psychological and emotional states outside of the self in the image, mirroring them, at the same time that it required and structured a response to others.[109] Tapping the conventional self-reflexivity of ekphrasis, Plath, for example, in "Disquieting Muses" (1957) used de Chirico's 1916 painting to depict the first-person speaker's personal psychological drama of societal and maternal expectations.[110] At the same time, the image is something the speaker and her companion/mother look at, and, of course, the image is something to which Plath's poem itself constitutes a response. Like a number of Plath's ekphrases, this is staged as a conversation:

Mother, mother, what illbred aunt
Or what disfigured and unsightly
Cousin did you so unwisely keep
Unasked to my christening, that she
Sent these ladies in her stead[111]

In Lowell's *History*, the ekphrastic sonnets are similarly striking for their conversational gestures: "you," he addresses Sir Thomas Moore; "Composed, you will say, for our forever friendship," he comments about "Cranach's Man-Hunt."[112]

The polyvocality of ekphrasis, obvious in Snodgrass' poem, present in Sexton's, undermines the notion of an authentic self the confessionals "get to" (as in the usual account of Plath's career) and calls attention to their use of masks.[113] While Sexton's poem seems driven and direct, it nevertheless contains the voices of Meyer Schapiro and Van Gogh. The possibility that the speaker is Van Gogh complicates our ability to locate Sexton in the poem, and highlights the confessionals' use of the inherently performative nature of ekphrasis. As critics have increasingly recognized,[114] the self is often consciously performed in confessional poetry (as Plath's "Lady Lazarus" declares), with all of the deliberate artifice that implies. Ekphrasis offered not only the drama of the ekphrastic situation itself, but often the drama depicted in the painting that the poet could unfold, as the conventions of the genre encouraged. In Plath's "Conversation among the Ruins" (1956) on de Chirico's 1927 painting of the same name, for example, the figures in the painting, like those in the paintings Durcan saw in the National Gallery of Ireland, play out a personal drama. Plath here envoices the painting's seated woman who, with her back to us, addresses another figure, a man dressed in a suit, who faces her: "Through portico of my elegant house you stalk/ With your wild furies."[115] That situation clearly maps the larger context of the poem, and perhaps the ekphrastic situation itself: the "you" is also a companion/lover whom the speaker/poet addresses (and could the "portico" be that of a museum?). As Hedley notes, Plath enthusiastically studied art history at Smith, and took advantage of her Fulbright to visit museums.[116] Like other modern poets, including Sexton and Snodgrass, she was steeped in museum culture and in the words already in circulation about the paintings she admired.

Following *After Experience*, the multi-voiced conversational poem tested in ekphrasis became the path of Snodgrass's poetry, most dramatically in *The Führer Bunker* (1977) and in *The Death of Cock Robin* (1989) and *W. D.'s Midnight Carnival* (1988).[117] These last two resulted from collaborations he undertook with the painter DeLoss McGraw, indicating the continued importance of images that encouraged him into other kinds of conversations about them. The same was true for Sexton, who conceived *Transformations* (1971), her acid retellings of Grimms' fairy tales, as a book with illustrations, perhaps in satiric acknowledgment of the long tradition of the tales as illustrated for children. In its production, she collaborated with her friend, the artist Barbara Swan, sending poems and pictures back and forth, talking on the phone as they worked through the book.[118] These collaborations point to the variety of ways the confessionals sought to establish their relationships to images, and they introduce the question of direct exchange between poet and artist, the subject of the next chapter.

5 | Ekphrasis in collaboration: Ted Hughes's and Leonard Baskin's *Cave Birds: An Alchemical Cave Drama*

> Down those dark streets which you can never see
> Shines just this much of light . . .
>
> (W. D. Snodgrass, "VAN GOGH:
'The Starry Night,'" 1968)[1]

The "you" of Snodgrass's "VAN GOGH: 'The Starry Night'" illustrates a common move in ekphrasis: the direct address of the artist whose painting or sculpture is its subject. "You do what I can only name," says Frank O'Hara to Larry Rivers.[2] "You were more interested/ in her swinging baroque tits / and the space between her thighs / than the expression on her face," says Vicki Feaver to Roger Hilton.[3] "Give me your hand," says W. S. Graham to Peter Lanyon.[4] Defined by a long lyric tradition, such apostrophes carry no expectation that the artist will speak back. And yet, the gesture is important, for it points to a sense of ekphrasis as a potential conversation with the artist. Whether in envy, complaint, or supplication, poets often address the painters and sculptors on whose work they write. In a more general way, the object of ekphrasis can be said to function as the opening line in a conversation that the poets pursue with varying degrees of directness and with varying strategies. "Listen for its opening words," says James Merrill.[5] The understanding that the artist makes a statement is what Williams addresses when he opens "Haymaking": 'The living quality of / the man's mind / stands out // and its covert assertions / for art, art, art!'[6] Williams responds with his own assertions. That he does so in a number of poems written over the years, a group of which he conceived as a sequence, suggests the desire for an ongoing relation. For the reader, the structure of "Pictures from Brueghel" is both a walk through a gallery and a conversation among multiple participants in which the painting named in each title in the sequence speaks back to the poem that precedes it as well as forward to the poem that follows: poem answers painting answers poem, and so on through ten exchanges. Such sequences are not unusual: one thinks of Robert Fagles on Van Gogh (*I Vincent*, 1978); or Irving Feldman on George Segal (*All of Us Here*, 1986); or Kevin Young's remarkable

300-page engagement with the life, work and times of Jean-Michel Basquiet
(*To Repel Ghosts*, 2001). The give and take of these sequences is orchestrated
by the poet. Despite the "living quality" his work may convey, the artist
does not respond to the poet in any literal sense.

But this is not the case in ekphrasis that arises from collaboration where
poet and artist often converse both literally and through their art. The
conversational model that has dominated recent discussions of literary
collaboration applies to verbal–visual collaboration as well.[7] In thinking
about ekphrasis we rarely recognize that born of the collaboration between
poet and artist, although such collaborations are an important part of the
histories of both literature and art in the twentieth century. Snodgrass'
extensive collaboration with the artist DeLoss McGraw that resulted in two
volumes of poems and paintings, *W. D.'s Midnight Carnival* (1988) and
The Death of Cock Robin (1989), depended on frequent conversation.[8]
"Together with letters, poems, slides and the telephone we concocted some
thirty-three poems and seventy paintings," explained McGraw about *The
Death of Cock Robin*.[9] The collaboration was, he said, a "dialogue."[10] In
working on *Transformations* (1971), Sexton and Barbara Swan exchanged
poems and pictures by mail, and talked frequently on the phone.[11] Of his
collaboration with Frank O'Hara on twenty-six gouache and ink "poem-
paintings" (1960), Norman Bluhm explained, "Frank would write
something on a sheet of paper [tacked to the studio wall] while I was in
another part of the studio, making a gesture on the paper. It was all
instantaneous, like a conversation between friends."[12] Collaboration is, one
commentator recently remarked, "a gregarious form."[13] Like the poet–
audience side of the ekphrastic triangle, the poet/poem–artist/work of art
side can be literally dynamic and interactive.

Often associated with the avant-garde, collaborations between poets and
painters are, as Marjorie Perloff has observed, "largely a twentieth-century
phenomenon."[14] Many of the century's artistic movements spawned
verbal–visual collaboration: Dada, surrealism, futurism, vorticism.[15] For
American poets, collaboration flourished conspicuously in the free-flowing
associations among writers and artists of the Harlem Renaissance (James
Weldon Johnson and Aaron Douglas collaborating on *God's Trombones*,
for instance)[16] and of the "New York School" of the 1950s and 1960s (Frank
O'Hara and Larry Rivers working over the same lithographic stone for
Stones, or Barbara Guest collaborating with June Felter, Richard Tuttle and
Ann Dunne, for example). LANGUAGE poetry, with its interest in the
visual and the material, has generated many collaborations, such as the
delightful *Bed Hangings* by Susan Howe and Susan Bee (2001). Often, such

collaborations were understood by those involved to be transgressive, and on at least two counts: as protests (often with political force) against the "myth of solitary genius" on which art and literary markets are founded, and as crossings of a verbal–visual line of demarcation.[17] But, as the examples of Snodgrass and Sexton suggest, the appeal of collaboration has been widespread and much of it has been carried on without the provocative oppositional stance of the avant-garde. For some poets, collaboration has been a one-time experiment; for others, such as Robert Creeley and Ted Hughes, it was an abiding, necessary method of working.[18]

A range of relationships commonly falls under the designation "collaboration." Often initiated and facilitated by a third party (a publisher/ printer, usually, but sometimes a gallery or museum), "collaboration" can include illustrated poems or ekphrases that involve no direct contact between poet and artist; those in which contact is minimal; those, as with Snodgrass' and Sexton's, in which there is much exchange and poet and artist work off of each other, but not on the same page or spatial field; and those, as with O'Hara's projects with Rivers and Bluhm, in which poet and artist work on the same page, often simultaneously and face to face.[19] To allow for the range of working relations, I would like to steer a middle course here and use "collaboration" to designate an exchange between poet and artist in which there is some contact and discussion between the collaborators (whether it be face-to-face or not) and in which at least one of the partners creates in response to the other's work (whether it be on the same page or not). Projects in which words and images are paired as appropriate by a third party would not, then, fall under this definition, nor would projects in which there is no contact between the writer(s) and the artist(s), even though such projects are often billed as collaborations.

The verbal–visual collaborative work presents special problems and opportunities for thinking about ekphrasis. It is often not immediately apparent whether a particular collaboration falls under the rubric of "ekphrasis" (words on images) or "illustration" (images on words) or something else. This is especially true of such projects as Larry Rivers' and Frank O'Hara's *Stones* where words and images intertwine on the same page; but even in collaborations in which poet and artist do not work on the same page, as in Creeley's and Susan Rothenberg's *Parts* (1993), it is not easy to tell the difference between ekphrasis and illustration. Most often, a project such as this will be called "illustrated," even though, in this last case, it is, in fact, ekphrasis. The distinction is important if priority (who responds to whom) matters, as it has, to our conceptions of the verbal–visual dynamics.

On the face of it, ekphrasis and illustration involve opposite relationships between words and images. They have different histories and carry different values, by which we read them. It is precisely the point of many collaborations to overcome those histories, to erase the priority of word or image on which the categories of "ekphrasis" and "illustration" depend, and to become a third, hybrid category (perhaps "imagetext" or "poem-painting"). In speaking of his collaboration with Rivers, O'Hara expressed their desire to overcome the "old fashioned: our unintegrated style."[20]

Should we try, then, to unravel what the artist and poet have so often tried to knit? I think that the answer is sometimes "yes," for the exercise can tell us something about the range of ekphrastic production in the twentieth century, about its intersections with other forms of verbal–visual productions, and about the uses and limits of "ekphrasis" (and "illustration") as interpretive categories. It suggests, among other things, that ekphrasis and illustration are not as distinct as they might seem, and that they can merge in disconcerting and exciting ways. The effort to trace the process of a collaboration, to see who did what in response to whom, also allows us to see how ekphrasis can arise from the literal, dynamic interaction between poet and artist.

Collaboration brings to the fore another important issue that has threaded beneath the discussions in the previous three chapters: the role of a text's material features in ekphrastic representation. Because the artist in the collaboration uses the material features of the product – whether it be a canvas, a sheet of paper, a book or some other structure – as his or her primary expressive medium, those features matter in ways that might not call out as loudly in other instances of ekphrasis. Drawing on the European modernist tradition of the *livre d'artiste*, many verbal–visual collaborations have been initiated by and/or produced in collaboration with small and fine arts presses whose aim is to use to their fullest the expressive possibilities of the material aspects of the page or the book.[21] *Stones* was the first project of Tatyana Grosman's now legendary Universal Limited Art Editions. Gemini published Creeley's collaboration with John Altoon, *About Women*. Granary, Gehenna, Arion and Black Sparrow (in the USA alone) are a few of the many presses specializing in verbal–visual collaborations. Poets on their own have been no strangers in the twentieth century to small and fine presses. Seeking greater control over the expressive potential and political valences of the material text, such poets as Yeats, Pound, Stein, Williams, Moore and Langston Hughes published with small and fine presses, some regularly, as have many, perhaps most, poets of the second half of the century, often taking an active role in the production of their books. Descendants of the fine press printing movement initiated by

William Morris (Kelmscott), Elkin Matthews and John Lane (Bodley Head) and others in the late nineteenth century – such presses as Elizabeth Yeats's Cuala Press in Dublin, William Bird's Three Mountain Press in Paris and Thomas Mosher in Maine in the early part of the twentieth century, and Cummington, Alcestis, Arion and Granary in the latter – have provided poets a way of resisting commercial publishing and the normalizing it represents. As this suggests, the genealogy of modern ekphrasis, which we've thought of as passing from the epics of Homer to the lyrics of Keats and Rossetti and on, also runs through the fine press movement of the nineteenth and twentieth centuries.

As editorial and textual theorists have been suggesting to us for the past fifteen years, a text comes with a material body, or, to use Jerome McGann's terms, a bibliographic code (paper, type face, shape, size, color, layout, decorations, illustrations, arrangements of contents, as well as the methods and means of distribution), as well as a linguistic code.[22] Both are signifying systems, in constant dialogue with each other.[23] In thinking about ekphrasis, we have tended to rely on a concept of verbal representation that takes textuality as essentially transparent – a window on the word–image dynamic, on the poet contemplating the work of art. Ekphrases published by small and fine presses call attention to the signifying aspects of material presentation, but even when ekphrasis appears from a commercial press, questions about material representation arise: what happens when an ekphrastic poem appears with or without a reproduction of the work of art; with other ekphrastic poems (as in a collection of such poems) or among poems on other subjects (as ekphrasis most frequently occurs); in a periodical or newspaper, like "The Man with the Hoe," or the series of ekphrastic poems published by *Art News* in the 1950s surrounded by advertisements, notices of shows, articles on artists? Paul Durcan's *Crazy About Women*, a glossy, full-color exhibition catalogue, raises these issues, as do the ways Yeats's and Auden's, Sexton's and Snodgrass' poems usually appear: in volumes of poems without images.

I've chosen Ted Hughes's and Leonard Baskin's *Cave Birds: An Alchemical Cave Drama* (1978) as an example of ekphrasis in collaboration, because it raises the question of the relation between ekphrasis and illustration, and, like many collaborations, self-consciously reflects upon the process of its own making. *Cave Birds* occupies an important position in Hughes's canon, although it is rarely read with reference to the images that occur on every spread. From the 1970s on, Hughes frequently collaborated on volumes of poems with visual artists, including photographers Fay Godwin (*Remains of Elmet*, 1979) and Peter Keen (*River*, 1983) and, most especially, the American graphic artist and sculptor Leonard Baskin, with whom he worked on more than ten projects. *Cave Birds* is a strange, forbidding book. Created over a number of years during the 1970s, it belongs to the controversial phase of Hughes's career following Plath's suicide (1963) and the deaths of his lover Assia Wevill and their daughter Shura (1967), when the precise observations of nature that had given his early poems their defining vividness gave way to the large, archetypal narratives of guilt and death in the volumes of his middle period: *Crow* (1970), *Gaudete* (1977) and *Cave Birds*. In her description of *Crow*, which began in a drawing by Baskin, biographer and poet Elaine Feinstein suggests the desperate terms of these poems:

Under the influence of Baskin, and Central European poets such as János Pilinszky and Vasko Popa, who understood the brutality of experience under totalitarian regimes, Hughes grappled with a darkness that few English poets of the time felt any necessity to allow into their poetry. His vision is comparable only to Beckett's in its bleakness.[24]

In its fullest elaboration, *Cave Birds* is a series of narratively linked poems and black-and-white drawings that tells the tale of a guilty, suffering and foolish hero (sometimes cockerel, sometimes crow) who is judged, sentenced, sacrificed and reborn. The poems are complex and allusive, an interweaving of pre-Christian (especially Egyptian) mythology with alchemy, shamanism, Blake and Jung. Although the poems are hardly autobiographical, they clearly proceed from personal struggle understood in mythical (and sometimes comic) terms.

If reading ekphrasis and other verbal–visual texts is, as Mary Ann Caws suggests, "stressed," it is especially so in the case of Hughes.[25] While many critics speak, often eloquently, to the power of images for Hughes and the importance of the collaborations in his life, there is ambivalence about both, and a marked hesitation to take them as part of the work or to read the poems in relation to them. Some studies of *Cave Birds*, including one on vision in the volume, do not mention the images that face the poems on every page.[26] It may be that making one's way through the dense, cryptic poems, and explicating Hughes's complex mythology is work enough. But the paucity of discussion of the images also seems due to the uncertain status of images in the modern printed book for grown-ups, and the perception, important to thinking about ekphrasis, that "dependence" on an image may hamper literary reputation. Some of Hughes's defenders have felt the need to repudiate an impression that he needed "outside" inspiration. Charting Hughes's career in the wake of Plath's death, Leonard Scigaj, one of Hughes's best critics and one sympathetic to his collaborations, nevertheless voices explicitly a powerful undercurrent in the criticism: "It would be untrue . . . to suggest that Hughes needs commissions [from Baskin], or myth or folklore texts to generate creative ideas . . ."[27]

The fear that the ekphrastic poem cannot stand on its own clearly speaks to the enduring power of the "myth of solitary genius" and of new critical understandings of the lyric. Poets have felt the need to defend themselves, as Paul Durcan did: "Art is not a prison with poetry in one cell, picture-making in another cell."[28] Such prejudices are beginning to break up as multi-media work becomes increasingly commonplace, especially in the electronic environment, and collaboration more valued. In what follows I'd like to show how fruitful the conversation through and about words and images was in the generation of *Cave Birds*, and how significant the relation of words and images is to the work. For Hughes and Baskin, the play of word and image opened an arena in which contemporary social and sexual dynamics could be explored. On one level, *Cave Birds* is about what Hughes called in an essay on Eliot "the spiritual tragedy of his epoch," in which "that ascendant spirit of totalitarian, secular control – sceptical, scientific, steeled, flexible, rational, critical – displays its victim."[29] The remedy, as it was for Lawrence, is union with the "other," the physical, instinctive, bodily and, of course, female. These are the familiar terms of ekphrastic *paragone*. The narrative of *Cave Birds* may be read not only in the verbal–visual story, but in the interplay of word and image across the page of the book: word, the agent of rational, critical thought in Hughes' and Baskin's drama, literally confronts the image, the physical, instinctive and female. While ekphrastic *paragone* defines the terms of this book, the engagement of word and image is aimed precisely at working through paragonal fear and antagonism to union in mutual exchange. More moving, I think, than the mythic, dramatic narrative of the cockerel-victim recovering his relation to his neglected other, the give and take of word and image on the page and in the collaboration that produced it plays out the provisional remedy for modern spiritual malaise *Cave Birds* offers. It also calls into relief the attitudes toward gender that readers have found so troubling in Hughes's work, and opens them into the history of gendered discourse about the arts that has so informed the ekphrastic tradition, as we have seen.

Ekphrasis in collaboration

Three weeks after Sylvia Plath's suicide in January, 1963, Leonard Baskin, in an effort to drive Hughes "from despair into activity," proposed that his

friend write a poem on one of his crow drawings to be printed at Baskin's
Gehenna Press.[30] The result, some seven years in the making, was *Crow*
(1970), the volume that placed Hughes firmly on the map of modern
poetry. We may know *Crow* as Hughes's, but he understood it as springing
from Baskin. During those years he periodically reminded Baskin in letters,
"After all, it was your idea originally" and "Crow was your suggestion
remember."[31] The gestures here are part of the negotiation of their
friendship. Appealing to their joint work during a time when their intimacy
seems strained, Hughes engaged Baskin in some more crow drawings for
the book. At one point (March 2, 1968), after two years of silence between
them, Hughes wrote Baskin proposing *Crow* as a long collaborative project
involving several books that would spur them both on: "What if," he asked
Baskin, "we do a short book now of some of these pieces, then perhaps
another book and another. Then finally when the whole epic is complete
your drawings would be a tremendous series, and if I can go on and finish as
I've started my part will also be OK."[32] Ideas for collaboration encouraged
them both as they built on each other's visions of possibility. Baskin warmly
wrote on New Year's Day, 1969: "Gehenna will print the :Crow:, in a great
illustrated edition, with crows alive & Dead flittering through the pages like
the humans they mimic so well."[33]

The grand scheme Hughes imagined did not materialize, but Baskin's
drawing helped precipitate a major shift in Hughes's style, and inaugurated
more than ten collaborations that include several children's books, *Cave
Birds: An Alchemical Cave Drama* (1978), and *Capriccio* (1990).[34] Their last
project, *Howls and Whispers*, an illustrated edition of eleven poems on
Hughes's relationship with Plath not included in *Birthday Letters* (1998),
appeared in 1998, the year of Hughes's death. A Baskin crow appears on the
dust cover of the first English edition of *Crow* (1970) and the dust-cover
and title page of the first American edition (1971). A second English
edition, published in 1973 in a limited edition by Faber and Faber, contains
twelve drawings by Baskin.[35]

Hughes had used the resources of ekphrasis early in his career to explore
the endurance of the past in the present, and to exercise the discipline of
observation so fundamental to his early poems. "Here see a man's
photograph," he says, using the ekphrastic deictic, indicating an image
immediate and present.[36] "First observe," he directs the painter of a water
lily.[37] Looking holds out the promise of finding what will satisfy, though it
often disappoints. In "February," the speaker searches images of wolves in
illustrations, a photograph and engravings, but "none suffice."[38] Ekphrastic
stillness pervades these early experiments in the genre. The "long-necked

lily-flower" "can be still/ As a painting."[39] In "Six Young Men" (1957), the stillness of the frozen image that "holds ... well" these men who died in World War I develops into the more active and dynamic trope of the picture that animates the past and makes it present:

That man's not more alive whom you confront
And shake by the hand, see hale, hear speak loud,
Than any of these six celluloid smiles are,
Nor prehistoric or fabulous beast more dead.[40]

Ekphrasis here opens the past of his father's traumatic wartime experience, at the same time that the presence and endurance of the image become a synonym for the past's vivid life in his father's mental present. For Hughes, the power of the image's stillness derives not from its artifice, as in his poetic forefather Yeats, but from its resemblance to the eternal presence of nature: "Pictured here, their expressions listen yet,/ And still that valley has not changed its sound/ Though their faces are four decades under the ground."[41]

Hughes had met Baskin during the year he and Plath spent in Northampton, Massachusetts (1957–1958) where Baskin was a colleague of Plath at Smith College. Baskin had, as an undergraduate at Yale, in 1942 already founded the Gehenna Press, which was to become one of the most important fine presses of the century. At one point, *Cave Birds* was to be produced at Gehenna, which has, through the years, offered the opportunity for many poets – including Anthony Hecht, Stanley Kunitz and Sidney Kaplan – to collaborate with artists.[42] A sculptor, printmaker and graphic artist, Baskin is perhaps best known to a broad public for his bronze bas-relief "The Funeral Cortege" for the FDR Memorial in Washington, DC. Deemed by Rudolf Wittkower "probably the most gifted all-round artist of his generation in America,"[43] Baskin is variously credited with reviving the art of the woodcut and spurring a renaissance of activity in small presses.[44] Baskin's abiding interest in human and animal forms set him "in direct opposition to the fashionable abstract expressionism of the 1950s," a condition that led, according to his champions, to his being "ignored or misinterpreted by the more influential critics" and opinion-makers of the day.[45] In Baskin's drawings of birds – alert, predatory, intense with "their tessera-like single-minded devotion to their ways of death," as Baskin describes their "allure,"[46] Hughes clearly found images of his own dark and violent vision.

Their collaboration, driven by friendship and a shared vision, also contained moments of envy and competition. When Hughes received a set of crow drawings (probably for the 1973 Faber and Faber limited edition), he wrote Baskin, "The Crow drawings are stupendous – my poor text wilts," voicing the sexual/botanical fear, so common to ekphrasis, that the image will overpower.[47] On his side, Baskin angled for better terms in the negotiations with Viking over the US edition of *Cave Birds*. He wrote George Nicholson, "I would like $4000 advance :Cave Birds: regardless of what you pay Ted. In the U. S. the book will sell for the drawings, principly [*sic*]. As in :Season Songs:. That is not to deny Ted's greatness, merely asserting a fact."[48] The need for cash (again, a persistent motive in modern ekphrasis) threads through their collaborations. Hughes saw the Gehenna books as a source of income. In 1995, he wrote to Baskin, wondering "Any chance of any cash from Capriccios? You've paid me so far on *twenty* copies. It would be a big favor right now. I'm chasing around for money (like most people), tongue out."[49]

Cave Birds

In January, 1979 Viking published *Cave Birds: An Alchemical Cave Drama*, "poems by Ted Hughes and drawings by Leonard Baskin"[50] from plates produced for Faber and Faber's London release of the volume in 1978. Baskin's weird, fierce anthropomorphic birds (Fig. 18) loom on every spread, opposite Hughes's poems, filling the page, often threatening with their direct stares and blatant, if sometimes indeterminate, sexuality (Fig. 19). On first approach, it is not clear exactly what *Cave Birds* is. Shaped like a children's picture-book, though clearly nothing of the kind, it looks for all the world like an illustrated text and is talked of as such in the standard bibliography and by early commentators on the work.[51]

Cave Birds, however, involves not only illustration, but ekphrasis. Indeed, it is mostly ekphrasis. On December 8, 1973, Baskin wrote Hughes reiterating various possibilities they had discussed for a next book together: "Did I suggest that *we* do a bird book … It wd be incredible if you were to write an epic in the wondrous minutiae of: the heavans in hollow flowers: & if i cd make parrallel [sp?] drawings."[52] Sometime before July, 1974, Baskin, then living in Devon to be near Hughes, showed Hughes nine bird drawings, and the collaboration was underway, not with parallel drawings, but with Baskin's images prompting Hughes's poems and those prompting more drawings. Hughes wrote nine poems on those first drawings (Round A). Baskin then responded with ten more drawings and Hughes with ten more poems (Round B). Hughes then wrote another twelve poems to which Baskin did ten illustrations (Round C). *Cave Birds* was composed, then, in

Figure 18 Leonard Baskin, drawing facing "The summoner."

three stages, two of ekphrasis and a final one of illustration.[53] But the division of ekphrasis and illustration is not so clear-cut. From the start, Baskin's images, like many ekphrastic objects, came with titles, his own acts of ekphrasis, so that Hughes's poems are both responses to Baskin's images and to his suggestive words about the images. As critics have noted, such titles as *A Hercules-in-the-Underworld Bird* (associated with the poem "The summoner," Fig. 18) and *A Tumbled Socratic Cock* ("The accused," Fig. 20) may well have set the initial direction for Hughes's epic, anti-Socratic narrative. However, within Round A, letters between Baskin and Hughes suggest that this last drawing was done in response to a request from Hughes: on July 29, 1974, he wrote Baskin, "You remember the bird-drawings, Leonard? Could you do one – same size etc – of a foolish-noble type of bird, an aspiring phoenix angel-simpleton bird? Necessary for the cast. The others have become a little drama."[54] If Baskin responded to order, *A Tumbled Socratic Cock* comes closest to what Hughes describes,

Figure 19 Leonard Baskin, drawing facing "The plaintiff."

which suggests that the explicitly Socratic element may have been introduced at the end of this initial exchange, and that the nature of Hughes's hero developed out of his response to, but was not depicted in, the first set of drawings. Baskin's response to Hughes's request marks a development of the collaboration's comic element, evident in many of the initial drawings, especially *An Oven-Ready Pirhana Bird* (Fig. 21), that Hughes had written into the "little drama" as the embodiment of the modern legal system in "The judge." "The accused," then, seems to be an ekphrastic poem written on a made-to-purpose image, which itself is a species of illustration in response to Hughes's written description.

The interplay of title and poem that occurs in Round A also occurs in the ekphrastic exchange of Round B. The title *A Monkey-Eating Eagle* ("A riddle") may have suggested the imagery of the poem "The gatekeeper": "monkey chatter/ Blurting from every orifice . . . And an eagle/ Is flying// To drop you into a bog or carry you to eagles."[55] In addition, while Baskin's images of Round B are the objects of further ekphrases, they may also be viewed as a species of illustration, or at least a visual extension of the verbal

Figure 20 Leonard Baskin, drawing facing "The accused."

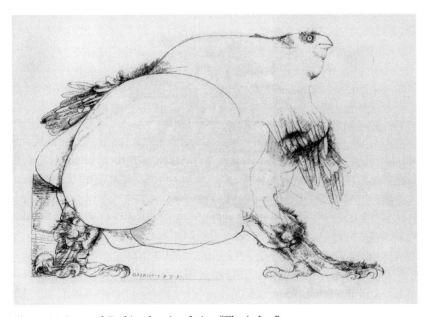

Figure 21 Leonard Baskin, drawing facing "The judge."

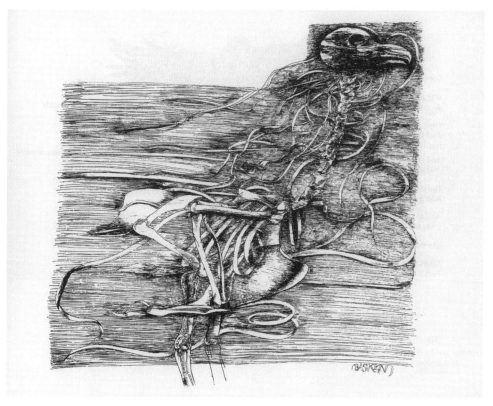

Figure 22 Leonard Baskin, drawing facing "The knight."

narrative that the poems of Round A set in motion. The picture of a crow's skeleton encircled by the remaining ribbons of (perhaps) tendons (Fig. 22, "The knight") responds to the narrative's demand for the death of the hero, whose resurrection has already been described in the picture and poem ("The risen") from the first round.

The poems of Round C fill in the narrative, mostly by expanding on the plight and reactions of the hero. They are rooted in both the verbal and visual texts already produced, poems that are ekphrastic as well as illustrated. "I came to loose bones/ On a heathery moor, and a roofless church"[56] takes off from traditional quest narratives as well as that set in motion in this book, and from the image of the skeleton–fossil from Round B, which would follow it in the final ordering of the book ("The knight"). The illustration, meanwhile, reinforces the classical heroic nature of the quest with the laurel branches circling the decaying bird's head, and, by depicting a partially decomposed body, adds a step in the narrative and visually prepares for the skeleton–fossil of the next spread.

Ekphrasis depends on "afterness," that condition of the word coming belatedly to the image that makes ekphrasis so fit for elegy and for explorations of history. But afterness, as *Cave Birds* suggests, is rarely, perhaps cannot be, absolute. Ekphrasis is *often* intertwined with illustration and often responds not only to the previous image but to previous words about the image, which may itself be an illustration of a previous text.

Along the way and subsequent to the collaboration, *Cave Birds* was offered to the public in various forms: a commissioned performance at the 1975 Ilkley Literature Festival where poems were read in front of the images projected on a screen; shortly after, a BBC radio broadcast on May 26, 1975 in which Hughes read thirty of the thirty-one poems with brief, explanatory comments connecting the narrative; a limited edition book of the ten images and ekphrastic poems from Round B produced by the Scolar Press for the Ilkley Festival;[57] and a trade edition of twenty-nine poems and twenty-eight images published by Faber and Faber in 1978 and Viking in 1979. Some of the poems appeared in subsequent editions of Hughes's selected poems, in which the images and claims for their importance gradually receded from the text.[58] The incarnations contain varying sets of the poems – some with images, some, as in the radio broadcast and selected poems, without – and, consequently, tell different stories that stand in different relation to the pictures.[59] The 1979 trade edition is the fullest elaboration of the collaboration and, for the purposes of thinking about ekphrasis, the richest and most suggestive.

Reading ekphrasis and illustration in *Cave Birds*

The *Cave Birds* collaboration contains two conversational exchanges: that of the collaboration itself as words responded to images that responded to words – the narrative itself being filled out and reworked through both poems and images – and that described by the order of words and images as they were finally arranged for publication. *Cave Birds: An Alchemical Cave Drama* (1978) contains twenty-eight of the poem–picture pairs produced in the course of collaboration, plus one unillustrated poem. The poem–picture pairs are arranged narratively, not in order of composition. The three compositional rounds are blended so that ekphrasis and illustration are intermixed throughout the volume.

Play of word and image across the page

To Hughes, Baskin's images seemed akin to the graphicality of written language.[60] In an important 1984 essay on Baskin, Hughes wrote that "his style springs from Hebrew script itself – all those Alephs, Bets, Lameds, Yods, crammed in a basketry of nerves, growing heads, tails, feelers, hair, mouths."[61] Hughes himself loved to draw and model (an interest he shared with Plath). In the 1960s, looking back over the origins of his poetics, he recalled his pleasure drawing as a child, remembering in particular his satisfaction when he copied animals from a book of "glossy photographs" his aunt had given him for his fourth birthday: "I can remember very vividly the excitement with which I used to sit staring at my drawings, and it is a similar thing I feel nowadays with poems."[62] Bearing witness to the way the graphic marks of language and of the visual arts flow in and out of each other for Hughes, some manuscript pages of his poems contain his drawings of animals, often fantastical, and he illustrated some of his own volumes of poems, occasionally intermixing word and image on the same page.

Such shared properties and easy intermingling of the arts perhaps held out the promise that the two might be joined into some other, third, form, neither one nor the other. Blake's imagetexts lie behind both Hughes's and Baskin's aesthetics. It can be argued that as in other modern volumes such as Anne Sexton's *Transformations* (illustrated by Barbara Swan) and Charles Simic's *Dime Story Alchemy* (on the work of Joseph Cornell), the transformation of word into image (illustration) and image into word (ekphrasis) in *Cave Birds* enacts the alchemy of the volume's subtitle, *An Alchemical Cave Drama*.[63] But in the final product, the poems are on the left, pictures on the right, spread after spread. The union that interests Baskin and Hughes in the end (and that the narrative itself charts) is not a seamless verbal–visual textuality, but sustained, engaged relation across difference.

Identifying the ekphrastic poems and reading them as such places them in a tradition whose conventions we can then see Hughes, like other ekphrastic poets, using and not using. Most of the poems proceed from initial description. Hughes plays on Baskin's birds, sometimes humorously interpreting them, as in the satiric characterization of Baskin's *An Oven-Ready Piranha Bird* as representative of western justice (Fig. 21):

The judge

The pondering body of the law teeters across
A web-glistening geometry.

Lolling, he receives and transmits
Cosmic equipoise.

The garbage-sack of everything that is not
The Absolute onto whose throne he lowers his buttocks.

Clowning, half-imbecile,
A Nero of the unalterable.[64]

Hughes employs a kind of ekphrastic imitation or mimicry as the couplets
teeter and loll, creating their own "cosmic equipoise" in each end-stopped
pair of lines, in comic echo of this grotesque bird's labored steps on the
wide-planted, gnarled legs on which Baskin has supported the immense
body. There seems fun, more than envy, in this imitation of the image. As
this passage suggests, the narrative impulse of ekphrasis operates less within
the single poem in *Cave Birds* than across the series as a whole: Hughes gives
the bird actions to perform, but it is the placement of this poem and image
in a sequence that makes clear what this judge does in the story. These
ekphrases, then, are related to ekphrases that play a part in a larger narrative
(as the description of Achilles' shield does in the *Iliad*); at the same time, as
lyric poems, they clearly participate in the tradition of the individual
ekphrastic poem we've been discussing.

Despite the volume's preoccupation with death, conventional ekphrastic
stillness features little here. There is not much sense that the images are still,
fixed and eternal while the words are moving and time-bound. For Baskin
and Hughes, both are dynamic, engaged in ongoing processes that are never
stilled, and in exchange with each other. So Baskin's skeleton–fossil
(Fig. 22), which should be the stillest of images, gives the impression of
great movement with its ribbons of tendons and entrails swirling around it,
and its background striated as though a strong wind blows or the skeleton
moves through the air. The poem's participles encourage the sense of
movement: "He is offering up his victory/ And unlacing his steel."[65]

In both the ekphrastic and illustrated poems, the relations among speaker,
image and audience are also dynamic. First-, second- and third-person voices
record the shifting relation, and distance, between reader, speaker,
protagonist and bird, playing out a drama of identification that implicates
all in the hero's trial, passage through death and rebirth. Sometimes, the
image is identified as the hero (as in "The knight") and described from a safe
distance in the third person. Sometimes the image is identified as one of the
agents of the court ("The summoner," "The interrogator," "The judge,"
"The executioner") or of the otherworld ("The baptist," "The gatekeeper"), a

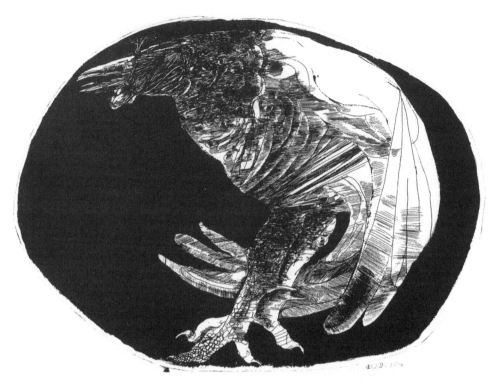

Figure 23 Leonard Baskin, drawing facing "A flayed crow in the hall of judgment."

"he" or "she" who often acts upon the "you," the guilty hero (and also, uncomfortably, us). Sometimes, in an act of prosopopoeia, the bird speaks directly to us in the first person, and we are inescapably "in" the narrative: "Why are you afraid?" "A green mother" demands, for example, and we are addressed as the flayed and guilty hero.[66] Sometimes the bird is the hero himself and speaks in direct self-expression: "A blot has knocked me down. It clogs me./ A globe of blot, a drop of unbeing" ("A flayed crow in the hall of judgment," Fig. 23).[67] The constantly shifting identification and distance among the terms suggests the psychological dance of the hero as he struggles to face his own guilt and death. For Hughes and Baskin, such variety also keeps the collaborative project fresh.

The poems and pictures of *Cave Birds* are, often wittily, interactive. In "After the first fright" from Round C, Baskin's comic riposte to Hughes's poem on moral evasion depicts a gruesome disembowelment as literal blank spaces in the body of a very lively looking bird. The ekphrastic poems are playfully aware of themselves as poems on images. "A blot has knocked me down," for example, describes the black oval in which Baskin's flayed crow is encased, interpreted in the poem as an egg

(Fig. 23). The crow asks, "Or am I under attention?" which, of course, he is – from us and from Hughes. Hughes puns on the image: the crow calls what is at the center of the oval/egg "This yoke of afterlife."[68] Light and darkness in the poems are deployed with their conventional associations of knowledge and ignorance, but refer, of course, also to the black and white of the drawings.

Some of the poems thematize looking, playing on the convention of sight as a way to knowledge. The necessary preparation for "revelation" is for the hero, as for other spiritual questers, a stripping bare of the self until, in Hughes's version, "Nothing remains of the warrior but his weapons//And his gaze." "His eyes darken bolder in their vigil" we're told, "As the chapel crumbles" ("The knight").[69] In "A flayed crow in the hall of judgment," "Darkness," the state in which sight cannot happen, is the condition of "nothingness," the opposite of revelation. There are none of the hesitations about the ethics of looking that we saw in Chapter 2, even when it is the searching stare of the predator. Looking here is associated with vigilance, with paying attention, and hence with living fully for both predator and prey. The compositional process of the poems themselves, of course, begins with looking: ekphrasis takes off from the knowledge attained by observation, and looking closely not only brings enlightenment, but relationship, the poems suggest.

Paragone *as narrative*

The purging and rebirth of the guilty hero of *Cave Birds* are set in the larger context of Hughes's critique of western man. The opening poem, "The scream," sets out the problem as manifested in the cockerel-hero who has led a life of complacent self-satisfaction:

Mountains lazed in their smoky camp.
Worms in the ground were doing a good job.

Flesh of bronze, stirred with a bronze thirst,
Like a newborn baby at the breast,
Slept in the sun's mercy.

And the inane weights of iron
That come suddenly crashing into people, out of nowhere,
Only made me feel brave and creaturely.

When I saw little rabbits with their heads crushed on roads
I knew I rode the wheel of the galaxy.[70]

Dissociation of sensibility under the pressure of western abstraction is for Hughes, as for Lawrence, the tragedy of modern man: the rational has suppressed the instinctual, the mind has gained ascendency over the body, human empathy has given way to the gratifying exercise of power. "The psychological stupidity, the ineptitude, of the rigidly rationalist outlook – it's a form of hubris, and we're paying the traditional price," Hughes said.[71] The hero of *Cave Birds* cracks under the strain of his own pride; he is brought up short at the end of the first poem, suddenly unable to talk, bereft of the language that had allowed him to rationalize and so evade "the inane weights of iron." He tries to speak, "But a silence wedged my gullet." He can voice only a primal cry: "The scream/ Vomited itself."[72]

As the first poem suggests, language, in Hughes's analysis, has been the instrument of the rationality that distances feeling and suppresses the physical life of the body. In the anti-Socratic argument, central not only to *Cave Birds* but to his larger poetic project, "idealistic attempts to isolate abstract conceptual principles" have historically worked by "identifying Good with God as Logos," as Graham Bradshaw has succinctly put it.[73] This is the familiar formulation, routinely accompanied through western history, as we know, with a valuation of the image as the word's challenging opposite.[74] The outline is worth reiterating here because of its importance to Hughes and Baskin. In the history of western discourse about the arts, the image as present, replete, silent and irrational is figured as opposite to the logical, symbolic and "civilizing" discipline of the word. "The history of culture," comments W. J. T. Mitchell, "is in part the story of a protracted struggle for dominance between pictorial and linguistic signs."[75] Fear of the power of the image (and what it might make man do) underlies the periodic episodes of iconoclasm that mark western history,[76] including, of course, the Reformation, origin for Hughes of modern dissociation. In their bodiliness, images make men desert rationality for base instinct. Blake, one of Hughes's main predecessors, voiced the familiar gendering: "Time [language] is a Man   Space [image] is a Woman," he said, echoing the common cultural notions that lie behind Gotthold Lessing's 1766 call in *Laocoön* for the arts to keep to their separate spheres.[77]

Baskin's and Hughes's narrative of modern man does not overturn the conventional terms of these dichotomies, but calls attention to and uses them. In *Cave Birds*, the terms in which the hero's problems are posed, and the insistent pairing of poems and images opposite each other, ask that we read the general relation of word and image in the context of this larger history of discourse about the arts: words, suggesting man's abstracting tendencies, are set in literal opposition to images insisting on the body. *Cave*

Birds participates in the common idea held by twentieth-century poets that images have an embodied presence that language lacks. In "The scream," Hughes's and Baskin's victim is all word with no image because he is the logical conclusion to centuries of rationalizing language misguidedly valued as the good and powerful. The reader turns the page, the trial begins, and there stands Baskin's summoner on the right (Fig. 18), a harsh corrective, "Spectral, gigantified,/ Protozoic, blood-eating" (as the poem on the left describes him), looking down on the reader, feathers stiffening into daggers, baroque talons menacing, demanding attention by his sheer physicality to the animal life the hero has criminally disregarded.[78] As the summoner calls the hero to account ("Sooner or later –/ The grip"),[79] the spread dramatizes the confrontation: image as body stands up to mind as word. There is no turning aside from Baskin's often sexually charged, physically confrontational images. They dominate most subsequent pairings of poem and image, commanding attention. Sometimes Baskin manipulates the angle of vision to position us at groin level, staring straight at the genitals of his human birds.

Some of the poem–picture pairs self-reflexively thematize the opposition of abstracting thought and physical body. When the protagonist gathers

Figure 24 Leonard Baskin, drawing facing "After the first fright."

himself in the third poem, "After the first fright," from Round C – "I sat up and took stock of my options./ I argued my way out of every thought anybody could think" – there is Baskin's answering illustration of the bird-body damaged by such rationalizing (Fig. 24).[80] The protagonist's linguistic evasions, full of the capitalized pieties Hughes and Baskin oppose, are met by the illustration's insistence on the literal cutting away of the body as their price.

When I said: "Civilisation,"
He began to chop off his fingers and mourn.
When I said: "Sanity and again Sanity and above all Sanity,"
He disembowelled himself with a cross-shaped cut.[81]

Later in the narrative in "The gatekeeper" when "remorse, promises, a monkey chatter" blurt "from every orifice" of the hero, the play of word and image emphasizes his attempt to talk his way out of death as a last-ditch effort to make rationalizing logos work against the physicality of life embodied in Baskin's double osprey, which fills the page, looking in two directions at once.[82]

The body as an active, insistent presence requiring recognition and acceptance is also figured in other aspects of the book's material features. Correspondence with the New York publishers shows that Baskin and Hughes were very much involved in the book's design. As early as 1976, Viking editor George Nicholson was writing Baskin, "[I] am very anxious to have your and Ted's ideas about format ... We want to honor the integrity of both your and Ted's work," and later Michael Loeb follows up, "George has asked me to reassure you that we will not proceed with production until we have your approval and blessing on the size and design."[83] From the start, *Cave Birds* is a suggestively physical book. There is little color: visually this is an earthy world of shades of brown and black, with the title (in the New York edition) in blood-red on the paper-bag-brown dust cover. The book is awkwardly rectangular, bound on the short end: it flops open in the hands, is difficult to hold, defies the usual physical balance of a modern open book and thereby calls attention to itself as an embodied text. Like a bird,[84] it flaps open, echoing the spread-winged raptor on the book's first page opposite the title. Like similarly constructed children's books, this may be a book for reading in the lap, increasing physical participation. The colors (deep cream paper, drawings and type in black ink, bound in a black cover with that brown and red dust jacket) and the matte, textured paper insist on earthiness.

The ritual of transformation is enacted both in the talismanic presence of visual images – recalling the invocation by images central to some rituals of Hughes's originary myths – and in the book's predictable, incantatory layout: poem on left, often in columns to fit on the page, picture on right.[85] With only a few exceptions, Baskin's birds either face the poem or stare straight at us, enforcing relationship, that central tenet of Hughes's mythology.

The volume contains references to its own status and characteristics as a book, most notably in the collaboration's finest poem, the ekphrastic "The knight," already mentioned above (Fig. 22). It details the protagonist's surrender to the earth :

The knight

Has conquered. He has surrendered everything.

Now he kneels. He is offering up his victory
And unlacing his steel.

In front of him are the common wild stones of the earth –

The first and last altar
Onto which he lowers his spoils.

And that is right.[86]

Here, in an elegiac and lyrical celebration of decomposition that identifies the cockerel's decaying body with the physical book, "The texts moulder," leaving only "his spine." "Here a bone, there a rag," recalls Yeats's "foul rag and bone shop of the heart," the origin of poetry, and also, as in Yeats's poem, the nineteenth-century shops that sold rags for the paper used in fine printing.[87]

Gender in Cave Birds

The narrative of *Cave Birds* climaxes in "Bride and groom lie hidden for three days" (Fig. 25) where the flayed and purified protagonist is reassembled in union with the neglected female in a ritual alchemical marriage. This is a product of Round C in which Baskin illustrated Hughes's poems. The poem charts a dance of mutual remaking as male and female create each other out of the world's refuse:

She gives him his eyes, she found them
Among some rubble, among some beetles

Figure 25 Leonard Baskin, drawing facing "Bride and groom lie hidden for three days."

He gives her her skin
He just seemed to pull it down out of the air
                        and lay it over her[88]

Male creation reciprocates female as "they bring each other to perfection,"
"gasping with joy, with cries of wonderment."[89] The poem's visual pattern
of urgently overlapping lines expresses the intertwining of their making,
repeated in the horizontal reach of the bird-man's outstretched leg across
the thigh of the bird-woman in Baskin's illustration, where their feathers
are nearly all stripped away, showing the human features beneath,
making explicit the volume's presiding anthropomorphism. Though
"superhuman" in its challenge, this three-day resurrection is accom-
plished by human hands, and it is consensual, mutual and earthy.[90]

   After fifty-five pages of poems and pictures, it is impossible not to read this
as also a description of the volume's collaboration, of the mutual bringing to
perfection of poet and artist, word and image constituting each other. Like
other collaborators (Frank O'Hara and Larry Rivers in *Stones*, for example)

and as in other poems already mentioned, Hughes and Baskin work self-reflexively. But Baskin's image makes evident the fact that the task he and Hughes set for themselves is formidable, and there are arguments to be made that the collaboration succeeds only partially. Elsewhere powerfully responsive to the written word,[91] Baskin, in Round C, produced some images that are, as Terry Gifford and Neil Roberts justly observe, "inferior."[92] (See also "His legs ran about" and "After there was nothing.") Ironically, the poem that celebrates the mutual creation of man and woman, word and image, inspired the least successful image in the volume. Functioning less as physical counter to the rationalizing word, the image tries here to embody their mutual constitution. Fascination with the hybrid, with the results of unions of difference, can easily shade into the grotesque, as it does here. Briefly, in 1984, Baskin and Hughes independently and simultaneously thought of going back to *Cave Birds* to rework it, to, in Hughes's words, "bring the weak makeshift pieces up to the quality of the 3 or 4 good ones."[93] The possibility generated a moving and eloquent meditation by Baskin on revisiting old work, but no further sustained efforts on *Cave Birds*.[94]

Part of the difficulty with the ultimate moment in the narrative involves the treatment of gender. Even a sympathetic feminist reader like Nathalie Anderson finds the terms of the mystic marriage unsatisfying. " 'Perfection,'" she notes of "Bride and groom," may "feel diminishing to a female reader": " 'she' characteristically *finds* the parts of his body ... while 'he' characteristically *devises* her parts."[95] Rarely in this volume does the main female character exist on her own: always she is understood as his victim, and the necessary component of his redemption. Apart from her desire to end the victimization, her need (does she, too, require reunion?) is never an issue.

The ekphrastic poems in *Cave Birds* in particular participate in the gendering of word and image in verbal–visual *paragone*. Exercising the license given ekphrasis to do what it will with the image, Hughes takes four of Baskin's most impressive raptors and genders them female: from Round A, "The interrogator" and "The plaintiff;" from Round B, "A green mother" and "A riddle." Probably working off Baskin's original title (*A Titled Vultress*), in "The interrogator" Hughes describes Baskin's vulture, solidly, implacably black on the page (Fig. 26), as carrying "a dripping bagful of evidence/ Under her humped robe."[96] The witty description of her body as "the sun's key-hole" carries a dark underside of voyeurism and of the threatening female that echoes back to "Crow's First Lesson": "And woman's vulva dropped over man's neck and tightened."[97] Hughes's vultress makes clear that there is "Small hope now for the stare-boned mule

Figure 26 Leonard Baskin, drawing facing "The interrogator."

of man/ Lumped on the badlands."[98] The force of those spondees conveys the inevitability of her intentions:

With her prehensile goad of interrogation
Her eye on the probe

Her olfactory x-ray
She ruffles the light that chills the startled eyeball.[99]

Adopting the conventional male gaze, the vultress uses sight (again the agent of knowledge) with scientific precision to locate and drag up the truth: "Investigation/ By grapnel."[100]

   In "The plaintiff," Hughes takes Baskin's ambiguously gendered owl (originally titled *A Hermaphroditic Ephesian Owl*) and turns it into the protagonist's suppressed female other come to claim her own (Fig. 19). He describes her oddly plush breast feathers:

Her feathers are leaves, the leaves tongues,
The mouths wounds, the tongues flames

The feet
Roots

Buried in your chest, a humbling weight
That will not let you breathe.

Your heart's winged flower
Come to supplant you.[101]

If Shelley's Medusa "turns the gazer's spirit into stone,"[102] this one asphyxiates. Both poems suggest powerful female figures, but unlike Rich's use of ekphrastic power, these emotionally turn more on the long ekphrastic tradition of fear of the threatening feminized image than on the liberation of women's voices.

In a thoughtful assessment of the "worrying" primitivism of *Cave Birds* and its "highly elaborate and 'intellectual ideology' of romantic retrospection," Graham Bradshaw usefully turns to the volume's two-line closing poem, "Finale": "At the end of the ritual/ up comes a goblin."[103]

The "Finale," itself a verbatim quotation from the *London Magazine* interview [with Hughes], reminds us that the problem confronts the poet as well as his protagonist; this suggests how Hughes has avoided or at least contained the danger of romantic retrospection and sophisticated primitivism, by recognizing it within his "alchemical cave drama." The protagonist is so evidently a modern man, sensitive to the strains and insufficiencies of contemporary life.[104]

While this goes some ways toward helping us understand Hughes's and Baskin's relationship to their own drama, the volume's gender dynamics continue to resist such containment within the narrative. The unpleasant thrill in the depictions of the threatening female and her lack of full agency are not recognized in the drama as a problem the protagonist (or the poet) faces.

Bradshaw's comments also return us to how the collaboration itself is featured in *Cave Birds* and point to a way of understanding the persistence of collaboration in Hughes's and Baskin's careers, and the particular relation of word to image in this volume. The repeated collaborations that have so marked both of their careers have the effect in one aspect of their lives of bringing their elaborate myth into the realm of practical activity. Collaboration grounds Hughes's great theme – the integration of damaged, rational man with the female principle, the recovery of empathy – in the real-world commitment to collaboration, a process that resists "romantic retrospection." Ideologically, collaboration suited their world view and was one means of living, in the day-to-day work on a project, the reintegration they thought necessary. This has less to do, I think, with any conscious collaborative program than a repeated response to the needs of the particular imaginations and temperaments that also gave rise to the myth originally.

Ekphrasis bred by collaboration speaks to changing conceptions of poetic production in the post-Romantic age. As artist Archie Rand said of working with Robert Creeley, "A collaborative medium goes so against the heroic isolated macho image of what an artist is in American culture."[105] If we take seriously the claims that generosity is a characteristic of collaboration, as David Herd suggests and Rand and Creeley affirm ("Now it is your turn, to continue," says Creeley),[106] then ekphrasis arising from collaboration may involve motives and feelings quite far from those that give rise to ekphrastic *paragone*. Collaboration allows for the possibility of shedding a macho kind of solitary creativity, and exercising generosity and humility, as it did for Hughes: "when the whole epic is complete your drawings would be a tremendous series, and if I can go on and finish as I've started my part will also be OK."[107] It also allows for a generosity that includes competition. Kenneth Koch describes his experience of collaboration: "You're competing with the person you are collaborating with and at the same time you are being inspired by that person and you're enjoying it and you are being appreciated."[108] Ekphrasis that arises from collaboration can define what poet John Yau describes in talking of Creeley, "the 'company' of friends and others with whom he shares mutual interests and concerns."[109] As it was in Baskin's and Hughes's collaboration, ekphrasis can be born of a need to find or create company, prompted by a utopian vision, and inevitably modified and complicated in practice.

As Catherine Paul has shown in her recent book *Poetry in the Museums of Modernism*, modernist poets responded to the great expansion of the museum age at the end of the nineteenth and beginning of the twentieth centuries by exploring "collecting, curating, exhibiting and visiting" as tropes for poetic composition and the assembly of poetic volumes.[1] For poets such as Williams, Moore, Stein and Pound the museum as model for the poetic volume linked lyric poetry to the broad cultural purposes of museums as definers and "preservers of the community's official cultural memory,"[2] which might be pursued with a revisionary agenda. Pound, for example, admitted to wishing he could provide "a 'portable substitute for the British Museum,'"[3] and developed what Paul calls his "exhibitionary method" as a way of displaying and illuminating by comparison the cultural artifacts he thought worthy.[4] The volume-as-art-museum suggested a way of extending the reach of the lyric: while it could honor the individuated poem – often set off, one poem to a page with plenty of space around it, like objects in a modern museum – it also offered a way to expand poetic scope by opening up the series. From the start of the century when museums began to reconceive their roles less as collectors than as presenters of objects to a public in need of education,[5] telling a coherent narrative through a series of objects (and words about them) has become the dominant mode of exhibitions. The movement from one object to the next helps construct the script whereby the objects are read. Juxtaposition and progression establish relationships and create narrative direction. While the art museum wrests artifacts from their places in daily life and displays them as isolated objects of contemplation, it also, as Philip Fisher contends, "orders objects systematically as part of a history, a world-view, a style or a biography. It converts objects into parts of a series."[6] The volume-as-museum marries the tradition of the poetic sequence to the cultural space and social and political functions of the modern art museum.

The volume-as-art-museum has its predecessors as far back as the Greeks – in Philostratus' *Imagines*, a series of instructive prose lessons on the works in his patron's art gallery – a line that comes up in poetry through Marino's *La Galeria* (1620), to the moderns mentioned and to William Carlos Williams' *Pictures from Brueghel and Other Poems* (1962), and such later volumes as Robert Lowell's *History* (1973). Most of these volumes contain ekphrases, and so implicitly raise the analogy to art museums; some, like *Imagines* and such modern descendants as Lawrence Ferlinghetti's *When I Look at Pictures* (1990), are exclusively ekphrastic, and, like the museum-commissioned volumes discussed in Chapter 1, explicitly conceive of textual space as museum space. Sometimes, the trope of the museum directs the arrangement of a series of ekphrastic poems within a volume – as in Williams' *Pictures from Brueghel and Other Poems* or Robert Fagles' *A Woman Unashamed and Other Poems* (1965) with its section "Poems on Art" pervaded by a consciousness of museums and the display of art. Sometimes, the trope works less explicitly, as in Robert Lowell's *History* (1973) with its frontispiece by Frank Parker (the subject and dedicatee of a number of the poems) and its sonnets (many ekphrastic) chronologically arranged according to subject as in an historical display.

In the history of ekphrasis, the museum's attention to the individuated work, set off "for contemplation or veneration in its own framed and labeled space," may have begotten, as James Heffernan argues, "the individual ekphrastic poem,"[7] completing the transformation of ekphrasis from description embedded in epic narrative to the free-standing poem we now know. Such a view neatly articulates with the focus on the isolated individual poem and its dynamics in recent studies of word–image relations in ekphrasis. But one of the implications of Paul's work for the study of ekphrasis is that we might well pay attention also to the model of the series offered by the museum. Whether in a volume that can be conceived in terms of a museum, or, as for most ekphrases, in volumes in which that trope is not at play, ekphrases work within a web of textual relations to other poems and their order. The poems of Baskin's and Hughes's *Cave Birds*, as we've seen, are part of an explicit narrative. In most volumes of, or containing, ekphrases, the relations between poems are less direct. In any case, those relations constitute an important aspect of the social dynamics of ekphrasis, complicating, conditioning, enlarging and defining the exchanges among poet, work of art and audience.

Throughout this book I've kept an eye on the larger texts to which the ekphrases discussed belong. I would like to conclude by focusing specifically on reading ekphrasis in a volume that mixes ekphrastic and non-ekphrastic poems. Many volumes could serve as illuminating case studies in how ekphrasis interacts with the other kinds of poems around it, and how it shapes and is shaped by the textual sequence to which it belongs – W. B. Yeats's *The Tower* (1928), Elizabeth Bishop's *North and South* (1946), Seamus Heaney's *North* (1975), for example. I've chosen Rita Dove's *Museum* (1983) – which contains, among other ekphrases, the extraordinary "Agosta the Winged Man and Rasha the Black Dove" – because it amplifies issues raised in Chapter 3 about feminist ekphrasis, opens race in relation to ekphrasis, and explicitly returns the discussion to where this book began, in the museum. A gathering of artifacts evoked in ekphrastic poems and poetic portraits, landscapes and genre scenes, Dove's volume clearly builds on the modernist poetic practices of collection and display that Paul charts. I want to indicate how the volume-as-museum offered Dove means to address in lyric poetry the issues of African American cultural heritage foregrounded by the Black Arts Movement of the 1960s and 1970s. Dove's museum joins the African American museums emerging from that movement as places where, as museum historian Fath Davis Ruffins observes, "alternative versions of the African American and African past can be debated and disseminated to a wider public."[8] The complex implications of Dove situating herself as a powerful black female viewer/curator revising an African American cultural program dominated by Afrocentric views are played out in the volume's central poem, "Agosta the Winged Man and Rasha the Black Dove." Its originating image, a 1929 painting by German modernist Christian Schad, is reproduced, at Dove's wish and with the artist's permission, on the cover (Fig. 28).

Museum and African American museums

In titling her volume *Museum* and joining the tradition of the volume-as-museum that stretches back to the Greeks, Dove directly engaged contemporary debates over African American heritage. Published in 1983, *Museum* comes at the end of a period from 1950 to 1980 that saw an astonishing growth of African American museums. Over ninety African American museums were founded in the USA and Canada during those thirty years, fueled by and contributing to the growing claims for cultural power and legitimacy arising from the Civil Rights and Black Power movements.[9] Many of the new museums "were founded by community activists who had worked in the Civil Rights movement at some level and now wanted to use that expertise for a cultural agenda."[10] As the Nation of Islam and other Black Power organizations drew ideas from African nationalists, Africa, viewed with ambivalence by most African Americans in the nineteenth century, came to be embraced as the origin of the distinctive qualities of African American culture, and a cultural legacy that could continue to feed African American art and life. Some of the new museums, like the National Museum of African Art, looked to explore and make visible the variety and complexity of that African heritage. Others, such as the Anacostia Museum, the National Center of Afro-American Artists (Boston) and the Minneapolis Afro-American History and Art Museum focused on collecting and preserving African American art, and the artifacts and stories of ordinary African Americans. By 1978, there were enough such museums to found the African American Museums Association.

Within a context in which "Afrocentricity has become the predominant ideology,"[11] Dove's *Museum* represents a revisionary voice, and a controversial and significant distancing from separatist and nationalist ideas of African American culture. It contributes to the body of the African American past the new museums had made visible, but refuses to be confined to it. Dove's response to the prescriptions of the Black Arts Movement is well known: while acknowledging the necessity for building "the base first . . . given the stereotypical ways in which the mainstream America looked at blacks," she wanted "more complexity": "don't fence me in," as she said in an interview.[12] Opening her museum with "The Hill Has Something to Say," a section of poems on the art, artifacts and classical monuments one might see on the European Grand Tour evoked by the volume's sightseeing motifs (a Greek pithos, the Citadel of Acrocorinthus, Nestor's bathtub, a tapestry in the Munich Hofbräuhaus, the painting by Christian Schad), Dove quietly but provocatively claims Europe as a legitimate part of an African American heritage. The section's title suggests an archeological voice that speaks through the excavated objects of the past. In its connotation of patient silence, it implies a buried life waiting and now wanting its turn to speak. That voice may be of African American culture silenced; and/or it may be the voice of Europe's relevance to African American culture suppressed in the drive to black pride and power. Next to the mainstream objects of western civilization, in the following three sections (or rooms) of her museum ("In the Bulrush," "My Father's Telescope," "Primer for a Nuclear Age"), she collects poems evoking, in addition to Europe, Israel, the African diaspora and, especially, objects of her own midwestern African American middle-class past (her father's telescope, grape sherbet, roses). Portraits of Champion Jack Dupree and Benjamin Banneker hang across from one of

Boccaccio, a scene of Acrocorinthus near one of a lawn in a medium-sized American town.

If ekphrasis was for Dove, as for other poets, a means of tapping an international culture, her use of it and of the volume-as-museum entered her into the debate about cosmopolitanism in African American culture ahead of its definition by Ross Posnock in 1998 in *Culture and Color*. As Malin Pereira argues, Dove belongs to what Posnock establishes as a tradition of the black public intellectual, not newly emerging in late century but beginning with DuBois. That tradition rejects "culture and politics conceived as private domains ruled by vested interests" and seeks "to develop a 'higher and broader and more varied human culture.'"[13] He calls DuBois's "effort" "cosmopolitan." "Though often misconstrued in our own time as a synonym for elitist privilege," Posnock contends, "the cosmopolitanism of modern black intellectuals presents a democratic challenge to the obdurate belief that high culture is a private citadel of white privilege."[14] Posnock begins his discussion with an example instructive for us: Zora Neale Hurston's 1950 "imaginary edifice," "The American Museum of Unnatural History," which displays in an "American Negro exhibit" two "typical" African Americans: one "seated on a stump picking away on his banjo and singing and laughing ... [t]he other ... a most amoral character before a share-cropper's shack mumbling about injustice."[15] Hurston's museum did not directly influence Dove's, but it suggests Dove's place in a line of effort to address the institutionalization of a limited, stereotypical African American role in American culture by focusing on the museum as the place where official history is displayed. Dove belongs in the company of the "literary artists" Posnock discusses who "devised ways to exit the 'American Museum of Unnatural History.'"[16] Dove exits by re-entering, recollecting, recurating. Her museum serves the democratic principles on which the first European museums were founded and which Posner understands underlie the efforts of black intellectuals in Du Bois's line.

The volume-as-museum became a way for Dove to expand significantly the idea of the cosmopolis to embrace midwestern African American culture as well as that of Africa, the Caribbean and the great cities of Europe, and to set those cultures in critical relation. Using juxtaposition, and the comparison and contrast it elicits, Dove's museum both recalculates the artifacts of European culture by setting them next to those of the African diaspora, and simultaneously claims value for African American artifacts by institutionalizing them in a museum. In poems such as "The Sailor in Africa" and the much anthologized "Parsley," the facts of racial oppression and of exploration and colonization (by, as Dove insists, both black and white Europeans) are brought into Dove's museum as telling artifacts themselves, reminders of the means by which so much of the "treasure" in early European museums got there. In taking a critical stance in relation to her European heritage, Dove participates directly in the work done by African American museums in raising to consciousness the criteria by which cultural artifacts are valued. Dove's museum might be seen as converging with the innovative exhibits curated in the 1980s by Susan Vogel at the Center for African Art, which raised awareness of the museum's methods of valuation and display by eschewing the "didactic" museum texts in favor of statements that are "personal, opinionated, and informal in tone."[17] In the show *Perspective: Angles on African Art* (1987), Vogel turned to non-curators (including James Baldwin) for display labels. The personal voice in both Dove's museum and Vogel's exhibits encourages awareness of the "drastic recontextualization" of objects in a museum,[18] and the inevitability and necessity of seeing those objects from inside a different subjectivity, time and place and, often, culture. Methods of display further the goal. What Vogel does to encourage viewers to see, really see, a Zande hunting net by displaying it on a platform bathed in light in a museum, Dove does for her father's grape sherbet by displaying it in her museum, labeled simply "Grape Sherbet." Duchamp's urinal surely echoes through both: in the curators' awareness of what the museum does to objects, in their desire to encourage their audiences to awareness, and in Dove's subtle irony (one can hardly imagine a memorial object less durable than sherbet). But unlike Duchamp, Dove and Vogel accept and use the powers of the institution to dignify the objects they display, and, most of all, to encourage close attention.

Mixing kinds of artifacts, drawing on high and low culture, Dove's is an eclectic museum: part art museum, part ethnographic museum, part natural history museum, part history museum. Its eclectic nature decenters her museum, keeps it from settling into established categories, and opens the possibility of admitting artifacts and narratives excluded from the mainstream modern museum. Dove consciously structured her museum to unsettle: "I'm trying to keep people from thinking that they know what's coming," she said in an interview.[19] Returning in some ways to the progenitor of the museum, the Renaissance curiosity cabinet, with its collections of assorted art, artifacts and "curiosities," Dove both reminds us of the historical moment when non-Europeans became the object of display in the wake of world exploration, and recaptures the possibilities for inclusiveness inherent in that moment but lost through the very idea of the "curiosity."[20] While not seeking to unwrite the history of the museum – her title embraces the modern public institution and her collection includes typical modern museum objects – she reanimates the openness to the variety and wonder that propelled the early collectors as, for example, when she sets on display a fantastic, magical image of her brother flying "over the house" on a summer night:

In the evening my brother
dips, a dark cross fluttering.
He hears the eaves
murmur; he watches the open

mouth of my father. Now
he smiles, sailing
over the roof, heading
straight for the blue cloud

of pine.[21]

Dove was highly conscious of the process of selection for her museum, and what selection does to the object or image:

There are some things which in fact are ideal museum objects – the fish in the stone, for instance, the fossil that we observe; but there are also people who become frozen or lifted out and set on a pedestal, a mental pedestal – like poems about Boccaccio's idealized love Fiammetta, who becomes an object of admiration. There's a whole section on my father; in a way that's the memory, childhood focusing on a father, what he seemed like to me then.[22]

Like the curators of many African American museums who collected and preserved the remnants of a local folk culture, Dove brings the ordinary objects of her childhood into the museum. But she knows the hazards of setting them on a pedestal, and the historical repercussions of an ethnographic impulse to display that kept whole peoples frozen as "others." The poems are full of concern with objectifying gazes. In *Museum*, this ethical-cultural impasse is negotiated by a lyric subjectivity that holds all the objects in a middle distance: ordinary objects are not elevated so high that they lose their connection to daily life, those already well-elevated are reseen as the domestic objects they once were. In "Nestor's Bathtub," for example, Nestor's bathtub becomes once more, for a moment, a bathtub. Colloquial speech ("But where was Nestor . . . ?"), familiar address to a sightseeing companion/reader ("But this heap of limestone/ blocks – look how they fell") and vivid attention to the object ("only the tub/ stands, tiny and voluptuous/ as a gravy dish") bring the tub from its perch as Classical Art into a viewing present in touch with the familiarly domestic.[23] Dove commented that she wanted both to "pay homage to important figures in history" and to see the "underside of history ... the side that no one sees when the lights are on." [24] In "Grape Sherbet," fond, ironic awareness of the rituals of the family cookout and the spare, tightly controlled lines help keep the titular object from becoming too remotely or sentimentally enshrined:

The day? Memorial.
After the grill
Dad appears with his masterpiece –
swirled snow, gelled light.
We cheer.[25]

While anticipating the new black aesthetic that Trey Ellis would announce some six years later in *Callaloo* (winter, 1989)[26] – born of the middle class and drawing on a mix of aesthetic influences, black and white, high and low culture – Dove's museum also recalls an earlier mixed, cosmopolitan cultural world evoked in Melvin Tolson's *Harlem Gallery* (1965), a volume that Dove has championed and whose place in the African American canon she has worked to recuperate.[27] In its implicit reference back to this and the other major influence, Hans Magnus Enzensberger's *Mausoleum* (1975), Dove's *Museum* creates, beyond the objects it collects and displays, a museum of its own muses. The first of a projected five-part epic of black experience in America, *Harlem Gallery, Book I: The Curator* appeared in 1965, the year before Tolson's death, in the midst of a burgeoning Black Arts Movement unsympathetic to his allusive portrait of a culturally various African America. As Dove wryly summarized the volume's reception, "Whereas many mainstream literati greeted it with enthusiasm, proclaiming it as the lyrical successor of *The Waste Land, The Bridge,* and *Paterson,* proponents of the rapidly solidifying Black Aesthetic – who had rejected 'white' literary standards – were less impressed." [28] In a passage Dove quotes, Tolson declared his working method, and a heritage that is also Dove's: "I, as a black poet, have absorbed the Great Ideas of the Great White World, and interpreted them in the melting-pot idiom of my people. My roots are in Africa, Europe, and America."[29] Centered on the comings and goings in and around the upscale Harlem Gallery, the volume "muses," as Dove observes, "on the predicament of being black and an artist in America"[30] by following the fortunes of three artists, all observed by "the curator" (the gallery owner), a mulatto of "Afroirishjewish" descent.[31] In a series of densely allusive poems organized according to the letters of the Greek alphabet, the curator offers vignettes of and commentary on the art and life around him:

The mecca Art is a babel city in the people's Shinar
      with a hundred gates
      and busybody roads
      that stretch beyond all dates,
   where sweating pilgrims fleshed in hallelujahs
      jostle like cars in a bumping race[32]

Dove's attraction to the multiple ways the "gallery" is put to poetic use in Tolson's work is evident in her explanation of the title:

Its primary meaning – the art gallery in Harlem which the Curator runs – is embellished by a host of secondary connotations: (1) the peanut gallery (cheaper balcony seats in a movie theater, where blacks were relegated in segregated establishments); (2) the art gallery as symbol, suggesting a reading of the poem as a series of portraits; and finally (3) the sense of gallery as a promenade where Tolson's characters can "exhibit" themselves.[33]

Less verbally extravagant than Tolson with his "golden, ostentatious lyricism,"[34] more tightly focused on her objects and the stories they reveal, less interested in a critique of an urban black community, and with no sense of being consigned to a peanut gallery, Dove in *Museum* nevertheless shares with Tolson the idea of the poetic series, an embrace of the cultural varieties of art, and a concept of the gallery as a central space in African American life where debates about the nature of African American culture are tested. Dove's museum, however, is specifically not the commercial art gallery, where the making and breaking of reputations happen in the scrappy, sometimes unscrupulous, exchange of money, status and power, where, in Tolson's gallery, the black bourgeoisie strut under the curator's satiric eye, "each ohing, ahing guest/ among the gobbler-breasted matrons and their spouses/ whose busheled taxes tax strange interludes of rest."[35] Dove is much more interested in a space where the legitimacy of black life and its artifacts can be institutionalized on a public, national and international scale, and be entered into the script of national life. Hers is a calm space for contemplation, not for bargaining, a space where objects have passed beyond Tolson's market-place with its "Cadillac Philistines"[36] and into history.

As a space for historical contemplation and education, Dove's museum shares more with Hans Magnus Enzensberger's *Mausoleum,* a series of poetic portraits of mathematicians, scientists, artists and, as Dove says, "other makers and shakers"[37] "who influenced history in some kind of way, often in a kind of ineffectual way or a negative way."[38] Published in 1975 and translated into English in 1976 (Dove read it in German), *Mausoleum* sat on Dove's desk as she wrote many of the poems of *Museum.* "After all," Dove remarked of its influence, "a museum is a mausoleum too."[39] Enzensberger helped give her entry to the idea discussed in Chapter 2 of the museum as memorial, as a place where the dead reside and where the living meet them and recall them into the present. Like Enzensberger's *Mausoleum,* Dove's *Museum* is a liminal space in which the living and the dead constitute each other. As Dove observed, Enzensberger's "subject matter is quite different and he writes in very long lines, while the poems in *Museum* are very skinny."[40] Enzensberger's chronological organization constructs his display of the past as a time-line with the viewer/reader following along in sequence. Dove's museum works only loosely on a chronological basis (beginning with the fossilized "Fish in the Stone" and ending in the Nuclear Age) with clusters of objects instead pressing readers/viewers into the active constructive role of discovering associations beyond chronology, of comparing and contrasting, of tracing the linguistic echoes for connection. But in both, a sense of vital, active exchange with the past animates the mausoleum and makes it a living space of discovery and memory. Both use direct address to the dead, rendering them immediate and present, sometimes familiar. "Do you remember," Enzensberger asks Mikhail Bakunin. "Always the same. Of course, you were a nuisance./ No wonder! And you're still one today. Understand?"[41] With the same linguistic gesture of understanding, more meditative in tone, slightly more distant, Dove addresses Catherine of Alexandria: "Deprived of learning and/ the chance to travel,/ no wonder sainthood/ came as a voice// in your bed."[42] Both weave in the words of the dead (Champion Jack Dupree, Dove's father, Bob Marley, Boris Karloff, Sir Henry Stanley, Chopin, Sir Marc Brunel), bringing their voices into the present. Using prosopopoeia, both project themselves into the dead. "I've watched them, mother, and I know/ the signs," says Fiammetta, speaking of the plague in Dove's *Museum.*[43] When the dead speak, their world flows into the space of the museum.

African American ekphrasis

Neither Enzensberger nor Tolson constructs his museum via ekphrasis, though both occasionally describe pictures (Enzensberger, Piranesi's engravings; Tolson, his artist John Taggart's painting *Black Bourgeoisie*).

Dove brings the possibilities offered by ekphrasis to the possibilities of the volume-as-museum these predecessors quickened in her imagination. If Anglo-American ekphrasis looks at first especially male, it also looks especially white. Born of education and access to culture, encouraged by the growth of museums, ekphrasis would appear to be a European-American middle- and upper-class activity. Few poets of color appear in discussions of the genre. But ekphrasis proves to have a healthy tradition in African American poetry, from Phillis Wheatley, "progenitor of the black literary tradition,"[44] through Gwendolyn Brooks, Robert Hayden, Yusef Komunyakaa, June Jordan, Kevin Young, Ntozake Shange, Maya Angelou, Elizabeth Alexander, Rita Dove and many others. As a genre and a cultural space that had been understood as predominantly European, ekphrasis was from the start for African American writers automatically charged with racial politics. In addition to the many other expressive purposes it served, ekphrasis opened an arena of cultural tensions and became one means of engaging them.

For Wheatley, for example, in "Niobe in Distress for Her Children Slain by Apollo," based on Ovid and a painting by the British landscapist Richard Wilson, ekphrasis provided an opportunity to demonstrate her cultural credentials to a largely white and skeptical audience. While Wheatley's poetic strategy has often been held up by critics as evidence of her co-option by the dominant culture, her ability to use the artifacts of that culture to express one of the horrors of slave life through the story of Niobe whose children are all taken from her suggests a remarkable turning of the genre to her own purposes.[45]

Remarkable, too, is the assertion of an active black creator and consumer of culture, which Wheatley's ekphrases constitute. Responding to a mainstream art world ruled almost exclusively by white males and slow to react to social change, claiming cultural power has been one of the most powerful motivations of African American ekphrasis up through the twentieth century, even, or especially, in the work of those who would reject Europe to claim an alternative black cultural heritage.[46] So Gwendolyn Brooks, her consciousness raised to new possibilities by the spring 1967 Second Black Writers' Conference that fired up the Black Arts Movement, spoke in August of that year at the dedication of the Chicago Picasso in the Civic Center Plaza, demonstrating in her poem on the sculpture her authority to interpret and question the status accorded the very "Art" (her word) the occasion meant to praise:

Observe the tall cold of a Flower
which is as innocent and as guilty,

as meaningful and as meaningless as any
other flower in the western field.
                  ("The Chicago Picasso," 1968)[47]

Part of Brooks's aim in this poem was to urge those uncomfortable before
art to extend themselves, to approach the Chicago Picasso as though it
were a flower.[48] Expanding the African American audience for art and
asserting the active participation by African Americans in the definition of
American culture became founding missions of the new African American
museums, whose directors "felt that museums could be instruments of
empowerment for the Black community."[49] Supported by a growing
movement, the rights Brooks claims for a knowledgeable black (and
female) critical consciousness open out in the ekphrastic poems of
succeeding generations, laying part of the foundation for Dove, for
example, to declare quite comfortably of the ruins of Nestor's palace in
the Peloponnese, "As usual, legend got it all/ wrong."[50]

   African American ekphrasis is also charged by the need to make present
in the cultural arena images of and by black people. As African American
museums displayed artifacts of black life in a program of cultural
preservation and pride, ekphrasis could help make visible what the
dynamics of slavery had sought to make invisible. If blackness was the
visible marker of otherness under slavery and a way for that "other" to be
identified, it was also a marker of what needn't be looked at. As black was
being declared beautiful, June Jordan's first volume *Who Look at Me* (1969)
undertook the recovery of dignity via the image in a series of ekphrastic and
illustrated poems accompanied by twenty-seven reproductions of works of
art by and of African Americans. This volume builds on the strategy
pioneered in the 1920s by such publications as the *Survey Graphic*, *Fire!* and
the many verbal–visual collaborations of the Harlem Renaissance to use
words and images together in order to overturn stereotypes and represent
African Americans as various and heterogeneous that they might be seen,
recognized and known as such.[51] June Jordan explained her volume:

We do not see those we do not know. Love and all varieties of happy concern
depend on the discovery of one's self in another. The question of every desiring
heart is, thus, WHO LOOK AT ME? In a nation suffering fierce hatred, the
question – race to race, man to man, and child to child – remains: WHO LOOK
AT ME? *We answer with our lives.* Let the human eye begin unlimited embrace of
human life.[52]

If in ekphrasis the image functions as other, it also, as Jordan suggests,
functions as mirror of the self. Ekphrasis can be brought to the aid of

self-definition and racial pride, a use that runs through the African American ekphrastic tradition and surfaces explicitly in such poems as Brooks's "The Wall," read two weeks after the "The Chicago Picasso," at another dedication: that of a mural on a Chicago South Side tenement building, "On Forty-third and Langley," depicting African Americans of accomplishment, including Du Bois, Rap Brown, Baldwin, Wilt Chamberlain and Brooks herself. Brooks's poem emphasizes the viewers – "hundreds of faces, red-brown, brown, black, ivory ... ready," she says, "to rile the high-flung ground"[53] – making images of them and calling into relief a mutually supporting ekphrastic exchange among poet, painter, viewer and reader.

Brooks's poem names the artists who painted the mural, using ekphrasis to address the need to recognize black artists, and to begin to correct the standard history of American art that had written an immense body of work out of existence. Ekphrasis offered African American poets a way to identify artists and, via description and praise, bring them to view and claim their importance. In the age of photographic reproduction, images of the originating works could accompany ekphrasis, as in Jordan's *Who Look at Me*, Maya Angelou's *Now Sheba Sings the Song* with "art by Tom Feelings" (1987), Ntozake Shange's *Ridin' the Moon in Texas* (1987), a "verbal dialogue"[54] with a variety of artists, and her collaborative project *from okra to greens* (1984) with Wopo Holup.

As both the poems and the number of verbal–visual collaborative projects suggest, African American ekphrasis displays remarkably little anxiety about word and image relations. From the beginning, the conception of the ekphrastic endeavor as a mutually helping hand runs especially deep in African American ekphrasis. Phillis Wheatley writing in 1773 "To S.M., a young *African* Painter, on seeing his Works" allied her poetic efforts in mutual support with those of Scipio Moorhead: "Still may the painter's and the poet's fire/ To aid thy pencil, and thy verse conspire!"[55] The strain runs right up through Kevin Young's book-long conversation with and about Jean-Michel Basquiet, *To Repel Ghosts* (2001), whose length and range of references make claims for the life and times and work of this 1980s art-world phenomenon whose paintings so often included and paid homage to words.

As Jordan's book suggests, African American ekphrasis is often charged by an acute consciousness of spectatorship and display. The other side of seeing and knowing is objectification. The dynamic of viewer and viewed inherent in the genre provides a means of drawing into lyric expression the historical and personal experience of blackness as a visible sign of difference, and its exhibition on the slave-auction platform, in the freak shows and other exhibitions of curiosities discovered by European expansion, and on the streets of modern European and American towns and cities. Ekphrasis has been an especially powerful tool to address the position of black women, the doubly looked-at. So Elizabeth Alexander uses ekphrasis in a black feminist protest to envoice the Venus Hottentot, the famous nineteenth-century African woman turned into a European traveling show recorded in the engraving "The Ball of Duchess DuBarry" (Fig. 27):[56]

In the engraving I lurch
toward the *belles dames*, mad-eyed, and
they swoon. Men in capes and pince-nez
shield them. Tassels dance at my hips.[57]

While language here reclaims the humanity taken away by the objectifying gaze recorded in the image, in Angelou's *Now Sheba Sings the Song*, Tom Feelings' drawings of black women, expressing as he said a "strength and beauty, so undervalued in the world,"[58] work with the ekphrases envoicing them to claim pride in the women's power to turn men's heads and, indeed, order the world:

My impertinent buttocks
(High, redolent, tight as dark drums)
Send the wind to shake tall grasses
Introduce frenzy into the hearts of small men.[59]

Recovery of pride in the black female body, estranged not only by the stares on the streets but by the discovery of African art by Europe in the nineteenth century and its elevation to a principle of vital primitivism, is addressed directly in Dove's own "Venus of Willendorf" in *On the Bus with Rosa Parks* (1999). Here the speaker, "one more exotic/ in the stream of foreign students/ invited to *Herr Professor's* summer house/ in the Wachau" in Austria, suffers a "gauntlet of stares" as the townspeople compare her ("a live black girl") to "the village miracle ... the legendary Venus of Willendorf ... unearthed/ not five kilometers from this garden shed" and now "entombed in a glass display" in the local inn.[60] Under the illicit pleasure of Herr Professor's desire for her, however, the unwelcome comparison soon melts into powerful identification with the Venus of Willendorf's "sprawling buttocks and barbarous thighs,/ breasts heaped up in her arms/ to keep from spilling":

and suddenly she understands what made
the Venus beautiful

Figure 27 *The Ball of the Duchess Du Barry,* popular engraving (1829).

was how the carver's hand had loved her,
that visible caress.[61]

Ekphrastic otherness becomes ekphrastic empathy in an unexpected and disconcerting way that admits the pleasures of being looked at, as it reckons fully how the male gaze entombs.

The issue of display runs throughout Dove's long interest in ekphrasis both explicitly and implicitly in her use of it to dismantle otherness, to reach out across the gaps between poet, image and audience. "Come here, I want to show you something," she says in "Sightseeing," a kind of *ars ekphrasis* from her first volume *The Yellow House on the Corner* (1980). Pointing to the broken, dismembered statues in a churchyard bombed in the war and left unreconstructed as a kind of museum, she sees "an arm gracefully upraised": "The hand will hold both of mine."[62] That sense of contact, of touch, the necessity of seeing and reimagining the remains of the past that they might hold our hands, and we theirs, animates her ekphrasis. For Dove, the ekphrastic power of the word is put to the service of connection that here and there, now and then, self and other not be isolated. Ekphrasis has been a steady resource for Dove, used in *Museum, Grace Notes* (1989), *Mother Love* (1995) and *On the Bus with Rosa Parks*. A number of these poems have significant lives in other venues. The poems of Section III of *Grace Notes* are selected from *The Other Side of the House* (1988), the collaboration Dove did with photographer Tamarra Kaida in 1988 and printed in a limited edition of fifty at the small press at Arizona State University. From *Rosa Parks*, "There Came a Soul" on Ivan Albright's remarkable painting *Into the World There Came a Soul Called Ida* was first published in the Art Institute of Chicago's collection of ekphrasis, *Transforming Vision*, edited by Edward Hirsch; and "Lady Freedom among Us" on Thomas Crawford's statue *Columbia, Goddess of Liberty* on the dome of the United States Capitol was read at the rededication of the monument after its restoration in 1993. The very language of the titles of these last two ("Came," "among Us") alone suggests the gestures Dove's ekphrases make to create a space shared by poet, object and audience. "Lady Freedom" also indicates Dove's use of ekphrasis to revise the stories of the past. First installed on the Capitol during the Civil War and originally intended to wear the "liberty cap," the marker of the freed slave, the statue may have been suggestive to Dove in early 1990s Washington and in her efforts as Poet Laureate to democratize poetry. Like Brooks encouraging the people to make the effort required of "Art," Dove urges sightseers to look: "don't lower your eyes ... consider her drenched gaze   her shining brow/ she who has brought mercy back into the streets/ and will not retire politely to the potter's field."[63] In a bit of ekphrastic conversation, Dove's sense of the statue living among us ("she is one of the many/ and she is each of us")[64] revises the symbolic, mythic vision of her as emblem of western expansion expressed in John James Piatt's poem "To the Statue on the Capitol: Looking Eastward at Dawn": "What sunken splendor in the Eastern skies/ Seest thou, O watcher, from thy lifted place? ... look, behind thee, where in sunshine lie/ Thy boundless fields of harvest in the West."[65] For Dove, ekphrasis needs to bring the distant close.

The private–public museum: Juxtaposition, "History" and "history"

Critics like to see the move in Dove's work from *Museum* to her next volume *Thomas and Beulah* (1986), about her grandparents' emigration to the northern industrial belt, as a move from History (with a capital H) to history (with a small h). But the two interpenetrate from the start of *Museum*, artifacts already carrying History set next to those trailing personal stories, history: History seen through the lens of personal observation or re-viewed as the ordinary experiences and objects they once were. Dove asks about Benjamin Banneker, "What did he do except lie/ under a pear tree, wrapped in/ a great cloak, and meditate/ on the heavenly bodies?"[66]

Juxtaposition as exhibition technique allows Dove, from the opening poems, to establish the public–private nature of her museum and its ability to hold History and history in a single hand, quietly and without overt comment. Placement carries her meaning. As the volume moves from the famous prefatory poem "Dusting" (which would later become part of *Thomas and Beulah*) to the first of the museum's four parts, the archeological "The Hill Has Something to Say," the ordinary, middle-class world of her grandmother opens into the world of European sightseeing and the museum. "Patient among knicknacks," Beulah "brings/ dark wood to life" with her "gray cloth." As she dusts, she remembers her girlhood, trying to uncover the name of "that/ silly boy at the fair."[67] The poem establishes the analogy of the public institutional space we enter through the volume's title to the private domestic world of Beulah's solarium; or rather, the move from the title of *Museum* to "Dusting" and from "Dusting" to the examination of the fossilized "Fish in the Stone" in the next poem enacts the way public and private spaces open into and out of each other. From "Dusting" the space of private life and private memory opens in "The Fish in the Stone" into the public museum and a public, historical past, just as the historical and public will in turn open into the private as the book moves from Part I's museum artifacts through to Part III, "My Father's Telescope." Dove's museum breaches the differences Susan Stewart articulated a year after the publication of *Museum* between the souvenir and the collection: "While the point of the souvenir may be remembering, or at least the invention of memory, the point of the collection is forgetting" so that the objects in the collection may be organized according to some principle that "supersedes the individual narratives that 'lie behind it.'"[68] Compelled by a desire like Paul Durcan's to draw works of art into relation to everyday life, though doing so in a very different way (whereas Durcan drafts objects into *his* story, Dove's attitude is listening to the stories the objects tell), Dove focuses precisely on the individual narratives in an effort not to forget the lives out of which these museum objects came. Dove's curatorial practices resist those of the conventional collection of which Stewart speaks, and which is embodied in mainstream art museums, and prod awareness that much art was once utilitarian. She thus paves the way for the incorporation of the ordinary artifacts and images of her own midwestern African-American childhood. Memory, not forgetting, is the point (memory, said Dove, "is a museum in itself"),[69] as it is in Dove's other work, and as it is in African American museums that seek to keep open and ready the memories of an African American culture that is rapidly disappearing and thus becoming unavailable as a source of racial pride. Remembering aids, not hinders, the larger narrative of a mixed heritage. Beulah's paradigmatic act of dusting and remembering is repeated again and again every time the sightseer/reader enters the past through the objects on display.

In "Dusting," Dove aligns herself with the curatorial pleasure in domestic objects of that subversive museum-goer Marianne Moore buying pictures (and plates, and candelabras, and hat-boxes) that will give her pleasure in her "average moments."[70] Whereas the quirks and oddities of objects please Moore, their tactile sensuousness pleases Dove: "Under her hand scrolls/ and crests gleam/ darker still."[71] In Dove's museum there are few interdictions against touch.

Beulah's average moments, so different from Moore's, are by no means so midwesternly provincial, or so dully middle-class, as the stereotype suggests. For one thing, they contain within them the Europe Dove's museum will go on to claim as her heritage. Beulah searches her memory for the name of a boy she once knew, "Not Michael –/ something finer." She finds it finally: "Maurice."[72] France, Dove suggests, lives deep inside Ohio, "complicating," as she said of Tolson, "our preconceived notions of cultural – and, by further comparison, existential – order."[73] From the beginning and at a very personal level, then, the strands of European and African American culture intertwine. That "Maurice" may be arrived in Ohio by way of the Caribbean offers the first reminder in Dove's museum that the artifacts of her cultural heritage are, at least in part, the legacy of colonization – not to reject that legacy, but to know it.

Is it useful to think of the culture "Dusting" describes, and of the museum it introduces, as hybrid? Perhaps, if "hybrid" can retain the rubs, the rich jostlings of difference that characterize Dove's museum. Dove places different objects next to each other to let their differences draw each other out: so, for example, a poem from Fiammetta's point of view follows one on her admiring would-be lover, Boccaccio, and, more disconcertingly and obscurely, Bob Marley, as we'll see, sings back to Fiammetta. The term "hybrid," as Jahan Ramazani uses it "to describe the intensified hybridization of already mixed and politically unequal cultures,"[74] clarifies Dove's importation of European, African and Caribbean traditions as amalgamating not pure cultures, but cultures already hybrid. Dove's black heritage already contains a France that lies too deep in memory and language to be purified by any return to African roots, which in any case are themselves mixed.

In moving from "Dusting" to the ekphrastic "The Fish in the Stone," one moves from the personal moment fixed as artifact to be placed in a museum, to one of "the ideal museum objects," reanimated, its personal life recovered. As emblem of all the objects taken out of daily life, resocialized and fixed in the museum, Dove's fossilized fish longs to re-enter the living stream:

The fish in the stone
would like to fall
back into the sea.

He is weary
of analysis, the small
predictable truths.
He is weary of waiting
in the open,
his profile stamped
by a white light.[75]

The juxtaposition of "Dusting" and "The Fish in the Stone" amplifies the metaphoric function of the two poems' fish: as the stove's heat thawed the goldfish frozen in its bowl in "Dusting," and Beulah's patient remembering unfroze the locked moment of the past so that it "swam free,"[76] so Dove in this volume will unfreeze the stilled artifacts of the past and return them, if only temporarily, to the living stream. Ekphrasis will be one of her means, as it is here. The metaphor of the frozen fish, indeed, suggests the conventional terms of ekphrasis: language animating the frozen moment of the object, freeing it from its silent stillness. In a general sense, then, the ekphrastic impulse is the presiding impulse of the volume.

Dove conceives of the artifacts in her museum as explicitly silent – "It's an inarticulate object," she says of the titular hill of the first section – and of the curator/poet's job as making their stories from what remains. The characters at the end of the first section, she says, "can't speak to us anymore . . . We have to go through what they've left behind and fashion it."[77] This last is important, for it indicates the attentiveness and humility required of the ekphrastic poet. For Dove, the poet may "fashion" the narrative, but the story is the object's. The poet/curator's task – a difficult one – is to listen closely: "The Hill Has Something to Say," we're told in the first section's title poem, "but isn't talking." "'The Hill Has Something to Say' ... if we would listen!"[78] Dove revises the conventional power dynamics of ekphrasis, imagining the poet not driving a narrative of her own devising, but open and receptive to a narrative given by the object, a narrative she will then "fashion." Whether the poems in this book – the curator's envoicing of the artifacts excavated from the hill – succeed in conveying the refreshing voices of the past or the "analysis" and "small/ predictable truths" of which the fish wearies remains uncertain, but Dove is ironically self-aware of the last possibility. She knows the potential foolishness of the ekphrastic endeavor, and its ethical liability: that we don't/can't get outside our own narratives to really hear (let alone convey) another's, and so remain predictable and narrowly analytical. But she also recognizes as human and legitimate the need of museum-goers, curators and poets to try to speak about what's in the museum. It may be, she knows, the necessity of knowing the others within us as much as those without: the wind that blows around the silent hill and makes the valley "groan ... amphoric," is "For all we know ... inside us, pacing/ our lungs."[79]

"The poems of *Museum*," Dove said, "are concerned with matters of art, matters of, I think, artifacts: how do you retain culture and make it available to another generation; what gets chosen and what doesn't?"[80] She could have added "And who chooses?" Importantly, Dove's *Museum* asserts, in its very being, the power of a black woman to listen to the artifacts, to say what gets handed on and to institutionalize its preservation in a museum. Dove belongs with such black women directors of African American Museums as Rowena Stewart (Rhode Island Black Heritage Society and the Afro-American Historical and Cultural Museum in Philadelphia) and Kinshasha Holman Conwill (Studio Museum). Her museum is revisionary not just in its choice of artifacts, but in her confident rewriting of official history: "As usual, legend got it all/ wrong," she says of "Nestor's Bathtub," and proceeds to give us a feminist revision: "Nestor's wife was the one/ to crouch under/ jug upon jug of fragrant water poured/ until the small room steamed."[81] Throughout the volume, Dove moves with aplomb among the varied experiences of sightseeing and the artifacts she's gathered, alive to herself as being in the world she inhabits and finding resonant chords in far distant cultures. Thus, for example, the Chinese Tou Wan building her husband's tomb of "four rooms/ hewn in the side of stone"[82] appears here not so very different from the poet–viewer–curator building this museum-house divided into four sections. Dove's own position as creator and viewer achieves the absolute presence Fanon defiantly articulated: "I am not a potentiality of something, I am wholly what I am ... My Negro consciousness does not hold itself out as a lack. It *is*."[83]

Dove's feminist consciousness speaks from the opening poem, which poses Beulah's dusting as the paradigmatic action (domestic and ordinary) of the museum-goer; through the reclaiming of the bathtub for Nestor's wife; to the feminizing of the copper beech at "the castle/ at Erpenberg" (holding her own, "Aristocrat among patriarchs");[84] to the portraits of Catherine of Alexandria, Catherine of Siena and Fiammetta; and the envoicing of Tou Wan. Like Rich, Dove rewrote myths from the perspective of women and engaged in the historical recovery of women's lives, recording the experiences of the saints Catherine, Fiammetta and Tou Wan, and humanizing them with intimate details. She was interested in women who chose alternatives to conventional domestic lives (sainthood, for example), as well as those who made space for themselves within their given worlds. Direct address and prosopopoeia help create relation between them and us, as they did in Rich: "You walked the length of Italy/ to find someone to talk to," Dove says to Catherine of Siena, offering her a kind of belated company.[85] The volume's poems also display another legacy of Moore's and Rich's feminist efforts: a female speaker self-confident in her looking and saying, skeptical of the directions of patriarchal power ("Contrary to/ tales you told us," Dove begins "Anti-Father").[86] The poems, however, are not complacent about the security of their achieved feminist ground. They reveal vulnerability to the old power of the commanding male, and fear of the humiliation that might come with succumbing. So, in "The Left-Handed Cellist,"

You came with a cello in one hand,
in the other, nothing.
Play, you said.

I played the scales of ignorant evening.
I played in high heels to be closer to you ...

Tell me that you did not profit from me,
you with the pewter hands.[87]

The volume's most vehement protest against such profit is voiced by Fiammetta, the untraced beloved of Boccaccio's early work, in

"Fiammetta Breaks Her Peace." Set during the 1348 plague in Florence (which the ten survivors leave behind in the *Decameron*), the poem imagines Fiammetta's horror at the death around her, and her outrage that in the midst of such suffering Boccaccio should try to still her into an object of compensatory beauty. As Rich had in her feminist ekphrasis, Dove recovers a lost female life and envoices the silent woman:

I've watched them, mother, and I know
the signs. The first day, rigor.
Staggering like drunks, they
ram the room's sharp edges
with the most delicate bodily parts
and feel no pain . . .

Day two is fever, the bright
stream clogged, eyes rodent
red. No one weeps anymore; just
waits, for appear they must –
in the armpits, at the groin –
hard, blackened apples . . .

And to think he wanted me
beautiful! To be his fresh air
and my breasts two soft
spiced promises. *Stand still*, he said
once, *and let me admire you.*

All is infection, mother – and avarice,
and self-pity, and fear![88]

Powerfully driven forward by rhythm and enjambment and contained by short lines and end-stopped stanzas, Fiammetta's sorrow and despair protest the same objectification that Christina Rossetti took on in "In the Artist's Studio." The image of the plague victims being stilled to death, then stiffening into rigor, highlights the deathliness of Boccaccio's command. And like Rich, Dove knows that such feminist protest exacts a terrible price: it breaks the peace, as the title tells us. In Dove's museum, which suggests connections via linguistic repetitions that create a web of relations crossing over those of juxtaposition, Fiammetta is linked to Beulah by the "promise" they represent to idealizing men.

Dove's challenge of the male gaze may be provoked not only by Boccaccio's idealization of Fiammetta and the literary tradition that preceded it, but also by its later manifestation in Rossetti's painting of

Fiammetta and his accompanying ekphrastic sonnet, "Fiammetta (For a Picture)" (1878).[89]

Behold Fiammetta, shown in Vision here.
  Gloom-girt 'mid Spring-flushed apple-growth she
    stands;
  And as she sways the branches with her hands,
Along her arm the sundered bloom falls sheer,
In separate petals shed, each like a tear;
  While from the quivering bough the bird expands
  His wings. And lo! thy spirit understands
Life shaken and shower'd and flown, and Death
    drawn near.

All stirs with change. Her garments beat the air:
  The angel circling round her aureole
  Shimmers in flight against the tree's grey bole:
While she, with reassuring eyes most fair,
A presage and a promise stands; as 'twere
  On Death's dark storm the rainbow of the Soul.[90]

In language that echoes Rossetti's, Dove's Fiammetta rails against being made to "stand" (repeated twice in Rossetti's poem) for a "presage and a promise" ("my breasts two soft/ spiced promises"), abstracted to a transcendent "vision," "reassuring" the living viewer/painter/lover in the midst of death. Dove's Fiammetta wants to live, not be transformed into Rossetti's symbolic "rainbow of the Soul" "On Death's dark storm," and so she and her mother retreat from the plague: "We shall sit quietly in this room/ and I think we'll be spared."[91]

She *won't* be spared, the foreboding tone tell us, perhaps precisely because she does retreat (and into a company of women?). In contrast to Fiammetta's fatal withdrawal, Dove in this volume seems to step out into a world of both men and women, and into a world that resists the identification of (racial) darkness with death. On the page facing the conclusion of "Fiammetta Breaks Her Peace," Part II of *Museum* begins with an epigraph that racializes Rossetti's "rainbow of the Soul" and expands its gender:

When the morning
gather the rainbow,
want you to know
I'm a rainbow, too.
  – *Bob Marley*[92]

In contrast to the role of rainbow imposed on Fiammetta, Marley (and
Dove) will take it on as actively chosen. The rainbow as symbol of release
from suffering into the peace of death is turned to metaphor for a new
day of social justice and empowerment arising from black culture. This
is not yet Jesse Jackson's rainbow coalition, but it's on its way. "To the
rescue/ Here I am," continues Marley's song. "Want you to know just if
you can, here I stand."[93] The delightful wittiness of Fiammetta and Bob
Marley sitting side by side displays Dove's delicate skill in organizing the
eclectic artifacts of her museum and the fruitfulness of her curatorial
method. The upbeat hopefulness of Marley's lyric contrasts with
Fiammetta's pulling in and shutting down. Dove will not claim that
black culture will find a way forward for the oppressed where European
culture represented by Fiammetta cannot, but there is recognition here
of vitality and energy that promise empowerment.

The black curator and the Black Dove

The strength and integrity of Dove's stand as a black feminist curator of a
cosmopolitan heritage are put to the test by the museum's various images
of black and female oppression, most spectacularly in "Agosta the
Winged Man and Rasha the Black Dove," on Christian Schad's painting
(Fig. 28). That she challenges herself to face the complex implications of
autonomy and power, is, I think, one measure of the courage of this
volume. The painting depicts two circus "freaks," professional performers who have turned their marginalization into art: a white man, his body
contorted with the deformity called "pigeon breast"; a black woman,
seated below him, whose only curiosity is the color of her skin. Both stare
directly at the viewer/painter. It is painted with "the icy-cool, objective
realism" of the *Neue Sachlichkeit* ("New Objectivity"), "which grew up
[during the 1920s in Germany] in defiance of the subjective, gestural
Expressionism practiced by the previous generation."[94] Dove first saw the
painting in 1980 at a retrospective of Schad's work at the Staatliche
Kunsthalle Berlin:

And we saw the painting and it was really riveting, and bought the catalog which
told a little bit about the two people. When I wrote the poem ... I sent it to
Christian Schad, just because I thought he should know. I didn't know if he knew
English, but it turned out he did. Then I met him afterwards and talked to him, and
he gave me permission to use the painting on the cover of the book. That was a year
before he died.[95]

Figure 28 Christian Schad, *Agosta the Pigeon-Breasted Man and Rasha the Black Dove* (1929).

Like other modern ekphrastic poets, Dove's sense of pictures is deeply informed by the museum and its textual commentary.

Faced with this painting, one might expect Dove to speak through her namesake, to give voice to the silenced object of the painter's objectifying gaze in an exercise of black, feminist power. Her choice of ekphrastic object, and the fact that she persuaded Carnegie Mellon to use it on the cover of the first edition, beg the identification of Dove herself and Schad's Black Dove (whom she looks remarkably like, as her young daughter remarked).[96] Dove recalls some of the impetus of *Museum* in her experiences as a Fulbright student in Tübingen, Germany: " ... they simply gawked at me or even pointed. It was amazing to me to be pointed out on the street like that, and it offended me in many ways ... I was so fed up with being on constant display."[97] Using the prerogative of ekphrasis to narrate and to move beyond the frame, Dove gives the Black Dove a life beyond the portrait, beyond display ("When the tent lights dimmed,/ Rasha went back to her trailer and plucked/ a chicken for dinner")[98] and so recovers the humanity of the objectified sitter.

But the implications of *Museum*'s claim for black curators and black viewers of culture prohibit a singular (and easy) identification. Dove steps back from the obvious ekphrastic moves of prosopopoeia or even telling the narrative from some position near Rasha. Dove is *not* powerless, though she, too, has felt the objectifying gaze. To speak as Rasha would not be to tell the whole truth, or even most of it, for all she has known Rasha's position. Accepting the position of power in the charged relation between painter and sitter, between the one who looks and the one who is looked at, Dove instead speaks from the point of view of the creator of this image, gets inside the imagination of the white male painter, explores it, and does not repudiate it. Other commentators on this poem have understood Schad as an essentially sympathetic figure, a painter deeply engaged with his sitters, one who "attends to the subjectivities of Agosta and Rasha" and finds "communion in art" with them.[99] But this is to rewrite Schad to make him a more acceptable mask for Dove. Schad is best known by art historians (some of whom Dove had read in the exhibition catalogue) for the ambiguous response to his sitters, a detached objectivity combined with voyeuristic fascination. His response may bear some relation to his uncertain attitude to Nazi power. While the work of his fellow artists of the New Objectivity, Beckman, Grosz and Dix, was displayed in Hitler's 1937 degenerate art show, Schad's appeared in Hitler's exhibit of great German art in Munich the same year. Schad seems not to have objected, though his "obsession with outsiders and deviants" came to be "viewed as a dangerous vice" and he "softened" his technique and eventually moved into photography.[100] Dove seems to me fairly clear-eyed in this poem about Schad's complex relations to his sitters. He is certainly the agonized artist pacing the studio, facing the "blank space," stuck inside his skin – like, presumably, Dove herself faced with the blank space of the poem.[101] But he is also distanced, cold and self-absorbed, "without passion," a man who likes things to run according to schedule and gets a thrill from Agosta's tales of "women/ trailing/ backstage to offer him/ the consummate bloom of their lust."[102] He rationalizes the mercilessness of his gaze by pointing the finger at the demands of art: "The canvas,// not his eye, was merciless."[103] When his two sitters stare back, he understands himself to be the victim: "Not/ the canvas," he concludes, "but their gaze,/ so calm,/ was merciless."[104]

In taking on Schad's perspective, Dove refuses to be the object of the gaze, refuses the role she might automatically be expected to inhabit. She also problematizes her own position as creator. Black power is not necessarily different from white power; nor is female power different from male. In this poem she looks steadily at and tries on the implications of being the powerful, viewing creator, including the analogies to the gawking spectators in the carnival where Agosta and the Black Dove display themselves for money (as they do to Schad), and to the medical students taking notes, describing, as Dove does too, the details of Agosta's deformity: "his torso/ exposed, its crests and fins/ a colony of birds, trying/ to get out … "[105] In a way, Dove tries on Schad's skin, as he had "painted himself in a new one,/ silk green, worn/ like a shirt" in *Self Portrait, 1927*.[106] Testing the powers of empathy with the not entirely admirable, she accepts her place as artist, not sitter. She will do this again, much more dramatically, in the volume's final famous poem, "Parsley," whose last section closes *Museum* with Dove stepping into and speaking through the persona of Rafael Trujillo, the dictator of the Dominican Republic who "ordered 20,000 blacks killed" "for a single beautiful word."[107]

In standing back with Schad, however, Dove can also begin to rewrite the assumptions about sitters: that those on display are entirely powerless, and that black females on display are doubly powerless. The looked-at, as we've seen before in ekphrasis, can have a power of their own, one that Dove, with her respect for the stories of her objects, does not minimize. Distance here allows Rasha and Agosta their autonomy; aligning herself with Schad allows Dove to record the force of their gazes. Her positioning sets up a complex web of relations that cross races and cultures, putting the dynamics of ekphrasis to her interracial, intercultural purposes. As

Therese Steffen has acutely observed, "the most astounding twist lies in the doubling of painter/poet and the models."[108] While I do not think we can see Dove as a co-creator of the painting, as Steffen does, Dove's alliance with Schad as creator speaks to her museum's insistence on a shared intercultural space of identification, exchange and conversation. It mirrors the alliance between Rasha and Agosta, connected by their shared professions as performers and models, and their bird-like qualities. But Dove rewrites here, too. Whereas Rasha is positioned at Agosta's feet (the pointed phrase is Dove's), the confidence with which Dove enters Schad's world places these two artists on a level. Whereas Schad seems to fear the stare that threatens to "turn the gazer's spirit into stone," Dove salutes it. No reversal of gender and racial power relations, Dove's claim firmly evens the balance. There is no collapsing of difference here either. "Rather, at stake in this poem," as Steffen suggests, "is a critique of the myth of 'universalist humanism'" in which "*différance* is integrated and leveled into a homogeneous world picture."[109] Dove's deployment of the ekphrastic dynamic here enables her to keep difference (between races, cultures, word and image) in play at the same time that she creates relation across difference. In "Agosta the Winged Man and Rasha the Black Dove," Dove's use of ekphrasis, involving her selective deployment of its conventions, is a means of resisting a reductive black solidarity (Dove/Rasha) while simultaneously refusing the universalist humanism so often posed as its only alternative within the rhetoric of the Black Arts Movement. Pereira calls Dove's a "revisionist universalism,"[110] and I think this is right if we take it to mean a faith in commonality that can be reached through positions of real racial, gender and cultural difference.

"Agosta the Winged Man and Rasha the Black Dove" lies at the exact center of *Museum*. With the following ekphrastic poem, "At the German Writer's Conference in Munich," it forms her museum's central core of ekphrastic engagement with the foreign culture that has most influenced her, echoed also in "The Copper Beech," "November for Beginners," "Reading Hölderlin on the Patio with the Aid of a Dictionary" and "Shakespeare Say." Together, they are the fulcrum of the sequence that balances Europe, which occupies most of the first two rooms, and the United States and the colonized world, which occupy most of the second two. If "Agosta" demonstrates Dove's stand with a white male German artist, "At the German Writer's Conference" reminds us of the multiplicity of her positions as she records once more the estranging effects of race and nationality. Here a banner announcing "Association of German/ Writers in the Union of Printers/ and Paper Manufacturers" stretches across the medieval tapestry decorating the wall of Munich's Hofbräuhaus.[111] It obscures the past image, competes with the text across the tapestry that tells of the marginalized artisans who perhaps made it ("Wives/ and Jewish Dyers") and reminds the speaker of her difference (it is "taut and white/ as skin (not mine)").[112] Yet, joining Rich and Moore in writing on a tapestry whose weaving sets up such resonance with writing ("textile"/"text," from "textus"), she nevertheless works with what "pokes out" and celebrates the visible remains: "those dainty shoes/ beneath the printed silk/ that first caught my eye,/ and the grotesquely bent/ fetlock-to-ivory hoof/ of the horse. And both/ are in flowers."[113] In verbal–visual communion (ironically echoed in her description of the "two doves [who] signify/ a union endorsed/ by God and the Church"),[114] Dove constructs her transcultural, transracial, cosmopolitan museum.

Why this interest, especially in the twentieth century, in the volume as museum? In addition to the opportunities it offers for the series as poetic model, it has something to do with poetry's sense of itself in relation to the continuity of culture. Dove's question, "*How* do you retain culture ... ?"[115] implies the question "*where* do you retain culture?" Through the nineteenth and twentieth centuries, for the work of art the answer increasingly became "the museum." Volumes of poems seem slight and fragile next to, say, the Metropolitan Museum of Art, the Natural History Museum, the Louvre. They seem not to have the institutional heft, the weight, the presence, the authority of these monumental marble and granite structures. They seem to speak to the personal more than the public. The volume-as-museum has been a way of imagining, or reimagining, poetry's role in the selection and preservation of culture in a public space.

Notes

Introduction. The engaging eye: Ekphrasis and twentieth-century poetry

1. Frank O'Hara, *The Collected Poems of Frank O'Hara*, ed. Donald Allen, rev. edn. (Berkeley, CA: University of California Press, 1995), p. 128.
2. W. D. Snodgrass [also known as S. S. Gardons], *After Experience: Poems and Translations* (New York, NY: Harper & Row, 1968), p. 57.
3. J. D. McClatchy, "Introduction" in J. D. McClatchy (ed.), *Poets on Painters* (Berkeley, CA: University of California Press, 1988), p. xiii.
4. Wallace Stevens, *The Necessary Angel: Essays on Reality and the Imagination* (New York, NY: Vintage, 1951), p. 169.
5. Paul Durcan, *Crazy About Women* (Dublin: National Gallery of Ireland, 1991), p. xi.
6. R. S. Thomas, "Threshold" in Dannie Abse and Joan Abse (eds.), *Voices in the Gallery* (London: The Tate Gallery, 1986), p. 40.
7. Richard Howard, "Henri Fantin-Latour, *Un Coin de Table* (1873)" in Edward Hirsch (ed.), *Transforming Vision: Writers on Art* (Boston, New York, Toronto, London: Bulfinch Press [Little, Brown & Co.] for The Art Institute of Chicago, 1994), p. 31; John Ashbery, "Self-Portrait in a Convex Mirror" in *Self-Portrait in a Convex Mirror* (New York, NY: Viking, 1975), p. 75; Vicki Feaver, "Oi yoi yoi" in Abse and Abse (eds.), *Voices*, p. 125.
8. William Carlos Williams, *The Autobiography of William Carlos Williams* (New York, NY: Random House, 1951), p. 148.
9. Perloff's explorations focus on the avant-garde and range across a wide variety of verbal–visual relations, including ekphrasis. See *Frank O'Hara: Poet among Painters* (Chicago, IL: University of Chicago Press, 1998 [1977]) and *The Futurist Moment: Avant-Garde, Avant Guerre, and the Language of Rupture* (Chicago, IL: University of Chicago Press, 1986). Less extensively focused on the visual arts are *The Poetics of Indeterminacy: Rimbaud to Cage* (Princeton, NJ: Princeton University Press, 1981) and *Radical Artifice: Writing Poetry in the Age of Media* (Chicago, IL: University of Chicago Press, 1991). See also Bram Dijkstra, *Cubism, Stieglitz and the Early Poetry of William Carlos Williams: The Hieroglyphics of a New Speech* (Princeton, NJ: Princeton University Press, 1969); Glen MacLeod, *Wallace Stevens and Modern Art: From the Armory Show to Abstract Expressionism* (New Haven,

CT: Yale University Press, 1993); and Linda Leavell, *Marianne Moore and the Visual Arts: Prismatic Color* (Baton Rouge, LA: Louisiana State University Press, 1995).

10. See my *Yeats and the Visual Arts* (New Brunswick, NJ: Rutgers University Press, 1986; rev. edn., Syracuse, NY: Syracuse University Press, 2003).

11. Ezra Pound, "A retrospect" in *Literary Essays of Ezra Pound*, ed. T. S. Eliot (New York, NY: New Directions, 1968), p. 4.

12. See Charles Altieri, *Painterly Abstraction in Modernist American Poetry: The Contemporaneity of Modernism* (University Park, PA: Pennsylvania State University Press, 1989). See also Wendy Steiner's semiotic study of the analogies between modern poetry and painting as poetic resource and critical strategy, *The Colors of Rhetoric: Problems in the Relation between Modern Literature and Painting* (Chicago, IL: University of Chicago Press, 1982).

13. Some of the best, including pieces by Moore, Lawrence, Bishop, Jarrell, Creeley and Strand, have been gathered in the collections by McClatchy (ed.), *Poets on Painters* (1988) and Daniel Halpern (ed.), *Writers on Artists* (San Francisco, CA: North Point, 1988).

14. W. J. T. Mitchell, *Picture Theory: Essays on Verbal and Visual Representation* (Chicago, IL: University of Chicago Press, 1994), pp. 11–34.

15. André Malraux, *Museum without Walls*, trans. Stuart Gilbert and Francis Price (New York, NY: Doubleday, 1967).

16. James Merrill, "Notes on Corot" in McClatchy (ed.), *Poets on Painters*, pp. 311–321 (p. 312).

17. Seamus Heaney, *Sweeney's Flight* (London: Faber, 1992), p. vii.

18. Mary Ann Caws, *The Art of Interference: Stressed Readings in Verbal and Visual Texts* (Princeton, NJ: Princeton University Press, 1983), p. 179.

19. Merrill, "Corot" in McClatchy (ed.), *Poets on Painters*, p. 313.

20. Richard Stein, *The Ritual of Interpretation: The Fine Arts as Literature in Ruskin, Rossetti, and Pater* (Cambridge, MA: Harvard University Press, 1975), p. 4.

21. Ibid.

22. Randall Jarrell, *The Complete Poems* (New York, NY: Noonday, 1969), p. 4.

23. Richard Wilbur, *The Poems of Richard Wilbur* (New York, NY: Harcourt Brace Jovanovich, 1963), p. 197.

24. Siegfried Sassoon, "'A View of Old Exeter'" in *Collected Poems 1908–1956* (London: Faber and Faber, 1971 [1961]), p. 242.

25. For an extended discussion of how "the artistic act itself, in establishing a relation between artist and object, is an ethical act" (p. 10), see Terence Diggory, *William Carlos Williams and the Ethics of Painting* (Princeton, NJ: Princeton University Press, 1991). Diggory argues that Williams sees in painting a solution to the violence of symbolism. With its "combination of material and signifying properties," painting "represents Williams's project" (p. 4) to hand to readers the things of the world interpreted, and so seen

anew, but not re-made by the poet/artist into something else. Description is William's means: it interprets but does not appropriate (pp. 9–10).

26. For a polemical defense of the "*intelligence* of sight," see Barbara Maria Stafford, *Good Looking: Essays on the Virtue of Images* (Cambridge, MA: MIT Press, 1996), p. 4; for a discussion of the "force" of looking, and the violence it does both object and observer, see James Elkins, *The Object Stares Back: On the Nature of Seeing* (New York, NY: Simon and Schuster, 1996), pp. 18–45.

27. See Mitchell, *Picture Theory*; James A. W. Heffernan, *Museum of Words: The Poetics of Ekphrasis from Homer to Ashbery* (Chicago, IL: University of Chicago Press, 1993); and Grant Scott, *The Sculpted Word: Keats, Ekphrasis, and the Visual Arts* (Hanover, NH: University Press of New England, 1994).

28. James Breslin, *From Modern to Contemporary: American Poetry, 1945–1965* (Chicago, IL: University of Chicago Press, 1984), p. 59.

29. Ibid., pp. 59–60.

30. I agree with James Longenbach's assessment "that Wilbur is that rare thing: a seriously misunderstood poet," that he is not elitist or reactionary or disengaged, as his affinity for poetic form has mistakenly prompted his detractors to see him (*Modern Poetry after Modernism* [Oxford: Oxford University Press, 1997], pp. 66–67).

31. Ashbery, "Self-Portrait," p. 81.

32. Breslin discusses, for example, Frank O'Hara's "On seeing Larry Rivers' *Washington Crossing the Delaware* at the Museum of Modern Art" (*From Modern to Contemporary*, pp. 225–230); James Longenbach, Jorie Graham's "At Luca Signorelli's Resurrection of the Body" (*Modern Poetry*, pp. 163–164); Helen Vendler, Robert Lowell's "For the Union Dead" (*The Given and the Made* [Cambridge, MA: Harvard University Press, 1995], pp. 13–17); and Marjorie Perloff, especially poems by O'Hara (*Frank O'Hara*).

33. Michael Fried, "Art and objecthood" in *Minimal Art: A Critical Anthology*, ed. Gregory Battock (Berkeley, CA: University of California Press, 1995), pp. 116–147 (p. 125).

34. Ibid. Fried's emphasis.

35. Ibid., p. 135.

36. For Fried, "theatricality" is a pejorative term. In *Absorption and Theatricality: Painting and Beholder in the Age of Diderot* (Berkeley, CA: University of California Press, 1980), he further develops his idea in historical terms by identifying the Rococco as the "theatrical" against which painting of the late eighteenth century reacted with strategies for denying the presence of the viewer to produce a painting that appears self-contained and "absorbed." Fried sees late eighteenth-century painting, culminating in the works of David, as the roots of modernist painting which was similarly concerned to develop internal relations among its parts and "neutralize the beholder's presence" (p. 68). He identifies this art with the "pictorial," as against the "theatrical," and associates it with "presentness," as opposed to the

"presence" achieved through objecthood characteristic of literalist art. For Fried, the great paradox of absorptive painting is that in denying the viewer it holds and moves the beholder (p. 68): "only by establishing the fiction of his [the viewer's] absence or nonexistence could his actual placement before and enthrallment by the painting be secured" (p. 103). The point of enthralling the viewer is, in the end, to overcome "alienation." This is also what modernist art, according to Fried, aims for. Literalist art keeps the beholder as a beholder, and thus necessarily at a distance. Fried made the stakes clear in "Art and objecthood": "We are all literalists most or all of our lives. Presentness is grace" (p. 147).

While ekphrasis is, by its very nature, theatrical, as I've suggested, the experience it most often records is precisely the kind of enthrallment Fried describes. Indeed, ekphrasis demands enthrallment, or at least engagement, as I've been arguing. There are few ekphrases on abstract art (much of which would fall under Fried's "pictorial" category), and few on minimalist art. It may be that the kind of engagement ekphrasis requires is elicited best by representational art, art that declares unequivocally its status as art rather than as object. Ekphrasis then may present a paradox of its own: the theatrical is a means of representing the experience of enthrallment, and may be a means of recreating it, or even inducing it, in an audience.

37. My argument here for continuity between modernism and postmodernism joins others, especially Marjorie Perloff's in *21st-Century Modernism: The "New" Poetics* (Oxford: Blackwell, 2002). Like Perloff, I understand the continuity (at least as ekphrasis demonstrates it) to be a matter of "openness," but I'm arguing that such openness can be achieved in ways other than the formal "Constructivist notions of 'laying bare the device,' of using material form – in this case, language – as an active compositional agent, impelling the reader to participate in the process of construction" that Perloff identifies as the link between the modernism of Stein and the early Eliot and the postmodern LANGUAGE poets (p. 26). For Perloff, the openness celebrated by those poets announced in Donald Allen's landmark collection *The New American Poetry* (New York, NY: Grove Press, 1960) is not the real openness achieved by the language poets, but, in hindsight, "a carrying on, in somewhat diluted form, of the avant-garde project that had been at the very heart of early modernism" (pp. 2–3). Jennifer Ashton, applying Fried's critique of literalism to the LANGUAGE poets, wants to reclaim the opposition between modernism and postmodernism on the basis of theatrical and non-theatrical (*From Modernism to Postmodernism: American Poetry and Theory in the Twentieth Century* [Cambridge: Cambridge University Press, 2005], p. 2).

38. See, for example, Mitchell, "Beyond comparison: picture, text, and method" in *Picture Theory* (pp. 83–107), and Wendy Steiner, *The Colors of Rhetoric*.

39. Other discussions of ekphrasis include: Katy Aisenberg, *Ravishing Images: Ekphrasis in the Poetry and Prose of William Wordsworth, W. H. Auden and*

Philip Larkin (New York, NY: Peter Lang, 1995); Andrew Sprague Becker, *The Shield of Achilles and the Poetics of Ekphrasis* (London: Rowman & Littlefield, 1995); Mario Klarer (ed.), *Ekphrasis*, special issue of *Word & Image* 15.1 (1999); Michael C. J. Putnam, *Virgil's Epic Designs : Ekphrasis in the Aeneid* (New Haven, CT: Yale University Press, 1998); Mack Smith, *Literary Realism and the Ekphrastic Tradition* (University Park, PA: Pennsylvania State University Press, 1995) on the tradition in fiction.

40. My discussion here is indebted to Ruth Webb's excellent essay on classical and modern definitions of "ekphrasis" (*"Ekphrasis* ancient and modern: The invention of a genre," *Word & Image* 15.1 [1999], 7–18). See also Scott, *The Sculpted Word*, pp. 29–41.

41. Leo Spitzer, "The 'Ode on a Grecian Urn,' or content vs. metagrammar" in Anna Hatcher (ed.), *Essays on English and American Literature* (Princeton, NJ: Princeton University Press, 1962), pp. 67–97 (p. 72).

42. "Ekphrasis" he reserved for those poems in which the work of art speaks (Jean Hagstrum, *The Sister Arts: The Tradition of Literary Pictorialism and English Poetry from Dryden to Gray* [Chicago, IL: University of Chicago Press, 1987 (1958)], pp. 17–18, esp. n. 34).

43. John Hollander, *The Gazer's Spirit: Poems Speaking to Silent Works of Art* (Chicago, IL: University of Chicago Press, 1995), p. 7.

44. Heffernan, *Museum*, p. 3.

45. David Carrier, *Artwriting* (Amherst, MA: University of Massachusetts Press, 1987). Svetlana Alpers first suggested that Vasari stood in a tradition of ekphrasis ("Ekphrasis and aesthetic attitudes in Vasari's *Lives*," *Journal of the Warburg and Courtauld Institutes* 23 [1960], 190–215), a construction of "tradition" that Webb questions ("Ekphrasis ancient and modern," p. 9).

46. See Hagstrum, *Sister Arts*, p. 25.

47. Gotthold Ephraim Lessing, *Laocoön: An Essay on the Limits of Painting and Poetry*, trans. Edward Allen McCormick (Baltimore, MD: Johns Hopkins University Press, 1984), p. 78.

48. Mitchell, *Picture Theory*, p. 160.

49. W. J. T. Mitchell, *Iconology: Image, Text, Ideology* (Chicago, IL: University of Chicago Press, 1986), pp. 95–115.

50. Mitchell, *Picture Theory*, p. 162.

51. Ibid., p. 156.

52. Heffernan, *Museum*, p. 7.

53. Mitchell, *Picture Theory*, p. 180.

54. Heffernan, *Museum*, pp. 1, 6.

55. See Scott, *The Sculpted Word*.

56. Gertrude Stein, "Pictures" in McClatchy (ed.), *Poets on Painters*, p. 97.

57. Ntozake Shange, *Ridin' the Moon in Texas: Word Paintings* (New York, NY: St. Martin's Press, 1987), p. 3.

58. Cole Swensen, "Interview" by Jon Thompson (http://english.chass.nscu/ freeverse/Archives/Winter_2003/Interviews/interviews [accessed October 1, 2005]). See, among other works, Swensen's *Such Rich Hour* (Iowa City, IA: University of Iowa Press, 2001).

59. W. S. Graham, "The Thermal Stair" in Abse and Abse (eds.), *Voices*, pp. 146, 148.

60. This sense of an expanded range of relations with "the other" underlies some recent explorations of literary ethics. See, especially, Derek Attridge, who insists that the work (of literature or any other art) be considered a "stranger" rather than "friend and companion" ("Innovation, literature, ethics: Relating to the other," *PMLA* 114.1 [January, 1999], 20–31 [p. 26]). While I would like to restore to discussions of ekphrastic relations the possibility of the work of art becoming friend or companion, I take an important part of these relations to be the "otherness" of friend or companion. Clearly, many (probably most) respectful relations across difference, those that do not participate in "*the domestication of the other*" or "*the violence or representation*" (Attridge, "Innovation, literature, ethics," p. 22, emphasis Attridge's), do not develop into companionship or friendship. I want to leave space in ekphrasis for these kinds of relations as well.

61. Murray Krieger, *Ekphrasis: The Illusion of the Natural Sign* (Baltimore MD: Johns Hopkins University Press, 1992), p. 10.

62. Ibid.

63. I thank Helen Vendler for drawing this to my attention.

64. Wallace Stevens, *The Collected Poems of Wallace Stevens* (New York, NY: Knopf, 1971), p. 239.

65. M. M. Bakhtin, *The Dialogic Imagination*, ed. Michael Holquist, trans. Carol Emerson and Michael Holquist (Austin, TX: University of Texas Press, 1981), p. 276.

66. Mary Ann Caws, "Looking: Literature's other," *PMLA* 119.5 (October, 2004), 1293–1314 (p. 1299).

67. See, especially, Mieke Bal, *Reading "Rembrandt": Beyond the Word–Image Opposition* (Cambridge: Cambridge University Press, 1991), and *Looking In: The Art of Viewing* (Amsterdam: G + B Arts, 2001). For a discussion of the dialogic in twentieth-century British poetry, see Ian Gregson, *Contemporary Poetry and Postmodernism* (New York, NY: St. Martin's Press, 1996).

68. Norman Bryson, "Introduction" to Bal, *Looking In*, pp. 1–39 (p. 15). For other efforts to move beyond the word–image opposition, see James Elkins, who suggests that we understand the relation "between pictures and writing … not as a duality with some imbrication, but as an articulated continuum of signs, so that every marked surface will have a measure of pictoriality and a measure of writing" (*On Pictures and the Words that Fail Them* [Cambridge: Cambridge University Press, 1998], p. 158); and Diggory, who articulates the "grounds for a critical practice that successfully resists

violence" by examining the relations William Carlos Williams found in painting. Diggory offers an alternative to the view of artistic creation as the successful "appropriation of one's materials, taking possession of them, exercising mastery over them" (*The Ethics of Painting*, pp. 5–6). Elkins is quite right to note that "it may not be meaningful or possible to move 'beyond' the word/image dichotomy – since it informs more accounts of pictures than we know how to identify," but claims that " 'word' and 'image' stop making sense as a pair when they are confronted with particular acts of seeing" (p. 129). I want to maintain the difference, recognizing a zone, rather than a line, of demarcation between them: relation, so crucial to ekphrasis, depends on difference.

69. What Jerome McGann has called a text's "bibliographic codes" (in, for example, *The Textual Condition* [Princeton, NJ: Princeton University Press, 1991]). For more on ekphrastic textuality, see my "Ekphrasis and textual consciousness," *Word & Image* 15.1 (January 1999), 76–96.

70. W. B. Yeats, *The Poems*, ed. Richard J. Finneran, rev. edn. (New York, NY: Macmillan, 1989), p. 214. The poem was first published in 1924. I quote the more familiar 1925 version. Both use "still." For other images on which the poem may draw, see Giorgio Melchiori, *The Whole Mystery of Art: Pattern into Poetry in the Work of W. B. Yeats* (New York, NY: Macmillan, 1961), pp. 153–163.

71. John Keats, *The Poems of John Keats*, ed. Jack Stillinger (Cambridge, MA: Harvard University Press, 1978), p. 373.

72. W. D. Snodgrass, *After Experience*, p. 64.

73. Keats, *Poems*, p. 372.

74. Yeats, *Poems*, p. 295; Robert Lowell, *Collected Poems*, ed. Frank Bidart and David Gewanter (New York, NY: Farrar, Straus and Giroux, 2003), p. 466.

75. Sylvia Plath, *Collected Poems*, ed. Ted Hughes (New York, NY: HarperCollins, 1981), p. 114.

76. Percy Bysshe Shelley, "On the Medusa of Leonardo da Vinci, in the Florentine Gallery," ed. Melissa J. Sites and Neil Fraistat (www.rc.umd.edu/editions/ shelley/medusa/medusa.html [accessed November 17, 2007]).

77. Rita Dove, *Museum* (Pittsburgh, PA: Carnegie Mellon, 1983), p. 13.

78. Ashbery, "Self-Portrait," p. 81.

79. Keats, *Poems*, p. 373. For a discussion of Keats's ekphrases and history, see Theresa Kelley, "Keats, ekphrasis and history" in Nicholas Roe (ed.), *Keats and History* (Cambridge: Cambridge University Press, 1995), pp. 212–237.

80. For a discussion of modern poetry including history, see James Longenbach, *Modernist Poetics of History: Pound, Eliot, and the Sense of the Past* (Princeton, NJ: Princeton University Press, 1987).

81. Lowell, *Collected Poems*, p. 458. For an excellent account of Lowell's use of painting, especially in *Day by Day*, see Helen Deese, "Lowell and the visual arts" in Steven Gould Axelrod and Helen Deese (eds.), *Robert Lowell: Essays on the Poetry* (Cambridge: Cambridge University Press, 1986), pp. 180–216.

82. Lowell, *Collected Poems*, p. 460.

83. Hayden, *Collected Poems*, ed. Frederich Glaysher (New York, NY: Liveright, 1996), p. 101; Lawrence Ferlinghetti, *When I Look at Pictures* (Salt Lake City, UT: Peregrine Books, 1990), p. 20.

84. Heffernan, *Museum*, pp. 137–138.

85. On the sequence, see M. L. Rosenthal and Sally M. Gall, *The Modern Poetic Sequence: The Genius of Modern Poetry* (New York, NY: Oxford University Press, 1983).

86. Ferlinghetti's *When I Look at Pictures* collects and arranges ekphrases from four previous volumes – *A Coney Island of the Mind* (1958), *Endless Life* (1981), *European Poems and Transitions* (1988) and *Love in the Days of Rage* (1988) – plus nine additional poems.

87. Keats, *Poems*, p. 373. This is the currently favored punctuation printed in the 1820 *Lamia*.

88. Willard Spiegelman has explored the varieties of pedagogical techniques in twentieth-century didactic poetry from Auden through James Merrill, noting ekphrasis among them, as, for example, in his discussion of Anthony Hecht. See *The Didactic Muse: Scenes of Instruction in Contemporary American Poetry* (Princeton, NJ: Princeton University Press, 1989), esp. pp. 66–78.

89. Plath, *Collected Poems*, p. 81.

90. Lowell, *Collected Poems*, p. 458.

91. William Carlos Williams, *Collected Poems of William Carlos Williams*, vol. 2, ed. Christopher MacGowan (New York, NY: New Directions, 1988), p. 385; Ashbery, "Self-Portrait," p. 68.

92. Elizabeth Bishop, *The Complete Poems, 1927–1979* (New York, NY: Farrar, Straus and Giroux, 1983), p. 12.

93. Ferlinghetti, *When I Look*, p. 8.

94. Quoted in Heffernan, *Museum*, p. 49.

95. Thom Gunn, *Positives* (London: Faber, 1973), p. 62.

96. Adrienne Rich, *Collected Early Poems 1950–1970* (New York, NY: Norton, 1993), p. 230.

97. For an excellent discussion of this development, see Carol T. Christ, *Victorian and Modern Poetics* (Chicago, IL: University of Chicago Press, 1984).

98. M. L. Rosenthal, "Some thoughts on Irving Feldman's poetry" in Harold Schweizer (ed.), *The Poetry of Irving Feldman: Nine Essays* (Lewisburg, PA: Bucknell University Press, 1992), pp. 29–39 (p. 34).

99. Michael North, *The Final Sculpture: Public Monuments and Modern Poets* (Ithaca, NY: Cornell University Press, 1985) and Kenneth Gross, *The Dream of the Moving Statue* (Ithaca, NY: Cornell University Press, 1992).

100. David Lehman, *The Last Avant-Garde: The Making of the New York School of Poets* (New York, NY: Doubleday, 1998), p. 293.

101. Michael Baxandall, *Patterns of Intention: On the Historical Explanation of Pictures* (New Haven, CT: Yale University Press, 1985).

1 Private lives in public places: Yeats and Durcan in Dublin's galleries

1. Sassoon, *Collected Poems*, p. 151.
2. Seamus Heaney, *North* (London: Faber and Faber, 1975), pp. 69–70.
3. Eavan Boland, *Outside History: Selected Poems 1980–1990* (New York, NY: Norton, 1990), pp. 104–105.
4. On the rise of the art museum, see Germain Bazin, *The Museum Age* (New York, NY: Universe Books, 1967); Philip Fisher, *Making and Effacing Art: Modern American Art in a Culture of Museums* (New York, NY: Oxford University Press, 1991); Kenneth Hudson, *Museums of Influence* (Cambridge: Cambridge University Press, 1987), pp. 39–64; and Andrew McClellan, *Inventing the Louvre: Art, Politics, and the Origins of the Modern Museum in Eighteenth-Century Paris* (Cambridge: Cambridge University Press, 1994).
5. Hollander, *The Gazer's Spirit*, p. 75.
6. Quoted in Carol Duncan, *Civilizing Rituals: Inside Public Art Museums* (New York, NY: Routledge, 1995), pp. 14–15.
7. Quoted ibid., p. 15.
8. Ibid., p. 16.
9. Quoted in Jean-Michel Rabaté, *The Ghosts of Modernity* (Gainesville, FL: University Press of Florida, 1996), p. 188.
10. Paul Valéry, "The problem of museums" in *The Collected Works of Paul Valéry*, ed. Jackson Mathews, 15 vols. (Princeton, NJ: Princeton University Press, 1956–1975), vol. 12, pp. 202–206 (p. 203).
11. John Wain, "The Shipwreck" in Pat Adams (ed.), *With a Poet's Eye: A Tate Gallery Anthology* (London: The Tate Gallery, 1986), p. 40.
12. Yeats, *Poems*, p. 340.
13. Wilbur, *Poems*, p. 125.
14. See Catherine Paul, *Poetry in the Museums of Modernism: Yeats, Pound, Moore, Stein* (Ann Arbor, MI: University of Michigan Press, 2002); and Susan Rosenbaum, "Elizabeth Bishop and the miniature museum," *Journal of Modern Literature* 28.2 (2005), 61–99.
15. See Fisher, *Making and Effacing Art*.
16. Seamus Heaney, *A Personal Selection* (Belfast: Ulster Museum, 1982).
17. Quoted in Duncan, *Civilizing Rituals*, p. 11.
18. Ibid., p. 12.
19. Bazin, *Museum Age*, p. 7.
20. Brian O'Doherty, *Inside the White Cube: The Ideology of Gallery Space* (Santa Monica, CA: The Lapis Press, 1986), p. 15.
21. William Carlos Williams, *Collected Poems of William Carlos Williams*, vol. 1, ed. A. Walton Litz and Christopher MacGowan (New York, NY: New Directions, 1986), p. 81.

22. Pierre Bourdieu and Alain Darbel, *The Love of Art: European Art Museums and Their Public*, trans. Caroline Beattie and Nick Merriman from *L'Amour de l'art* (1969). (Stanford, CA: Stanford University Press, 1990), p. 18.

23. Ferlinghetti, *When I Look*, p. 20.

24. Malraux, *Museum without Walls*, p. 9.

25. Duncan, *Civilizing Rituals*, p. 1.

26. The academy has also played a role in the proliferation of ekphrasis through the flourishing of art history as an academic discipline, so closely allied with the growth of the modern art museum. In the preface to his influential collection of essays, *Beyond Culture: Essays on Literature and Learning* (New York, NY: Viking, 1965), Lionel Trilling observed the articulation of the academy and art museums in the growing importance of the "critical agent" to affect radically our understanding of culture (p. xv).

    The museum and the academy have long been linked by the academic training of curators and the art-historical narrative that has tended to structure museum exhibitions. The further tie to poetry produced in the academy is neatly pointed up by the collection of poems on Edward Hopper, *The Poetry of Solitude: A Tribute to Edward Hopper* (New York, NY: Universe, 1995), gathered by Hopper's biographer and frequent curator, Gail Levin. Most of the poets teach at colleges and universities, and many of the poems arose from poets' experiences with specific exhibitions of Hopper's work, often curated by Levin, and from the general rise of Hopper's reputation, for which Levin, a professor at Baruch College and CUNY Graduate School, is partly responsible. D. G. Kehl's anthology of ekphrastic poems, *Poetry and the Visual Arts* (Belmont, CA: Wadsworth, 1975), was intended for the classroom.

27. Irving Feldman, *All of Us Here* (New York, NY: Viking, 1986), p. 3.

28. Ibid., p. 7.

29. For discussions of Yeats's interactions with the visual arts, see Edward Engelberg, *The Vast Design: Patterns in W. B. Yeats's Aesthetic*, 2nd edn. (Washington, DC: Catholic University Press, 1988); T. R. Henn, *The Lonely Tower: Studies in the Poetry of W. B. Yeats*, rev. edn. (London: Methuen, 1965); and my *Yeats and the Visual Arts*.

30. W. B. Yeats, *Autobiographies*, ed. William H. O'Donnell and Douglas Archibald (New York, NY: Scribner, 1999), p. 163.

31. W. B. Yeats, *Under the Moon: The Unpublished Early Poetry*, ed. George Bornstein (New York, NY: Scribner, 1995), p. 36.

32. Ezra Pound, *Literary Essays of Ezra Pound*, ed. T. S. Eliot (New York, NY: New Directions, 1968), pp. 4, 3.

33. Williams, *Collected Poems*, vol. 2, p. 55.

34. J. D. McClatchy, "Introduction" in McClatchy (ed.), *Poets on Painters*, p. xi.

35. Yeats, *Poems*, p. 193.

36. Ibid.

37. Ibid., p. 214.

38. Rossetti's *Astarte Syriaca* in Manchester.

39. John Hollander notes "the class of 'gallery poems' . . . In these, a walk through a sequence of pictures itself occasions a quasi-narrative expository structure" (*Gazer's Spirit*, p. 75). For a discussion of Yeats's "Municipal Gallery" as a "poetic visit" that likens the space of the poem to the space of the museum, see Paul, *Poetry in the Museums of Modernism*, pp. 39–64.

40. As Catherine Paul notes (*Poetry in the Museums of Modernism*, p. 246 n. 11), not all of the pictures referred to in the poem can be identified with certainty for there are no records of what was on display in the museum in 1937. Richard Finneran in the notes to *Poems* (pp. 677–678) offers a set of likely possibilities: Sean Keating, *The Men of the West* (1915, "An ambush"); Sir John Lavery, *St. Patrick's Purgatory* (1929–1930, "pilgrims at the water-side"); Lavery, *The Court of Criminal Appeal* (1916, "Casement upon trial"); Lavery, *Arthur Griffith* (1921); Lavery, *Kevin O'Higgins*; Lavery, *The Blessing of the Colours* ("a revolutionary soldier kneeling"); perhaps John Singer Sargent, *Lady Charles Beresford* ("a woman's portrait"), although drafts show Yeats was also thinking of Lady Lavery (Wayne Chapman, " 'The Municipal Gallery Re-visited' and its writing," *Yeats Annual* 10 [1993]), 159–187 [p. 177]); Charles Shannon, *Robert Gregory*; probably Sargent, *Sir Hugh Lane* (1906); probably Lavery, *Portrait of Lady Lavery*, though possibly also *Hazel Lavery* and *Lady Lavery* ("living"); Lavery, *The Unfinished Harmony* (1934, "dying"); Antonio Mancini, *Lady Gregory* (1908); John Butler Yeats, *John M. Synge* (1905). The Municipal Gallery has suggested some additional possibilities in its two exhibitions of the poem with its images (1959 and 1996): Lavery, *Michael Collins*: *"Love of Ireland"* (1922), a more politically charged match with "An ambush"; Lavery, *La Dame aux Perles* (1901, "a woman's portrait"); and Lavery, *Hazel, Lady Lavery at an Easel* (*c.* 1905, "living"). The gallery published a slide pack for the 1996 exhibition. For excellent readings of "The Municipal Gallery Re-visited" with different emphases from my reading here, see Paul, *Poetry in the Museums of Modernism*, pp. 39–64 and Maureen Murphy, "Back to the Municipal Gallery: W. B. Yeats and modern Ireland" in *Conflicting Identities: Essays on Modern Irish Literature*, ed. Robbie B. H. Goh (Singapore: UniPress, 1997), pp. 121–143.

41. Yeats, *Poems*, p. 319.

42. Ibid., p. 320.

43. Ibid., p. 321.

44. Ibid., pp. 319, 320.

45. Ibid., p. 320.

46. W. B. Yeats, *The Variorum Edition of the Poems of W. B. Yeats*, ed. Peter Allt and Russell K. Alspach, corrected 3rd printing (New York, NY: Macmillan, 1966), p. 839; Yeats, *Poems*, p. 321.

47. Yeats, *Poems*, p. 320.

48. Duncan, *Civilizing Rituals*, p. 8.
49. Quoted in James White, *National Gallery of Ireland* (New York, NY: Praeger, 1968), p. 35.
50. For a reading of "September 1913" in its varying bibliographical and political manifestations, see George Bornstein, *Material Modernism: The Politics of the Page* (Cambridge: Cambridge University Press, 2001), pp. 55–64.
51. Yeats, *Poems*, p. 108.
52. Lucy McDiarmid, *The Irish Art of Controversy* (Ithaca, NY: Cornell University Press, 2005), p. 37.
53. Yeats fought the English claim by citing the importance of art in shaping an emerging nation: "I have based my whole life on the conviction that it is more important to give fine examples of high art to a country that is still plastic, still growing, than to an old country where national character has been formed for centuries" (*Uncollected Prose*, vol. 2, ed. John P. Frayne and Colton Johnson [New York, NY: Columbia University Press, 1976], p. 418). For Yeats, Hugh Lane's French pictures would educate the nation's young out of provincialism and create a national culture ready to take its place on the international stage. Culturally, the museum as a local habitation of the international allowed for Yeats the yoking of nationalism to international modernism.
54. See McDiarmid for details of further refinements of the agreement that recognized, increasingly, Dublin's claim on the pictures (*The Irish Art of Controversy*, p. 48).
55. Yeats, *Poems*, p. 321.
56. Malraux, *Museum without Walls*, p. 9.
57. Murphy, "Back to the Municipal Gallery," pp. 131, 139; Yeats, *Poems*, p. 319.
58. W. B. Yeats, *Senate Speeches*, ed. Donald R. Pearce (Bloomington, IN: Indiana University Press, 1960), p. 119.
59. Paul, *Poetry in the Museums of Modernism*, pp. 51–52.
60. See, for example, Seamus Deane, "The literary myths of the Revival" and "Yeats and the idea of revolution" in *Celtic Revivals: Essays in Modern Irish Literature, 1880–1890* (Winston-Salem, NC: Wake Forest University Press, 1987 [1985]), pp. 28–37, 38–50; and Richard Kearney, "Myth and motherland" in *Ireland's Field Day* (Notre Dame, IN: University of Notre Dame Press, 1986 [1983]), pp. 61–80. Kearney's influential critique in "Myth" that Yeats promoted (in "Easter 1916" and elsewhere) a "mythic attitude" (p. 62) to Irish history and nationality by elaborating a "sacred rite of blood-sacrifice whereby" Ireland would reclaim its identity by entering "the sacred time which transcends historical time" (p. 70) depends on an uncomplicated reading of Yeats's work and a view of his thought as unchanging across his career. The terms of Kearney's argument – Yeats's tendency to "piety" in the tradition of "*pius Aeneas*" rather than "secularity" (pp. 62–63) – seem to play out in Yeats's sacralizing of the images of his friends in "The Municipal Gallery," except that, as I argue, Yeats's own

attitude to the attitude of "piety" is acutely and painfully ambivalent. David Lloyd's reading of "Easter 1916" as "one of Yeats's earliest reflections upon the obsessive rituals of repetition by which nation states assure the legitimacy of their foundations and maintain their equilibrium" (*Anomalous States: Irish Writing and the Post-Colonial Moment* [Durham, NC: Duke University Press, 1993], p. 70) is provocative for thinking about the repetition highlighted in the title of Yeats's poem.

61. See Helen Vendler, "Four elegies" in A. Norman Jeffares (ed.), *Yeats, Sligo and Ireland* (Totowa, NJ: Barnes and Noble, 1980), pp. 216–231, and Jahan Ramazani, *Yeats and the Poetry of Death: Elegy, Self-Elegy and the Sublime* (New Haven, CT: Yale University Press, 1990).

62. Ramazani, *Yeats and the Poetry of Death*, p. 153.

63. Yeats, *Poems*, p. 321.

64. Fisher, *Making and Effacing Art*, p. 7.

65. "To the extent that the Louvre embodied the Republican principles of Liberty, Equality, and Fraternity, all citizens were encouraged to participate in the experience of communal ownership, and clearly many did ... Foreign visitors were struck by the presence of 'the lowest classes of the community'" (McClellan, *Inventing the Louvre*, p. 9).

66. Ferlinghetti, "Monet's Lilies Shuddering" in *When I Look*, p. 20.

67. Such anxiety is part of a larger picture of changes in cultural production that began in the early part of the century as writers tried to reckon with mass culture and the implications of art's commodification. Lawrence Rainey's materialist revision of literary modernist history is helpful here on the extent to which patron–collectors invested in literary modernism by underwriting little magazines and investing in limited editions of modernist works (*Institutions of Modernism: Literary Elites and Public Culture* [New Haven, CT: Yale University Press, 1998]):

> Literary modernism constitutes a strange and perhaps unprecedented withdrawal from the public sphere of cultural production and debate, a retreat into a divided world of patronage, investment, and collecting. Uneasiness concerning the ethical legitimacy of patronage, corresponding efforts to assimilate patronage to concepts of investment and profit, and the concomitant attempt to objectify literary value in the form of the rare book or deluxe edition – all these trace a profound change in the relations among authors, publishers, critics, and readerships. (p. 75)

> Yeats knew well the world of limited editions and their patrons: his sister owned and ran the Cuala Press, of which he was literary executor and, occasionally, financier. As a small-press production itself, the first edition of "The Municipal Gallery Re-visited" already opens the question of who would support and patronize both museums and poems. Rainey goes on to observe, "To a remarkable degree, modernist literature was an experiment in adopting exchange

and market structures typical of the visual arts, a realm in which patronage and collecting can thrive because its artisanal mode of production is compatible with a limited submarket for luxury goods." It is, indeed, "no accident" that "paintings repeatedly figure as metaphors for the literary work in this period" (p. 75).

68. Yeats, *Variorum Poems*, p. 839.
69. Bakhtin, *The Dialogic Imagination*, p. 23.
70. Durcan, *Crazy*, p. 3.
71. Established by an Act of Parliament in 1854, opened in 1864, inaugurated by the Lord Lieutenant, the Earl of Carlisle, the National Gallery of Ireland was the product less of private collections made public than of subscriptions given by Ireland's wealthy Anglo-Irish. Part of the initial collection was purchased (some in Rome from the "celebrated collection" of Cardinal Fesch) with money lent by the Lord Chancellor, Maziere Brady. For a history of the gallery, see Raymond Keaveney, "Introduction" in Raymond Keaveney, Michael Wynne, Adrian Le Harivel, Fionnuala Croke and Sergio Benedetti, *National Gallery of Ireland* (London: Scala, 1998 [1990]), pp. 6–9. For a discussion of Durcan's response to the violence in the North, including a reading of "Riding School" from *Crazy*, see Edna Longley, "Paul Durcan and the North: Recollections" in Colm Tóibín (ed.), *The Kilfenora Teaboy: A Study of Paul Durcan* (Dublin: New Island Books, 1996), pp. 102–113.
72. McClellan, *Inventing the Louvre*, p. 9.
73. See Durcan, *Crazy*, p. x and Colm Tóibín, "Portrait of the artist as a spring lamb" in Tóibín (ed.), *The Kilfenora Teaboy*, pp. 7–25 (p. 11).
74. Durcan, *Crazy*, pp. x–xi.
75. For discussions of Durcan's ekphrases before *Crazy*, see Kathleen McCracken, "Canvas and camera translated: Paul Durcan and the visual arts," *The Irish Review* (Fall, 1989), 18–29; and Kathleen McCracken Gahern, "Masks and voices: Dramatic personas in the poetry of Paul Durcan," *Canadian Journal of Irish Studies* 13.1 (1987), 107–120.
76. Wilbur, *Poems*, p. 125.
77. Ibid.
78. Adams (ed.), *With a Poet's Eye*; Abse and Abse (eds.), *Voices*; Edward Hirsch (ed.), *Transforming Vision*; Paul Durcan, *Give Me Your Hand* (London: National Gallery, 1994). Other similar efforts include the Armand Hammer Museum in Los Angeles, which sponsored a 1996 exhibition of René Magritte's paintings accompanied by specially commissioned poems on them by six poets (Jorie Graham, John Hollander, Deborah Greger, Richard Howard, J. D. McClatchy and Rosanna Warren) published as *Lines = Lignes; Réflexions = Reflections* (Los Angeles, CA: Armand Hammer Museum, 1996), and Richard Tillinghast (ed.), *A Visit to the Gallery* (Ann Arbor, MI: University of Michigan Museum of Art, 1997), containing twenty-four commissioned ekphrases on the University of Michigan Art Museum's collection.

79. Lowell, *Collected Poems*, p. 460.
80. Durcan, *Crazy*, pp. 89, 37.
81. Ibid., p. 103.
82. Eamon Grennan, "Prime Durcan: A collage" in Tóibín (ed.), *The Kilfenora Teaboy*, pp. 42–74 (p. 66).
83. O'Doherty, *Inside the White Cube*, pp. 35–64.
84. Durcan, *Crazy*, p. 138.
85. Ibid., p. 139.
86. Ibid., p. 63.
87. Ibid., p. 137.
88. Ibid., p. 59.
89. Ibid., p. 61.
90. Ibid., pp. 74–75.
91. Ibid., p. 87.
92. Ibid., p. 19.
93. Ibid., p. 41.
94. Derek Mahon, "Orpheus ascending: The poetry of Paul Durcan" in Tóibín (ed.), *The Kilfenora Teaboy*, pp. 163–170 (p. 168).
95. Durcan, *Crazy*, p. 45.
96. Fisher, *Making and Effacing Art*, p. 10.
97. Durcan, *Crazy*, p. 5.
98. Ibid.
99. Ibid., p. 7.
100. Ibid.
101. Ibid., p. 121.
102. Hilde S. Heine, *The Museum in Transition: A Philosophical Perspective* (Washington, DC: Smithsonian Institution Press, 2000), pp. 6, 5.
103. Raymond Keaveney, "Acknowledgements" in Durcan, *Crazy*, p. vii. The museum had some second thoughts when Durcan delivered the manuscript: "Suddenly the National Gallery of Ireland had to face the situation that it was about to engage in a project that challenged its public on non-artistic issues. Paul's poems . . . described vividly the act of love-making, referred to homosexual love, to AIDS, to the fondness of some men for little girls, and also to making love in the grass, sharing a bath with a lover, jumping into bed in the middle of the day. This would be no ordinary National Gallery exhibition and accompanying publication" (Brian Kennedy, "*Crazy About Women*: Poems about paintings" in Tóibín (ed.), *The Kilfenora Teaboy*, pp. 155–162 (pp. 158–159).
104. Brian Kennedy, "Foreword" in Durcan, *Crazy*, p. ix.
105. Ibid.
106. Durcan, *Crazy*, p. x.
107. Ibid., p. 23.
108. Kennedy, "Poems about paintings," pp. 160–161.

109. Marianne Moore, *Becoming Marianne Moore: The Early Poems, 1907–1924*, ed. Robin G. Schulze (Berkeley, CA: University of California Press, 2002), p. 101.
110. Yeats, *Poems*, p. 175.
111. Quoted in Rabaté, *Ghosts*, p. 188.

2 Bystanding in Auden's "Musée"

1. Michael Hamburger, "A Painter Painted" in Abse and Abse (eds.), *Voices*, p. 128.
2. Jarrell, *Complete Poems*, p. 332.
3. See Kenneth Gross for a discussion of ekphrasis and statues of the dead (*Dream of the Moving Statue*, esp. pp.143–146). For a discussion of Yeats's ekphrases and death, see Ramazani, *Yeats and the Poetry of Death*, pp. 152–161.
4. Hayden, *Collected Poems*, p. 101.
5. M. L. Rosenthal, "Some thoughts on Irving Feldman's poetry" in Harold Schweizer (ed.), *The Poetry of Irving Feldman: Nine Essays* (Lewisburg, PA: Bucknell University Press, 1992), pp. 29–39 (p. 34).
6. Heaney, *North*, pp. 35–36.
7. Ernest Becker, *The Denial of Death* (New York, NY: Free Press, 1973).
8. Philippe Ariès, *The Hour of Our Death*, trans. Helen Weaver (New York, NY: Knopf, 1981), pp. 559–601.
9. Ibid., p. 571.
10. Jay Ruby, *Secure the Shadow: Death and Photography in America* (Cambridge, MA: MIT Press, 1995), pp. 17, 12.
11. Susan Sontag, *On Photography* (New York, NY: Farrar, Straus and Giroux, 1977), pp. 19–20.
12. Ferlinghetti, *When I Look*, p. 8.
13. U. A. Fanthorpe, "The Doctor" in Adams (ed.), *With a Poet's Eye*, pp. 62–63.
14. Feldman, "The Bystanders at the Massacre" in *All of Us Here*, p. 14.
15. Shelley, "On the Medusa of Leonardo da Vinci."
16. Edward Hirsch, *For the Sleepwalkers* (Pittsburgh, PA: Carnegie-Mellon University Press, 1998), pp. 76–77.
17. Heaney, *North*, p. 38.
18. Ariès, *Hour of Our Death*, p. 575.
19. Geoffrey Gorer, "The pornography of death" in *Death, Grief, and Mourning* (New York, NY: Doubleday, 1965), pp. 192–199.
20. See, e.g., Ernest Gilman, *Iconoclasm and Poetry in the English Reformation: Down Went Dagon* (Chicago, IL: University of Chicago Press, 1986); Mitchell, *Iconology*; Ronald Paulson, "English iconoclasm in the eighteenth century" in James Heffernan (ed.), *Space, Time, Image, Sign: Essays on Literature and the Visual Arts* (New York, NY: Peter Lang, 1987), pp. 41–62.
21. Stafford, *Good Looking*, p. 12.

22. Quoted in David Freedberg, *The Power of Images: Studies in the History and Theory of Response* (Chicago, IL: University of Chicago Press, 1989), p. 4.

23. Duncan, *Civilizing Rituals*, p. 56.

24. See, e.g., Caws, *Interference*, pp.179–193; Heffernan, *Museum*, pp. 146–152.

25. James V. Mirollo cites Gisbert Kranz's extensive *Meisterwerke in Bildgedichten* as listing more than forty twentieth-century ekphrastic responses to Brueghel's *Fall of Icarus* ("Bruegel's *Fall of Icarus* and the poets" in Amy Golahny [ed.], *The Eye of the Poet: Studies in the Reciprocity of the Visual and Literary Arts from the Renaissance to the Present* [Lewisburg, PA: Bucknell University Press, 1996], pp. 131–153). Robert J. Clements discusses eighteen modern poems on Brueghel's painting, fifteen coming after Auden ("Brueghel's *Fall of Icarus*: Eighteen modern literary readings," *Studies in Iconography* 7–8 [1981–1982], 253–268). To his list we can add Randall Jarrell's "Old and New Masters," a direct response to Auden though not on *Icarus*, and Dannie Abse's "Brueghel in Naples," both discussed below.

26. W. H. Auden, *Another Time* (New York, NY: Random House, 1940), p. 33.

27. Marsha Bryant, *Auden and Documentary in the 1930s* (Charlottesville, VA: University Press of Virginia, 1997), p. 7.

28. Ibid., pp. 7–8.

29. Auden, *Another Time*, p. 80.

30. Bryant, *Auden and Documentary*, p. 66.

31. W. H. Auden and Louis MacNeice, *Letters from Iceland* (London: Faber and Faber, 1937), p. 32.

32. Auden and Christopher Isherwood, *Journey to a War* (New York, NY: Random House, 1939), p. 19.

33. Quoted in Edward Mendelson, *Early Auden* (Cambridge, MA: Harvard University Press, 1983), p. 321 n.

34. Ibid., p. 321.

35. Auden, *Another Time*, p. 98. Auden radically revised "Spain 1937" for inclusion in *Another Time*, removing the passages that connect acts of war with natural processes. "Necessary murder" has been changed to "fact of murder," but "the conscious acceptance of guilt" remains. See Mendelson, *Early Auden*, pp. 322–323, and George Mills Harper, " 'Necessary murder': The Auden circle and the Spanish Civil War" in Vereen Bell and Laurence Lerner (eds.), *On Modern Poetry: Essays Presented to Donald Davie* (Nashville, TN: Vanderbilt, 1988), pp. 67–80.

36. See Lucy McDiarmid, *Saving Civilization: Yeats, Eliot, and Auden between the Wars* (Cambridge: Cambridge University Press, 1984).

37. For Heffernan's discussion of how the museum's words, including its titling of Brueghel's picture, shape the poem, see *Museum*, pp. 146–152.

38. Auden, *Another Time*, p. 34.

39. Heffernan (*Museum*, p. 146) follows Long and Cage's identification of the pictures and makes the point that Auden "assembled" his Musée by

importing *Massacre of the Innocents* from Vienna to Brussels (Beverly Whitaker Long and Timothy Scott Cage, "Contemporary American poetry: A selected bibliography," *Text and Performance Quarterly* 9 [1989], 286–296 [p. 287]). But Hollander notes that the Brussels museum has a copy of the *Massacre* on canvas by his son Pieter Brueghel the Younger (*Gazer's Spirit*, p. 251). There was no need to import the original.

40. Auden, *Another Time*, p. 34.
41. See Heffernan, *Museum*, p. 150.
42. Williams, *Collected Poems*, vol. 2, p. 386.
43. Elizabeth Bishop, *One Art*, ed. Robert Giroux (New York, NY: Farrar, Straus and Giroux, 1994), p. 170.
44. Jarrell, *Complete Poems*, p. 332.
45. Ibid.
46. Caws, *Interference*, p. 185.
47. Harold Schweizer, "Lyric suffering in Auden and Feldman," *English Language Notes* 31.2 (December 1, 1993), 66–74 (p. 67).
48. Irving Feldman, *Teach Me, Dear Sister* (New York, NY: Viking, 1983), p. 34.
49. Auden, *Another Time*, p. 33.
50. João Ferreira Duarte, "Auden's Icarus and his fall: Vision, super-vision and revision" in Robert Clark and Piero Boitani (eds.), *English Studies in Transition: Papers from the ESSE Inaugural Conference* (London: Routledge, 1991), p. 240.
51. Auden, *Another Time*, p. 34.
52. Ashbery, "Self-Portrait," p. 70.
53. Reported in a study of American museums conducted from 1925 to 1927. The longest time spent at any one given picture averaged between 25 and 52 seconds (Edward Stevens Robinson, *The Behavior of the Museum Visitor* [Washington, DC: Publications of the American Association of Museums, new series no. 5, 1928], pp. 28–30). Robinson reports the average time spent in a given art museum visit as 15 to 25 minutes. Times were longer in Bourdieu's 1969 study of European museums: 22 minutes for working-class visitors, 35 minutes for middle-class visitors, and 47 minutes for upper-class visitors (Bourdieu and Darbel, *The Love of Art*, pp. 37–38).
54. Paul Valéry, "The problem of museums," p. 203.
55. Michael Riffaterre, "Textuality: W. H. Auden's 'Musee des Beaux Arts'" in Mary Ann Caws (ed.), *Textual Analysis: Some Readers Reading* (New York, NY: Modern Language Association, 1986), pp. 1–13 (p. 8).
56. John Fuller, *W. H. Auden: A Commentary* (Princeton, NJ: Princeton University Press, 1998), p. 266.
57. As Heffernan notes, Gustave Gluck's 1936 *Peter Brueghel* suggests that the corpse illustrates the German proverb "No plough comes to a standstill because a man dies," a book and saying Auden might have known; he certainly knew it from Blake's *Marriage of Heaven and Hell* as "Drive your cart and your plow over the bones of the dead" (*Museum*, pp. 219–220 n. 16).

58. Auden also expressed this in one of the sonnets from the sequence "In Time of War," part of *Journey to a War* and possibly a comment on his photograph "The Innocent": "They are and suffer; that is all they do . . . And lie apart like epochs from each other . . . And are remote as plants; we stand elsewhere" (Auden and Isherwood, *Journey to a War*, p. 275).

59. Auden, *Another Time*, p. 94.

60. Dannie Abse, "Brueghel in Naples," *Poetry Review* 79.2 (1989), 26.

61. Sontag, *On Photography*, p. 12.

62. Caws, *Interference*, p. 186.

63. Bryant, *Auden and Documentary*, pp. 130–142.

64. Heaney, *North*, p. 70.

65. Diggory, *Ethics of Painting*, p. 50.

66. Susan Sontag, "Looking at the unbearable" in Hirsch (ed.), *Transforming Vision*, p. 91.

67. Mendelson, *Early Auden*, p. xiv.

68. Ibid., p. 364.

69. Ibid., p. xvii.

70. He did go on, however, to review *The Complete Letters of Vincent Van Gogh* in 1959 and, two years later, edit his own selection of Van Gogh's letters: W. H. Auden (ed.), *Van Gogh, a Self-Portrait: Letters Revealing His Life as a Painter* (London: Thames & Hudson, 1961).

71. As in the 1969 "Ballad of Barnaby," written for students at a prep school and handed out at Auden's memorial service in 1972, with illustrations by Edward Gorey. See Lucy McDiarmid, *Auden's Apologies for Poetry* (Princeton, NJ: Princeton University Press, 1990), pp. 3–8.

3 Women looking: The feminist ekphrasis of Marianne Moore and Adrienne Rich

1. Mitchell, *Picture Theory*, p. 168.

2. Keats, *Poems*, p. 372.

3. Mitchell, *Picture Theory*, p. 168.

4. Ibid., p. 181.

5. See Cathryn Vasseleu's argument that Irigaray's position is more complicated and not as hostile to sight as others, notably Martin Jay, perceive ("Illuminating passion: Irigaray's transfiguration of night" in Teresa Brennan and Martin Jay (eds.), *Vision in Context: Historical and Contemporary Perspectives on Sight* [New York, NY: Routledge, 1996], pp. 127–137). See Martin Jay, *Downcast Eyes: The Denigration of Vision in Twentieth-Century French Thought* (Berkeley, CA: University of California Press, 1993). For an excellent overview of the role of vision in western thought, see Evelyn Fox Keller and Christine R. Grontkowski, "The mind's eye" in Evelyn Fox Keller and Helen E. Longino (eds.), *Feminism and Science* (Oxford: Oxford University Press, 1996), pp. 187–202.

6. Discussions of particular women poets' ekphrastic practices are accumulating. See, for example, Jane Hedley, Nick Halpern and Willard Spiegelman (eds.), *In the Frame: Women's Ekphrastic Poetry from Marianne Moore to Susan Wheeler* (Newark, DE: University of Delaware Press, 2008); Kristin Bluemel, "The dangers of eccentricity: Stevie Smith's doodles and poetry," *Mosaic* 31.3 (September, 1998), 111–132; Barbara K. Fischer, *Museum Meditations: Reframing Ekphrasis in Contemporary American Poetry* (New York, NY: Routledge, 2006); Jane Hedley, "Sylvia Plath's ekphrastic poetry," *Raritan* 20.4 (2001), 37–73; Donna K. Hollenberg, "'History as I desired it': Ekphrasis as postmodern witness in Denise Levertov's late poetry," *Modernism/Modernity* 10.3 (2003), 519–537; Sherry Lutz Zivley, "Sylvia Plath's transformations of modernist paintings," *College Literature* 29.3 (Summer, 2002), 35–56; and, especially, Sara Lundquist, "Reverence and resistance: Barbara Guest, ekphrasis, and the female gaze," *Contemporary Literature* 38.2 (1997), 260–286. For a brief account of the importance of the sister arts analogy (and the use of ekphrasis) to nineteenth-century feminism, see Michele Martinez, "Women poets and the sister arts in nineteenth-century England," *Victorian Poetry* 41.4 (Winter, 2003), 621–628.

7. As Linda Nochlin so succinctly summarizes in *Women, Art, and Power and Other Essays* (New York, NY: Harper & Row, 1988), p. 30. For some of the same questions asked in relation to Plath, see Hedley, "Plath's ekphrastic poetry."

8. Griselda Pollock, *Vision and Difference: Femininity, Feminism and Histories of Art* (London: Routledge, 1988), p. 85.

9. See Scott, *Sculpted Word*, p. 17, on Baillie's teapot in relation to Keats's urn.

10. Edna St. Vincent Millay, *Collected Sonnets* (New York, NY: Harper & Row, 1988), p. 67.

11. For an overview of the feminist response (to 1990) to women looking at images of women, see Lynne Pearce, *Woman/Image/Text: Readings in Pre-Raphaelite Art and Literature* (Toronto, ON: University of Toronto Press, 1991).

12. Bonnie Costello, *Marianne Moore: Imaginary Possessions* (Cambridge, MA: Harvard University Press, 1981), p. 192. On the importance of the visual arts to Moore, see also Leavell, *Marianne Moore and the Visual Arts*; and Elisabeth Joyce, *Cultural Critique and Abstraction: Marianne Moore and the Avant-Garde* (Lewisburg, PA: Bucknell University Press, 1998).

13. Revised version, as it appears in Marianne Moore, *The Complete Poems of Marianne Moore* (New York, NY: Macmillan, 1982 [1967]), p. 47.

14. Marianne Moore, *The Complete Prose of Marianne Moore*, ed. Patricia C. Willis (New York, NY: Viking, 1986), p. 215.

15. Cristanne Miller, *Marianne Moore: Questions of Authority* (Cambridge, MA: Harvard University Press, 1995), p. ix.

16. Mitchell, *Picture Theory*, p. 156.

17. Ibid.

18. Heffernan, *Museum*, p. 7.

19. See Margaret Dickie, "The maternal gaze: Women modernists and poetic authority" in Linda Marie Brooks (ed.), *Alternative Identities: The Self in Literature, History, Theory* (New York, NY: Garland, 1995), pp. 221–242; and Paul's discussion of Stein (*Poetry in the Museums of Modernism,* pp. 200–203).

20. Though none have placed Moore in the ekphrastic tradition, many critics have explored Moore's efforts to undermine conventional, gendered attitudes toward the world, especially the natural world. See, especially, Jeanne Heuving, *Omissions Are Not Accidents: Gender in the Art of Marianne Moore* (Detroit, MI: Wayne State University Press, 1992). For a discussion of how Moore's "use of Chinese painting theory and philosophy [and Chinese art] . . . enabled her to explore alternatives . . . to western ways of narrating visual experience," see Cynthia Stamy, *Marianne Moore and China: Orientalism and a Writing of America* (Oxford: Oxford University Press, 1999), p. vii.

21. For a discussion of women's colleges, see Helen Lefkowitz Horowitz, *Alma Mater: Design and Experience in the Women's Colleges from Their Nineteenth-Century Beginnings to the 1930s* (New York, NY: Knopf, 1984); and, of Bryn Mawr in particular, William H. Welch, "Contribution of Bryn Mawr College to the higher education of women," *Science* 56 (July 7, 1922), 1–8. On women and the sciences, see Margaret W. Rossiter, *Women Scientists in America: Struggles and Strategies to 1940* (Baltimore, MD: Johns Hopkins University Press, 1982). On women entering the art world, see Linda Downs, "A recent history of women educators in art museums" in Jane R. Glaser and Artemis A. Zenetou (eds.), *Gender Perspectives: Essays on Women in Museums* (Washington, DC: Smithsonian Institution Press, 1994), pp. 92–96; Kathleen D. McCarthy, *Women's Culture: American Philanthropy and Art, 1830–1930* (Chicago, IL: University of Chicago Press, 1991); Claire Richter Sherman with Adele M. Holcomb, "Precursors and pioneers (1820–1890)" and Claire Richter Sherman, "Widening horizons (1890–1930)," both in Claire Richter Sherman with Adele M. Holcomb (eds.), *Women as Interpreters of the Visual Arts, 1820–1979* (Westport, CT: Greenwood, 1981), pp. 3–26 and pp. 27–59 respectively; and Kendall Taylor, "Pioneering efforts of early museum women" in Glaser and Zenetou (eds.), *Gender Perspectives,* pp. 11–27.

22. Susanna Terrell Saunders, "Georgiana Goddard King (1871–1939): Educator and pioneer in medieval Spanish art" in Sherman with Holcomb (eds.), *Women as Interpreters of the Visual Arts,* pp. 209–238 (p. 218). See also Charles Molesworth, *Marianne Moore: A Literary Life* (New York, NY: Atheneum, 1990).

23. The poem also draws on Elizabethan maps, Leonardo's *St. Jerome,* and ekphrastic descriptions of the "embroideries" adorning Queen Elizabeth's dresses. Moore's notes point us to Violet A. Wilson's *Queen Elizabeth's Maids of Honour and Ladies of the Privy Chamber* (London: John Lane, 1922) as the source for the account of voyagers encountering and returning with

evidence of sea unicorns (Arctic narwhals) and land unicorns, as well as the quoted phrases (some exact, some modified) used to describe the "embroideries." They are phrases Wilson herself quotes from Mary Scudamore's inventory of Queen Elizabeth's embroidered dresses (pp. 131–132) and although they mention "greene satten, embrodered all over with sylver, like beasts, fowles, and fishes" (p. 132), there is no mention of Moore's "fourfold combination." For two of the fourfold combination, those described in lines 39–43 ("the lion standing up against this screen of woven air/ which is the forest:/ the unicorn also, on its hind legs in reciprocity"), we can turn to the Cluny tapestries, three of which depict the lion and unicorn on their hind legs. The pursuit of the unicorn by the dogs is depicted in the famous *The Hunt of the Unicorn* series of the Metropolitan Museum (The Cloisters), exhibited at the Anderson Galleries in 1922. Moore could have known them from this time. In 1923 the tapestries twice made headline news in *The New York Times* as John D. Rockefeller negotiated their purchase. He later donated them to the Metropolitan, which displayed them at The Cloisters, opened in 1938 (Janet Sullivan, "Encountering the unicorn: William Carlos Williams and Marianne Moore," *Sagtrieb: A Journal Devoted to Poets in the Imagist/Objectivist Tradition* 6.3 [Winter, 1987], 147–161 [pp. 154–155]). The Cloisters tapestries also depict other animals, including the lion, but no sea lions or sea unicorns. The final image of the unicorn tamed by the lady is made up of elements of Queen Elizabeth's dresses ("improved 'all over slightly with snakes of Venice gold,/ and silver, and some O's'") and other medieval and early Renaissance depictions of the unicorn with its head in the virgin's lap. In some depictions, the story serves as an allegory of the annunciation, hence the unicorn's association with "dress of Virgin-Mary blue" (Moore, *Becoming Marianne Moore*, p. 135). See Margaret B. Freeman, *The Unicorn Tapestries* (New York, NY: Metropolitan Museum, 1976), pp. 49–51.

24. Moore, *Becoming Marianne Moore*, p. 134.
25. Costello, *Marianne Moore*, p. 154.
26. Moore, *Becoming Marianne Moore*, pp. 134–135.
27. Ibid., p. 133.
28. Moore, *Complete Prose*, p. 218.
29. Many of the ethical questions Moore faces she shared with William Carlos Williams, who also sought to work them out in relation to visual arts (including The Cloisters tapestries) and by some of the same means. *Paterson V*, in particular, focuses on the virgin and the unicorn. See Diggory's analysis of Williams' ethics in relation to those of Julia Kristeva, especially his chapter on the virgin (*Ethics of Painting*, pp. 82–102).
30. Moore, *Becoming Marianne Moore*, p. 102. For Moore and humility, see Jeredith Merrin, *An Enabling Humility: Marianne Moore, Elizabeth Bishop, and the Uses of Tradition* (New Brunswick, NJ:Rutgers University Press, 1990).
31. Moore, *Complete Poems*, p. 231.

32. Moore's use of quotations also, however, raises in another way the ethical issue she was trying to resolve. On the one hand, her free use of them brings the words of others into close dialogue with the poet, refusing a distancing reverence; on the other, as Taffy Martin says, "she is less gracious when it comes to acknowledging and respecting the integrity of the words she borrows," often without attribution. She "has mastered the skill of appropriating" (*Marianne Moore: Subversive Modernist* [Austin, TX: University Texas Press, 1986], p. 108).

33. Costello, *Marianne Moore*, p. 200. The poem was first titled "In Einer Jonsson's 'Cow.'" In another example, "The Magician's Retreat" names the house designed by Jean-Jacques Lequeu, which Moore saw on the cover of *Arts Magazine*, but the poem describes the house in a painting by René Magritte called *Domain of Lights*. See Patricia Willis, "Discoveries: 'The Magician's Retreat,'" *Marianne Moore Newsletter* 1.2 (Fall, 1977), 2–5 (p. 2); and Margaret Holley, *The Poetry of Marianne Moore: A Study in Voice and Value* (Cambridge: Cambridge University Press, 1987), p. 180.

34. *Voices and Visions: Program 8 – Marianne Moore*, videocassette (New York, NY: The New York Center for Visual History, 1988).

35. Moore, *Becoming Marianne Moore*, p. 101.

36. Moore was herself a collector of objects, and the pleasures of possession are everywhere present in her sitting room, preserved at the Rosenbach Museum and Library, and in the poems. "A kleptomaniac of the mind," Costello calls her, referring to her passion for clipping from newspapers, magazines, catalogues, and keeping detailed notes of what she read, gathering bits and pieces of material (*Marianne Moore*, p. 5). She treated her own poems as objects in a collection, organizing them for display in the space of the book (see Paul, *Poetry in the Museums of Modernism*, pp. 168–193). Moore's resistance to the dark ethical side of collecting and possessing is founded in her own knowledge of its pleasures and her recorded fascination with its excesses. Critics have remarked that the first section of "The Jerboa" – which registers Moore's skepticism about collecting, her recognition of the indulgence of acquisition, and the abuse of other cultures and misuses of resources that support it – nevertheless brings before us in detail the amassed art and artifice of Rome and Egypt (Costello, *Marianne Moore*, pp. 197–199; and Paul, *Poetry in the Museums of Modernism*, pp. 162–163).

37. The colored postcard was given to her in January, 1962 by Laurence Scott. She sent to the museum for more postcards, and also got two booklets. As Willis notes ("Charity Overcoming Envy," *Marianne Moore Newsletter* 3.1 [1979], 2–6), one of them, the *Scottish Art Review*, displays the tapestry on the cover and contains an article on it by William Wells that provides the quotations (some altered) in Moore's poem, and the phrase ("chest armour over chain mail") altered and not in quotations. "Chain-armour" is Wells's phrase. Wells also provides another important phrase not in quotations: "the

problem is mastered." The problem to which Wells refers is "the problem of representing three-dimensional space" in tapestries, mastered in one later tapestry in the Burrell Collection, but not in *Charity Overcoming Envy* (William Wells, "Two tapestries in the Burrell Collection," *Scottish Art Review* 6.3 [1957], 7–10, 29 [p. 29]). Three-dimensional space does not interest Moore; the issue of mastery does.

38. Moore, *Complete Poems*, p. 216.
39. The scroll reads *Ividi dolor animi cepru peris est proximi – gaudens eius de malis/ ut canis – sed hoc elephas nescit vincit et hoc nephas caritas fraceri*. Thanks to Judith Hollett and Gregory Staley (University of Maryland) and Jeffrey Hammond (St. Mary's College) for help with the translation. Hollander provides a slightly different translation based on a transcription differing from that offered in the literature on the tapestry (*Gazer's Spirit*, p. 299). Wells's essay does not mention the inscription. I have not been able to discover whether Moore read a translation elsewhere, but she probably had enough Latin to get the drift of this difficult passage. In any case, Wells's essay argues for reading the tapestry as a depiction of the conventional and popular theme of "the conflict between the [Christian] Virtues and the [pagan] Vices" (p. 7), a theme Moore left behind in early drafts of the poem.
40. Moore, *Complete Poems*, p. 216.
41. Quoted in Willis, "Charity Overcoming Envy," p. 5.
42. Elisabeth Joyce suggested this sense of "master" to me. Private correspondence, November 2002.
43. Willis, "Charity Overcoming Envy," p. 6.
44. Moore, *Complete Poems*, p. 217.
45. Moore, *Becoming Marianne Moore*, p. 124.
46. Moore, *Complete Poems*, p. 216.
47. See, especially, "The Black Earth" (*Becoming Marianne Moore*, pp. 87–89) and Costello's discussion (*Marianne Moore*, pp. 57–62).
48. Adrienne Rich, *On Lies, Secrets, and Silence: Selected Prose 1966–1978* (New York, NY: Norton, 1979), p. 39.
49. Tillie Olson, *Silences* (London: Virago, 1978), p. 10.
50. Miller, *Marianne Moore*, p. iv.
51. Rich, *On Lies*, pp. 14–15.
52. Rich, *Collected Early Poems*, p. 287.
53. Adrienne Rich, *Blood, Bread, and Poetry: Selected Prose 1979–1985* (New York, NY: Norton, 1986), p. 182.
54. Susan R. Van Dyne, "The mirrored vision of Adrienne Rich," *Modern Poetry Studies* 8 (1978), 140–173 (p. 146).
55. Albert Gelpi, "Adrienne Rich: The poetics of change," in Barbara Charlesworth Gelpi and Albert Gelpi (eds.), *Adrienne Rich's Poetry and Prose*, rev. edn. (New York, NY: Norton, 1993), p. 283.

56. Elaine Showalter, "Towards a feminist poetics" in Mary Jacobus (ed.), *Women Writing and Writing about Women* (New York, NY: Barnes and Noble, 1979), pp. 22–41 (p. 28).

57. Marianne Whelchel, "Mining the 'earth-deposits': Women's history in Adrienne Rich's poetry" in Jane Roberta Cooper (ed.), *Reading Adrienne Rich: Reviews and Re-visions, 1951–1981* (Ann Arbor, MI: University of Michigan Press, 1984), pp. 51–71 (pp. 52–53).

58. Rich, *Collected Early Poems*, p. 29. Historians now believe the tapestry was commissioned by Odo, the Bishop of Bayeux and half-brother of William, and produced by the famous embroidery works in Winchester, England (Lynn Harry Nelson, www.ku.edu/Kansas/medieval/108/lectures/bayeux_tapestry.html [accessed August 1, 2003].)

59. See Ibis Communications, "Invasion of England, 1066," www. eyewitnesstohistory.com/bayeux.htm (accessed February 20, 2004).

60. Rich, *Collected Early Poems*, p. 29.

61. Ibid.

62. Rich, *On Lies*, p. 43.

63. Kate Millett, *Sexual Politics* (Garden City, NY: Doubleday, 1970), pp. 54–58.

64. Rich, *Blood, Bread, and Poetry*, p. 146.

65. Rich, *On Lies*, pp. 14–15.

66. Rich, *Collected Early Poems*, p. 29.

67. Ibid.

68. Ibid., p. 41.

69. Ibid., p. 64.

70. David Kalstone, *Five Temperaments: Elizabeth Bishop, Robert Lowell, James Merrill, Adrienne Rich, John Ashbery* (New York, NY: Oxford University Press, 1977), p. 131.

71. Rich, *Collected Early Poems*, p. 64.

72. Ibid., p. 113.

73. Ibid.

74. Laura Mulvey, *Visual and Other Pleasures* (Bloomington, IN: Indiana University Press, 1989), pp. 32–33.

75. See Pearce, *Woman/Image/Text*, p. 19.

76. Rich, *Collected Early Poems*, p. 113.

77. Adrienne Rich, *A Wild Patience Has Taken Me This Far: Poems 1978–1981* (New York, NY: Norton, 1981), p. 4.

78. Ibid., p. 5.

79. For other discussions of "Mourning Picture" as ekphrasis, see John Dixon Hunt, *Self-Portrait in a Convex Mirror: On Poems on Paintings* (London: Bedford College, 1980), pp. 1–4; and Heffernan, *Museum*, pp. 136–137.

80. Rich, *On Lies*, p. 181.

81. In *Collected Early Poems*, the poem is missing the part of the headnote printed in *Necessities of Life* that reads "The picture was painted by Edwin Romanzo

Elmer (1850–1923) as a memorial to his daughter Effie. In the poem, it is the dead girl who speaks" (Adrienne Rich, *Necessities of Life: Poems 1962–1965* [New York, NY: Norton, 1966], p. 72).

82. Rich, *Collected Early Poems*, p. 230.
83. Ibid.
84. Ibid., p. 231.
85. Ibid.
86. Rich, *On Lies*, p. 263.
87. *Folk Art in America – A Living Tradition: Selections from the Abby Aldrich Rockefeller Folk Art Collection, Williamsburg, Virginia* (Atlanta, GA: High Art Museum, 1974), pp. 37–41.
88. Adrienne Rich, *Dream of a Common Language: Poems 1974–1977* (New York, NY: Norton, 1978), pp. 76, 77.
89. Rich, *On Lies*, p. 248.
90. Rich, *Dream*, p. 20.
91. Paul Fry, *A Defense of Poetry: Reflections on the Occasion of Writing* (Stanford, CA: Stanford University Press, 1995), p. 85.

4 Ekphrasis in conversation: Anne Sexton and W. D. Snodgrass on Van Gogh

1. Charles Tomlinson, "The Miracle of the Bottle and the Fishes" in Adams (ed.), *With a Poet's Eye*, p. 88.
2. Elkins, *On Pictures*, p. 209.
3. Stein, *Ritual of Interpretation*, pp. 4, 8.
4. Mitchell, *Picture Theory*, p. 164.
5. "The loose nominatives, the choppy phrases, the frequent parentheses are," Arthur Fairbanks observes, "apparently intended to give the illusion of a casual conversation about the paintings" ("Introduction" in Philostratus, *Imagines/Callistratus: Descriptions*, trans. Arthur Fairbanks [New York, NY: Putnam, 1931], p. xxiii). Philostratus' instructive descriptions of the works of art in his pupil's father's collection are also full of direct addresses to the son, many in response to *his* responses – and his anticipated responses – to the paintings and the tutor's explanations.
6. Moore, *Complete Poems*, p. 216.
7. Ashbery, "Self-Portrait," p. 68.
8. Heffernan, *Museum*, p. 141.
9. Ibid., pp. 139–145.
10. Feldman, *Teach Me*, p. 34.
11. For an account of this event, and its contribution to Hearst's vice-presidential aspirations, see W. A. Swanberg, *Citizen Hearst* (New York, NY: Scribners, 1961), pp. 172–176.
12. Hollander, *Gazer's Spirit*, p. 230. For Cheney's poem, see p. 231.

13. Gertrude Stein, "Pictures" (1935) in McClatchy (ed.), *Poets on Painters*, pp. 87–88.

14. For a discussion of the various material presentations of this poem, see Bornstein, *Material Modernism*, pp. 15–23.

15. Anne Sexton, *The Complete Poems* (Boston, MA: Houghton Mifflin, 1981), p. 53.

16. Ibid., pp. 53–54.

17. Ibid., p. 54.

18. A. Alvarez, *The Savage God: A Study of Suicide* (New York, NY: Random House, 1972), p. 210.

19. Quoted in Robert Phillips, *The Confessional Poets* (Carbondale, IL: Southern Illinois University Press, 1973), p. 18.

20. Quoted ibid., p. 76.

21. M. L. Rosenthal, *The New Poets: American and British Poetry since World War II* (New York, NY: Oxford, 1967), p. 15.

22. Ibid., p. 7.

23. John Berryman, *77 Dream Songs* (New York, NY: Farrar, Straus and Co., 1964), p. 83.

24. Phillips, *Confessional Poets*, p. 6. See also Rosenthal, *New Poets*, p. 131; and Laurence Lerner, "What is confessional poetry?" *Critical Quarterly* 29:2 (Summer, 1987), 46–66 (p. 52).

25. Alvarez, *Savage God*, pp. 257–258.

26. Phillips, *Confessional Poets*, p. 14.

27. Alvarez, *Savage God*, p. xiv.

28. Ibid., p. 26.

29. Ibid.

30. Quoted in Phillips, *Confessional Poets*, p. 15.

31. Concerted critical efforts to undermine the term "confessional" have been surprisingly rare. For the most thorough examination of its limitations, see Thomas Travisano, *Midcentury Quartet: Bishop, Lowell, Jarrell, Berryman and the Making of a Postmodern Aesthetic* (Charlottesville, VA: University Press of Virginia, 1999).

32. Denise Levertov, "Light Up the Cave," in Denise Levertov, *Light Up the Cave* (New York, NY: New Directions, 1981), pp. 80–86 (pp. 80–81).

33. Ibid., p. 83.

34. Ibid., p. 84. *Levertov* quotes from Alvarez's jacket blurb for John Berryman's *Delusions, etc.* (1972). Adrienne Rich saw it in feminist terms: "We have had enough suicidal women poets, enough suicidal women, enough self-destructiveness as the sole form of violence permitted to women" (*On Lies*, p. 122).

35. Griselda Pollock, "Artists' mythologies and media genius, madness and art history," *Screen* 21:3 (1980), 57–96 (pp. 64, 60).

36. Ibid., pp. 64, 70.

37. For an account of the rise of Van Gogh's reputation in the United States following the 1935 blockbuster exhibition at the Museum of Modern Art, see

Steve Spence, "Van Gogh in Alabama, 1936," *Representations* 75 (Summer, 2001), 33–60. The success of the Van Gogh show established the six-year-old museum's place in American culture. Spence suggests that the Van Gogh so popular in the 1930s was based on the artist's early paintings, often dark in color, depicting peasants and other laborers in Belgium and the Netherlands, which struck a chord in Depression-era America. By contrast, the post-impressionist Van Gogh of vibrant colors and landscapes is the Van Gogh best known after World War II.

38. Pollock, "Artists' mythologies," p. 59.

39. Ibid., p. 64.

40. Albert Boime, "Van Gogh's *Starry Night*: A history of matter and a matter of history," *Arts Magazine* 59:4 (December, 1984), 86–103 (p. 87).

41. William Packard, "Craft interview with Anne Sexton (1970)" in J. D. McClatchy (ed.), *Anne Sexton: The Artist and Her Critics* (Bloomington, IN: Indiana University Press, 1978), pp. 43–47 (p. 47).

42. A selection of Van Gogh's letters to his brother Theo, edited by Irving and Jean Stone, had been available since 1937 (Irving Stone and Jean Stone (eds.), *Dear Theo: The Autobiography of Vincent Van Gogh* [Garden City, NY: Doubleday, 1937]).

43. A. M. Hammacher, "Van Gogh and the words," in J. B. de la Faille, *The Works of Vincent Van Gogh* (New York, NY: Reynal, 1970), pp. 10–37.

44. Hammacher discusses Aurier, Rilke, Artaud, Stone and Miller (ibid., p. 9). See also René Char, *Les voisinages de Van Gogh* (Paris: Gallimard, 1985); Robert Fagles, *I, Vincent* (Princeton, NJ: Princeton University Press, 1978); Paul Durcan, *Give Me Your Hand*, pp. 135–136; and Derek Mahon, *Selected Poems* (New York, NY: Viking, 1991), p. 20. Artaud's essay mattered to the Beats: "Van Gogh: The man suicided by society" (trans. Bernard Fretchman) was reprinted in the Beat publication *The Trembling Lamb* (John Fles [ed.], *The Trembling Lamb* [New York, NY: H. Gantt, n.d. (1959?)]), prefaced by a letter from Gregory Corso to Allen Ginsberg, and containing essays by Carl Solomon on chess and LeRoi Jones on Dante.

45. Ronald Pickvance, *Van Gogh in Saint-Rémy and Auvers* (New York, NY: The Metropolitan Museum of Art/Harry N. Abrams, 1986), pp. 312, 315 n. 3. Pickvance's book contains the text of Aurier's essay and some commentary (Appendix III, pp. 310–315).

46. W. D. Snodgrass, *In Radical Pursuit: Critical Essays and Lectures* (New York, NY: Harper & Row, 1975), pp. 88–89.

47. Vincent Van Gogh, *Complete Letters of Vincent Van Gogh*, 3 vols. (Greenwich, CT: New York Graphic Society, 1958), vol. 1, p. liii.

48. W. D. Snodgrass, "VAN GOGH: 'The Starry Night' " in *After Experience*, p. 69.

49. See Claus Cluver, "On intersemiotic transposition," *Poetics Today* 10:1 (Spring, 1989), 55–90 (pp. 64–65 and n. 6).

50. Meyer Schapiro, *Vincent Van Gogh* (New York, NY: Abrams, 1950), p. 33.

51. Ibid., p. 100.
52. Ibid., p. 33.
53. Sexton, *Complete Poems*, p. 54.
54. W.H. Auden, "Calm even in catastrophe" in McClatchy (ed.), *Poets on Painters*, p. 128.
55. Ibid.
56. It seems certain that Van Gogh was, in fact, not mad, but that he suffered bouts of epilepsy. Since Pollock's 1980 essay, art historians have turned away from biographically determined readings of Van Gogh. See, for example, Pickvance's catalogue for a 1986–1987 Van Gogh show at the Metropolitan Museum in New York: Van Gogh's "pictures are neither graphs of his so-called madness nor primarily indicators of his mental state" (Pickvance, *Van Gogh*, p.15).
57. Rosenthal, *New Poets*, p. 137.
58. Sexton, *Complete Poems*, p. 53.
59. Ibid., p. 54.
60. Ibid.
61. Ibid., p. 53.
62. Cluver also makes his point ("On intersemiotic transposition," p. 66).
63. *The Starry Night* was painted in the asylum at Saint-Rémy where Van Gogh lived and painted from May 1889 to May 1890. It was one of 129 paintings Van Gogh sent his brother Theo from Saint-Rémy. There were several other night scenes among those paintings to which Sexton might be referring (including *Landscape with Couple Walking and Crescent Moon* and *Road with Cypress and Star*), though *The Starry Night* is the most well known and the only one for which there is evidence that Sexton knew it. For the paintings Van Gogh did at Saint-Rémy, see Pickvance, *Van Gogh*, Appendix II.
64. Anne Sexton, *Anne Sexton: A Self-Portrait in Letters*, ed. Linda Gray Sexton and Lois Ames (Boston, MA: Houghton Mifflin, 1977), p. 291.
65. Sexton, *Complete Poems*, p. 374.
66. Ibid., pp. xxx–xxxi.
67. Diane Wood Middlebrook, *Anne Sexton: A Biography* (Boston, MA: Houghton Mifflin, 1991), p. 231.
68. Sexton, *Complete Poems*, p. 53.
69. Ibid.
70. Sexton, *Self-Portrait*, p. 97.
71. *The Hudson Review* 13:1 (Spring, 1960), 11–20. Snodgrass's poems appear on pp. 20–25.
72. Frederick Seidel, "Robert Lowell" in Malcolm Cowley (ed.), *Writers at Work: The "Paris Review" Interviews*, Series 2 (New York, NY: Viking Press, 1963), pp. 337–368 (p. 347).
73. Middlebrook, *Anne Sexton*, p. 82.
74. Sexton, *Self-Portrait*, p. 107.

75. Snodgrass, *In Radical Pursuit*, p. 63.

76. W. D. Snodgrass, "MATISSE: 'The Red Studio.' " *ARTNews Annual* 3 (1960), 90–91.

77. When he republished "VAN GOGH: 'The Starry Night' " as part of "Poems About Paintings" in *In Radical Pursuit* (1975), Snodgrass revised the poem, emphasizing the sexual nature of the sky. My discussion uses the version that appeared in *After Experience* (1968), which is contemporaneous with Sexton's. "MANET: 'The Execution of the Emperor Maximilian' " was published in the *Hudson Review* (16.2 [Summer, 1963], 246–248), as was "VUILLARD: 'The Mother and Sister of the Artist' " (this last under the pseudonym S. S. Gardons, *Hudson Review* 13.4 [Winter, 1960–1961], 514–516).

78. Snodgrass, *In Radical Pursuit*, p. 71.

79. Ibid., p. 76.

80. W. D. Snodgrass to Anne Sexton, January 26, 1961; W. D. Snodgrass–Anne Sexton Correspondence, The Harry Ransom Humanities Research Center, Austin, TX.

81. Snodgrass, *In Radical Pursuit*, pp. 88–89.

82. W. D. Snodgrass to Anne Sexton, "Friday night," n.d. [September, 1958]; W. D. Snodgrass–Anne Sexton Correspondence, The Harry Ransom Humanities Research Center, Austin, TX.

83. W. D. Snodgrass to Anne Sexton, June 23, 1959; W. D. Snodgrass–Anne Sexton Correspondence, The Harry Ransom Humanities Research Center, Austin, TX. Later, on February 6, 1961, Sexton wrote Snodgrass, telling him how "great" his poems in the *Hudson Review* were (Anne Sexton to W. D. Snodgrass, February 6, 1961; W. D. Snodgrass papers, University of Delaware Library, Newark, DE). Those would be "To a Child" and "VUILLARD: 'The Mother and Sister of the Artist,' " published in the winter, 1960–1961 issue under the pseudonym S. S. Gardons, a fiction of which Sexton was aware.

84. E. g. W. D. Snodgrass to Anne Sexton, December 10, 1960; W. D. Snodgrass–Anne Sexton Correspondence, The Harry Ransom Humanities Research Center, Austin, TX.

85. Telephone interview with Elizabeth Bergmann Loizeaux, October, 2001. Snodgrass thought he recalled that at some point, possibly when *After Experience* appeared, Sexton commented in a letter to him that they were now in competition over Van Gogh. I have not found such a letter in the repositories of Sexton's and Snodgrass's correspondence.

86. Snodgrass, *After Experience*, p. 64.

87. For details of which letters Snodgrass has quoted in the poem, see Philip Hoy, "*The Starry Night*: Snodgrass's Van Gogh reconsidered," *Agenda* 34:1 (1996), 22–111.

88. Snodgrass, *After Experience*, p. 64.

89. Ibid., pp. 66, 68.

90. Ibid., pp. 64, 65.

91. Snodgrass, *In Radical Pursuit*, pp. 63–70.
92. Ibid., p. x.
93. Ibid., p. 62.
94. Ibid., p. 62 n.
95. Snodgrass, *After Experience*, p. 64.
96. Ibid., p. 65.
97. Ibid., p. 66.
98. Ibid.
99. Ibid., pp. 67–68.
100. Ibid., pp. 66–67.
101. Ibid., pp. 68–69.
102. Ibid., p. 69.
103. See, for example, Christina Britzolakis, *Sylvia Plath and the Theatre of Mourning* (Oxford: Oxford University Press, 1999); Marsha Bryant, "Plath, domesticity, and the art of advertising," *College Literature* 29.3 (Summer, 2002), 17–34; and Deborah Nelson, *Pursuing Privacy in Cold War America* (New York, NY: Columbia University Press, 2002).
104. Paul Gaston, *W. D. Snodgrass* (Boston, MA: Twayne, 1978), p. 120.
105. Ibid.
106. Hedley, "Plath's ekphrastic poetry," p. 51.
107. Vendler, *Given and the Made*, p. 22.
108. Lowell, *Collected Poems*, p. 625.
109. Such use of ekphrasis was part of the Romantic heritage, dating back at least to 1806 when Wordsworth addressed George Beaumont and found in the ruined seaside castle and raging storm of *Peele Castle* an image of his own grief at his brother's death at sea. See Heffernan, *Museum*, pp. 94–107.
110. On Plath's ekphrastic poetry, see Hedley, "Plath's ekphrastic poetry"; Zivley, "Sylvia Plath's transformations"; and Leonard Scigaj, "The painterly Plath that nobody knows," *Centennial Review* 32.3 (1988), 220–249.
111. Plath, *Collected Poems*, p. 74.
112. Lowell, *Collected Poems*, pp. 458, 460.
113. In this way ekphrasis functioned for the confessionals in much the same way as translation (Snodgrass and Lowell) or Sexton's retellings of the Grimms' fairy tales in *Transformations* (1971): a means to express the self through and in the words of others. In *After Experience*, Snodgrass combined ekphrasis and translation: the volume's Part II, composed of translations, follows the five ekphrastic poems and contains three translations of ekphrases by Rilke, two from "Sonnets to Orpheus" (on "Antique sarcophagi" and "The Tapestry of the Lady with the Unicorn") and the famous "An Archaic Torso of Apollo," with its closing tutelary address to the poet and reader, "You must change your life" (p. 86).
114. See, for example, Britzolakis, *Sylvia Plath*.
115. Plath, *Collected Poems*, p. 21.

116. Hedley, "Plath's ekphrastic poetry," pp. 46, 42.

117. W. D. Snodgrass, *The Death of Cock Robin* (Newark: University of Delaware Press, 1989); and *W. D.'s Midnight Carnival* (Encinitas, CA: Artra, 1988).

118. See Barbara Swan, "A reminiscence" in Steven E. Colburn (ed.), *Anne Sexton: Telling the Tale* (Ann Arbor, MI: University of Michigan Press, 1988), pp. 39–45.

5 Ekphrasis in collaboration: Ted Hughes's and Leonard Baskin's *Cave Birds: An Alchemical Cave Drama*

1. Snodgrass, *After Experience*, p. 67.

2. O'Hara, *Collected Poems*, p. 128.

3. Vicki Feaver, "Oi yoi yoi" in Abse and Abse (eds.), *Voices*, p. 125.

4. W. S. Graham, "The Thermal Stair" in ibid., p. 146.

5. Merrill, "Corot" in McClatchy (ed.), *Poets on Painters*, p. 313.

6. William Carlos Williams, *Pictures from Brueghel and Other Poems* (New York, NY: New Directions, 1962), p. 8.

7. See, for example, Lisa Ede and Andrea Lunsford, *Single Text/Plural Authors: Perspectives on Collaborative Writing* (Carbondale, IL: Southern Illinois University Press, 1990). For an excellent, brief overview of the scholarship on collaborative writing, see Linda Hutcheon and Michael Hutcheon, "A convenience of marriage: Collaboration and interdisciplinarity," *PMLA* 116:5 (October, 2001), 1364–1376.

8. Two other projects, an *Alphabet* and *A Dance Cycle*, were not completed. The collaborations began when McGraw approached Snodgrass in December, 1981 about using his name in the titles of a number of works he had already done in response to the "world" of Snodgrass' poems. McGraw has also done paintings and sculptures in response to other writers including Blake, Yeats, Faulkner and Marquez. See the exhibition catalogue *DeLoss McGraw: As a Poem, So Is a Picture* (Scottsdale, AZ: Scottsdale Center for the Arts, 1997). See also Snodgrass' brief discussion of the collaboration in *After-Images: Autobiographical Sketches* (Rochester, NY: BOA Editions, 1999), pp. 192–193.

9. DeLoss McGraw, "Two statements on collaborating with W. D. Snodgrass" in Stephen Haven (ed.), *The Poetry of W. D. Snodgrass: Everything Human* (Ann Arbor, MI: University of Michigan Press, 1993), pp. 297–300 (p. 298).

10. Ibid.

11. Sexton had already written one poem on Swan's work ("To Lose the Earth" from *Live or Die* [1966] for which she won the Pulitzer Prize) and would write another ("Jesus Walking" from *The Death Notebooks* [1974]). Swan and Sexton collaborated on the cover illustrations for *The Book of Folly* (1972), *Live or Die* and *The Death Notebooks*. When contemplating a series of poems from Grimm, Sexton had asked Swan for suggestions for an illustrator, and ended up working with Swan herself. As Swan describes the

process of creating *Transformations*, Sexton would send her a poem, Swan would "absorb each poem individually, do a drawing, and then await the next poem." In between "there would be a phone call [a favorite medium of communication for Sexton] and I would tell Anne my visual reaction to the poem, what I felt I could express," in other words, a kind of ekphrasis, Swan's own description of what she had drawn, which became part of the mix out of which Sexton's next poem would come. "Always my reactions intrigued her," reported Swan ("A reminiscence," pp. 43–45).

12. Quoted in Russell Ferguson, *In Memory of My Feelings: Frank O'Hara and American Art* (Berkeley, CA: University of California Press [Museum of Contemporary Art, Los Angeles], 1999), p. 60.

13. Paul Violi, "Introduction" in Kenneth Koch, *Kenneth Koch: Collaborations with Artists* (Ipswich: Ipswich Borough Council, 1993), unpaginated.

14. Perloff, *O'Hara*, p. 96.

15. On collaboration as avant-garde practice, see David Herd, who argues for the importance of the circumstances of collaboration for elaborating a theory of it ("Collaboration and the avant-garde," *Critical Review* 35 [1995], 36–63).

16. On the verbal–visual collaborations of the Harlem Renaissance, see Anne Carroll, *Word, Image, and the New Negro: Representation and Identity in the Harlem Renaissance* (Bloomington, IN: Indiana University Press, 2005); and Martha Jane Nadell, *Enter the New Negroes: Images of Race in American Culture* (Cambridge, MA: Harvard University Press, 2004).

17. For collaboration and the myth of solitary genius, see Jack Stillinger's seminal *Multiple Authorship and the Myth of Solitary Genius* (New York, NY: Oxford University Press, 1991); Bette London, "Introduction: Seeing double," in *Writing Double: Women's Literary Partnerships* (Ithaca, NY: Cornell University Press, 1999), pp. 1–32; and Holly Laird, *Women Coauthors* (Urbana, IL: University of Illinois Press, 2000). For literary collaborations as homoerotic, see, for example, Wayne Koestenbaum, *Double Talk: The Erotics of Male Literary Collaboration* (New York, NY: Routledge, 1989); and Susan Leonardi and Rebecca Pope, "(Co)Labored li(v)es: Love's labors queered," *PMLA* 116:3 (May, 2001), 631–637.

18. For accounts of Creeley's collaborations, see Amy Cappellazzo and Elizabeth Licata (eds.), *In Company: Robert Creeley's Collaborations* (Chapel Hill, NC: University of North Carolina Press, 1999).

19. For an overview of efforts to synthesize the arts (not just poetry and painting), see Thomas Jensen Hines, *Collaborative Form: Studies in the Relations of the Arts* (Kent, OH: Kent State University Press, 1991). He uses the term "collaborative form" to designate both the composite work in which the "contributing arts" can be said to collaborate, and the acts of collaboration by artists. Marjorie Perloff, in writing about Frank O'Hara, reserves "collaboration" for when poet and artist "work simultaneously on

the same spatial area, playing off words against visual images so as to create new forms" (*O'Hara*, p. 99). John Yau, writing on Robert Creeley's collaborations, distinguishes between the "poem-paintings" Perloff discusses (in which poet and painter work on the same field), those collaborations following the *livre d'artiste* tradition (in which an artist works off of pre-existing words, what I've been calling more loosely illustration), and what Creeley strives for in most of his collaborations from the late 1960s on: "the writing should neither be a foil to, nor translation of, the art . . . the writing should extend from the art, not be reactive to, or descriptive of, it" ("Active participants: Robert Creeley and the visual arts" in Cappellazzo and Licata [eds.], *In Company*, pp. 45–82 [p. 48]). *Livres d'artistes* are a development of the late nineteenth century when painters were commissioned, often by their dealers, to illustrate small editions of books by major authors. Among the celebrated *livres d'artistes* of the twentieth century are Henri Matisse's illustrated version of Stéphane Mallarmé's *Poésies* (1932) and Sonia Delaunay-Terk's illustrated version of Blaise Cendrars's *La prose du transsibérien et de la petite Jehanne de France* (1913). See Riva Castelman, *A Century of Artist's Books* (New York, NY: Museum of Modern Art, 1994).

20. Quoted in Perloff, *O'Hara*, p. 105.

21. I am using the term "fine press" or "fine printing" in the broad sense Johanna Drucker describes: "The term 'fine printing' is generally associated with letterpress, handset type, and limited editions, but also can be used to describe carefully produced work in any print medium" ("The artist's book as idea and form" in Jerome Rothenberg and Steven Clay [eds.], *A Book of the Book: Some Works & Projections about the Book & Writing* [New York, NY: Granary, 2000], p. 380). Most fine presses are small, but the reverse is not necessarily the case.

22. McGann, *Textual Condition*, pp. 66–67 and passim. George Bornstein has suggested that "contextual code" be added to designate the varying arrangements of the contents of a text, say, of poems within a volume ("What is the text of a poem by Yeats?" in George Bornstein and Ralph Williams [eds.], *Palimpsest: Editorial Theory in the Humanities* [Ann Arbor, MI: University of Michigan Press, 1993], pp. 168–193 [p. 179]).

23. For further essays on textual criticism and verbal–visual studies, see the special issue of *Word & Image* on "Genetic criticism," 13.2 (1997), and Elizabeth Bergmann Loizeaux and Neil Fraistat (eds.), *Reimagining Textuality: Textual Studies in the Late Age of Print* (Madison: University of Wisconsin Press, 2002).

24. Elaine Feinstein, *Ted Hughes: The Life of a Poet* (New York, NY: Norton, 2001), pp. 160–161.

25. Caws, *Interference*, p. 3.

26. For important exceptions to the tendency to shy away from the images, see Elizabeth Maslen, "Counterpoint: Collaborations between Ted Hughes and three visual artists," *Word & Image* 2.1 (January–March, 1986), 33–44; and,

itself a collaboration, Terry Gifford and Neil Roberts, *Ted Hughes: A Critical Study* (London: Faber and Faber, 1981).

27. Leonard Scigaj, *Ted Hughes* (Boston, MA: Twayne, 1991), p. 13. As Maslen pointed out more than twenty years ago, "this focus on Hughes' own achievements has tended to obscure the fact that collaborations with visual artists have been an integral part of his work for well over twenty years" ("Counterpoint," p. 33). The fact that Baskin was a persistent collaborator, as well as the fact that he worked in the "lower" arts of sculpture, drawing and print-making, and in a figurative tradition, may well have hampered Baskin's reputation. Beside two extensive treatments of his sculpture and graphic works, by Jaffe and by Fern and O'Sullivan, serious scholarship on his work is scarce; few efforts have been made to account for his position in the art of his generation. See Irma B. Jaffe, *The Sculpture of Leonard Baskin* (New York, NY: Viking, 1980) and Alan Fern and Judith O'Sullivan (eds.), *The Complete Prints of Leonard Baskin* (Boston, MA: Little Brown, 1984).

28. Durcan, *Crazy*, p. xi.

29. Ted Hughes, "The poetic self: A centenary tribute to T. S. Eliot" (1988) in Hughes, *Winter Pollen: Occasional Prose*, ed. William Scammell (New York, NY: Picador, 1995), pp. 273–274.

30. Leonard Scigaj, *The Poetry of Ted Hughes: Form and Imagination* (Iowa City, IA: University of Iowa Press, 1986), p. 144. Accounts of Baskin's invitation differ. Keith Sagar suggests the invitation came in 1966 (*The Laughter of Foxes: A Study of Ted Hughes* [Liverpool: Liverpool University Press, 2000], p. xxii). Feinstein dates it 1967 (*Ted Hughes*, p. 160).

31. Ted Hughes to Leonard Baskin, n.d. [1969–1970?], Leonard Baskin Collection, British Library, London; Ted Hughes, *The Letters of Ted Hughes*, ed. Christopher Reid (London: Faber and Faber, 2007), p. 300.

32. Hughes, *Letters*, p. 280.

33. Leonard Baskin to Ted Hughes, January 1, 1969; Ted Hughes Collection, Manuscript, Archives, and Rare Book Library, Emory University, Atlanta, GA.

34. The collaborations range from the coupling of their works, as in the numerous books by Hughes that contain a drawing by Baskin, to the more extensive give-and-take that is usually implied by the term "collaboration." In addition to *Cave Birds*, *Capriccio* and *Howls and Whispers*, these latter include: the limited edition of *Crow* with twelve drawings by Baskin (London: Faber and Faber, 1973); *Season Songs* (New York, NY: Viking, 1975); *Moon-Whales and Other Moon Poems* (New York, NY: Viking, 1976); *A Primer of Birds* (Lurley: Gehenna Press, 1981); *Makomaki* (Leeds, MA: Eremite Press, 1985); and *Flowers and Insects* (London: Faber and Faber, 1986).

35. An "augmented" sixth printing of the first English edition contains seven additional poems. The second English edition (1973), with the twelve drawings by Baskin, contains still three more poems. See Keith Sagar and Stephen Tabor, *Ted Hughes: A Bibliography 1946–1980* (London: Mansell, 1983), pp. 44–46.

36. Ted Hughes, *Selected Poems 1957–1994* (New York, NY: Farrar, Straus and Giroux, 2002), p. 18.

37. Ibid., p. 31.

38. Ibid., p. 24.

39. Ibid., p. 32.

40. Ibid., pp. 17–18.

41. Ibid., p. 18.

42. For details, see *The Gehenna Press: The Work of Fifty Years. 1942–1992* (Dallas, TX: Bridwell Library and Gehenna Press, 1992), entries 13, 17, 53 (Hecht), 76 (Kunitz) and 81 (Kaplan).

43. Quoted in Jaffe, *Sculpture of Leonard Baskin*, p. 6.

44. Alan Fern, "Foreword" in Fern and O'Sullivan (eds.), *The Complete Prints of Leonard Baskin*, pp. 7–9 (pp. 7–8).

45. Ibid., p. 8.

46. Leonard Baskin, *Sculpture, Drawings & Prints* (New York, NY: Braziller, 1970), p. 16.

47. Ted Hughes to Leonard Baskin [*c.* 1971–1972], Leonard Baskin Collection, British Library, London.

48. Leonard Baskin to George Nicholson, July 3, 1976; Leonard Baskin Collection, British Library, London.

49. Ted Hughes to Leonard Baskin, March 25, 1995; Leonard Baskin Collection, British Library, London.

50. Ted Hughes and Leonard Baskin, *Cave Birds: An Alchemical Cave Drama* (New York, NY: Viking, 1978), title page. Although published in 1979, the book bears the 1978 publication date. The New York and London trade editions differ slightly in their physical features and significantly in the text offered on the dust-jacket. See Sagar and Tabor, *Ted Hughes: A Bibliography*, pp. 67–69.

51. Sagar and Tabor, *Ted Hughes: A Bibliography*, pp. 67–69.

52. Leonard Baskin to Ted Hughes, December 8, 1973; Ted Hughes Collection, Manuscript, Archives, and Rare Book Library, Emory University, Atlanta, GA. Punctuation, spelling and brackets are Baskin's.

53. See Keith Sagar, *The Art of Ted Hughes*, 2nd edn. (Cambridge: Cambridge University Press, 1978), pp. 243–244, for an overview of the collaboration. Sagar counts only eight illustrations to the twelve Hughes poems in Round C, but there are ten. The Round A poems are: "The summoner," "The interrogator," "The judge," "The plaintiff," "The executioner," "The accused," "The risen," "Finale" and one that was not included ("The advocate"). The Round B poems are: "The knight," "The gatekeeper," "A flayed crow in the hall of judgment," "The baptist," "A green mother," "A riddle," "The scapegoat," "The guide," "Walking bare," "The owl flower." The Round C poems are "The scream" (with no accompanying image), "After the first fright," "She seemed so considerate," "Your mother's bones wanted to speak"

(not published in the New York or London trade editions), "In these fading moments I wanted to say," "First, the doubtful charts of skin," "Something was happening," "Only a little sleep, a little slumber," "As I came, I saw a wood," "After there was nothing there was a woman," "His legs ran about," "Bride and groom lie hidden for three days."

54. Ted Hughes to Leonard Baskin, July 29, 1974; Leonard Baskin Collection, British Library, London.
55. Hughes and Baskin, *Cave Birds* (1978), p. 32.
56. Ibid., p. 26.
57. Hughes and Baskin, *Cave Birds: Poems* (Ilkley: Scolar Press, 1975).
58. In Hughes's *New Selected Poems* (New York, NY: Harper & Row, 1982), selections from *Cave Birds* appear without the images but with a foreword by Hughes explaining that the poems were "written to accompany drawings – of imaginary birds – by Leonard Baskin," briefly describing the missing images and asserting their importance: "throughout the original sequence the interdependence between drawings and verses is quite close" (p. xi). In subsequent versions, reference to the images gradually shrinks until in *New Selected Poems 1957–1994* there are no images, and no contextualizing notes of any kind (London: Faber and Faber, 1995; published in New York as *Selected Poems 1957–1994* [Farrar, Straus and Giroux, 2002]).
59. See Gifford and Roberts, *Ted Hughes*, p. 199. For a discussion of the Scolar Press and trade editions in the context of Hughes's interest in the material properties of his books, see my "Reading word, image and the body of the book: Ted Hughes' and Leonard Baskin's *Cave Birds*," *Twentieth Century Literature* 50.1 (Spring, 2004), 18–58.
60. The term is Morris Eaves's ("Graphicality: Multimedia fables for 'textual' critics" in Loizeaux and Fraistat (eds.), *Reimagining Textuality*, pp. 99–122).
61. Ted Hughes, "The hanged man and the dragonfly (note for a panegyric ode on Leonard Baskin's *Collected Prints*)" (1984) in Hughes, *Winter Pollen*, pp. 84–102 (p. 86).
62. Ted Hughes, "Poetry in the making: Three extracts" (1967) in Hughes, *Winter Pollen*, pp. 10–24 (p. 11).
63. For a summary and analysis of the volume's alchemical background and quest, see Timothy Materer, *Modernist Alchemy: Poetry and the Occult* (Ithaca, NY: Cornell University Press, 1995), pp. 141–155. For the poem's ritual and mythic origins, see Stuart Hirschberg, *Myth in the Poetry of Ted Hughes: A Guide to the Poems* (Totowa, NJ: Barnes and Noble, 1981), pp. 152–177. Materer and Hirschberg do not discuss the pictures or the collaboration. In exploring the possibility of psychological criticism based on Sufism and Gurdjieff, Nick Bishop notes the relation of the "principle of alchemy" to the " 'layered' compositional process" of *Cave Birds* (Nick Bishop, *Re-making Poetry: Ted Hughes and a New Critical Psychology* [New York, NY: St. Martin's Press, 1991], p. 178).

64. Hughes and Baskin, *Cave Birds* (1978), p. 16.
65. Ibid., p. 28.
66. Ibid., p. 40.
67. Ibid., p. 34.
68. Ibid.
69. Ibid., p. 28.
70. Ibid., p. 7.
71. Quoted in Ekbert Faas, *Ted Hughes: The Unaccommodated Universe* (Santa Barbara, CA: Black Sparrow, 1980), p. 200.
72. Hughes and Baskin, *Cave Birds* (1978), p. 7.
73. Graham Bradshaw, "Creative mythology in *Cave Birds*" in Keith Sagar (ed.), *The Achievement of Ted Hughes* (Athens: University of Georgia Press, 1983), pp. 210–238 (p. 215).
74. See, for example, Mitchell, *Iconology*; Paulson, "English iconoclasm in the eighteenth century" and Ernest Gilman, *Iconoclasm and Poetry in the English Reformation*.
75. Mitchell, *Iconology*, p. 43.
76. See, for example, Freedberg, *Power of Images*.
77. Quoted in Mitchell, *Iconology*, p. 95, spacing Blake's. Such thinking is so pervasive that the conventional figuring of the image as female and subversive can be seen in the criticism of *Cave Birds* itself. Explaining what he finds the uneven quality of the poems in the volume, one critic remarks, "the story, seduced no doubt by Baskin's drawings, seems to lose its way, dissipating the energy" (Sagar, *Art of Ted Hughes*, p. 179).
78. Hughes and Baskin, *Cave Birds* (1978), p. 8.
79. Ibid.
80. Ibid., p. 10.
81. Ibid.
82. Ibid., p. 32.
83. George Nicholson to Leonard Baskin, January 14, 1976; Leonard Baskin Collection, British Library, London. Michael Loeb to Leonard Baskin, March 28, 1977; Leonard Baskin Collection, British Library, London.
84. Thanks to Randall McLeod for this point.
85. In other collaborative books, this arrangement, which might appear "natural," is not followed: in *River*, for example, Keen's photos are sometimes grouped together in a visual sequence, sometimes interspersed through a longer poem and sometimes paired face-to-face with a poem. See Maslen, "Counterpoint," p. 40.
86. Hughes and Baskin, *Cave Birds* (1978), p. 28.
87. Yeats, *Poems*, p. 348. See Jerome McGann for a reading of the final lines of "The Circus Animals' Desertion" as an allusion to the commerce of the paper industry (Jerome J. McGann, *Black Riders: The Visible Language of Modernism* [Princeton, NJ: Princeton University Press, 1993], p. 5).

88. Hughes and Baskin, *Cave Birds* (1978), p. 56.
89. Ibid.
90. Ibid.
91. Not only in other collaborations with Hughes, but in his numerous illustrations to other writers including Shakespeare, Euripides, Poe, Blake, Tennyson, James Baldwin, Anthony Hecht and Ruth Fainlight. For a suggestive partial list, see the exhibition brochure, *Caprices, Grotesques and Homages: Leonard Baskin and the Gehenna Press – A Library of Congress Exhibition* (Washington, DC: Library of Congress, 1994).
92. Gifford and Roberts, *Ted Hughes*, p. 200.
93. Ted Hughes to Leonard Baskin, August 15, 1984; Leonard Baskin Collection, British Library, London.
94. Leonard Baskin to Ted Hughes, August 26, 1984; Ted Hughes Collection, Manuscript, Archives, and Rare Book Library, Emory University, Atlanta, GA.
95. Nathalie Anderson, "Ted Hughes and the challenge of gender" in Keith Sagar (ed.), *The Challenge of Ted Hughes* (New York, NY: St. Martin's Press, 1994), pp. 91–115 (pp. 107, 106).
96. Hughes and Baskin, *Cave Birds* (1978), p. 12.
97. Ted Hughes and Leonard Baskin, *Crow: From the Life and Songs of the Crow* (London: Faber and Faber, 1974), p. 20.
98. Hughes and Baskin, *Cave Birds* (1978), p. 12.
99. Ibid.
100. Ibid.
101. Ibid., p. 18.
102. Shelley, "On the Medusa of Leonardo da Vinci."
103. Bradshaw, "Creative mythology," p. 237; Hughes and Baskin, *Cave Birds* (1978), p. 62.
104. Bradshaw, "Creative mythology," pp. 237–238.
105. Amy Cappellazzo, Reine Hauser, Seth McCormack and Elizabeth Licata, "The collaborators talk" in Cappellazzo and Licata (eds.), *In Company*, pp. 22–27 (p. 27).
106. David Herd, "Collaboration and the avant-garde," p. 54. Creeley, quoted in Elizabeth Licata, "Robert Creeley's collaborations: A history" in Cappellazzo and Licata (eds.), *In Company*, pp. 11–21 (p. 21).
107. Hughes, *Letters*, p. 280.
108. Koch, *Collaborations*, p. 7.
109. Yau, "Active participants," p. 54.

6 Ekphrasis in the book: Rita Dove's African American museum

1. Paul, *Poetry in the Museums of Modernism*, p. 4.
2. Duncan, *Civilizing Rituals*, p. 8.

3. Pound, *Literary Essays of Ezra Pound*, p. 16.

4. Paul, *Poetry in the Museums of Modernism*, pp. 65–139.

5. Ibid., p. 15.

6. Fisher, *Making and Effacing Art*, p. 166.

7. Heffernan, *Museum*, p. 138.

8. Fath Davis Ruffins, "Mythos, memory, and history: African American preservation efforts, 1820–1990" in Ivan Karp, Christine Mullen Kreamer and Steven D. Lavine (eds.), *Museums and Communities: The Politics of Public Culture* (Washington, DC: Smithsonian, 1992), pp. 506–611 (p. 567).

9. Ruffins, "Mythos," p. 557.

10. Ibid.

11. Ibid., p. 563.

12. Malin Pereira, *Rita Dove's Cosmopolitanism* (Urbana, IL: University of Illinois Press, 2003), p. 174.

13. Ross Posnock, *Color and Culture: Black Writers and the Making of the Modern Intellectual* (Cambridge, MA: Harvard University Press, 1998), pp. 2, 3.

14. Ibid., p. 3.

15. Ibid., p. 4.

16. Ibid., p. 5.

17. Susan Vogel, "Always true to the object, in our fashion" in Ivan Karp and Steven D. Lavine (eds.), *Exhibiting Cultures: The Poetics and Politics of Museum Display* (Washington, DC: Smithsonian, 1991), pp. 191–204 (p. 193).

18. Ibid.

19. Stan Sanvel Rubin and Judith Kitchen, "Riding that current as far as it'll take you" (1985), in Earl Ingersoll (ed.), *Conversations with Rita Dove* (Jackson: University of Mississippi Press, 2003), pp. 3–14 (p. 8).

20. For curiosity cabinets, see Susan A. Crane, "Curious cabinets and imaginary museums" in Susan A. Crane (ed.), *Museums and Memory* (Stanford, CA: Stanford University Press, 2000), pp. 60–90.

21. Dove, *Museum*, p. 53.

22. Rubin and Kitchen, "Riding that current," p. 6.

23. Dove, *Museum*, p. 16.

24. Grace Cavalieri, "Brushed by an angel's wings" in Ingersoll (ed.), *Conversations with Rita Dove*, p. 143.

25. Dove, *Museum*, p. 47.

26. Trey Ellis, "The new black aesthetic," *Callaloo* 12.1 (1989), 233–251.

27. See Rita Dove, "Rita Dove on Melvin B. Tolson" in Elise Paschen and Rebekah Presson Mosby (eds.), *Poetry Speaks* (Naperville, IL: Sourcebooks, 2001), pp. 139–140; and "Telling it like it I-S *IS*: Narrative techniques in Melvin Tolson's Harlem Gallery," *New England Review/Bread Loaf Quarterly* 8 (Fall, 1985), 109–117.

28. Dove, "Rita Dove on Melvin B. Tolson," pp. 139–140.

29. Ibid., p. 140.

30. Ibid.

31. Melvin B. Tolson, *"Harlem Gallery" and Other Poems of Melvin B. Tolson*, ed. Raymond Nelson, introduction by Rita Dove (Charlottesville, VA: University Press of Virginia, 1999), p. 217.

32. Ibid. p. 216.

33. Rita Dove, "Introduction" in Tolson, *"Harlem Gallery,"* pp. xi–xxv (p. xxiii).

34. Dove, "Rita Dove on Melvin B. Tolson," p. 140.

35. Tolson, *"Harlem Gallery,"* p. 247.

36. Ibid.

37. Mohamed B. Taleb-Khyar, "Gifts to be earned" (1991) in Ingersoll (ed.), *Conversations with Rita Dove*, pp. 74–87 (p. 85).

38. Gretchen Johnson and Richard Peabody, "A cage of sound" in Ingersoll (ed.), *Conversations with Rita Dove*, p. 26.

39. Ibid.

40. Taleb-Khyar, "Gifts to be earned," p. 85.

41. Hans Magnus Enzensberger, *Mausoleum*, trans. Joachim Neugroschel (New York, NY: Urizen Books, 1976), p. 104.

42. Dove, *Museum*, p. 23.

43. Ibid., p. 27.

44. Henry Louis Gates, Jr., "Foreword: In her own write" in Phillis Wheatley, *The Collected Works of Phillis Wheatley*, ed. John C. Shields (New York, NY: Oxford University Press, 1988), pp. vii–xxii (p. x).

45. Wheatley, *The Collected Works*, pp. 101–113.

46. As late as 1993, American art museums' "romance with Europe" remained a hot issue. See *Race, Ethnicity and Culture in the Visual Arts: A Panel Discussion* (New York, NY: American Council for the Arts, 1993), p. 4.

47. Gwendolyn Brooks, *In the Mecca* (New York, NY: Harper & Row, 1968), p. 41.

48. Gwendolyn Brooks, *Report from Part One* (Detroit, MI: Broadside, 1972), p. 148.

49. Ruffins, "Mythos," p. 565.

50. Dove, *Museum*, p. 16.

51. See Carroll, *Word, Image, and the New Negro*; and Nadell, *Enter the New Negroes*.

52. June Jordan, *Who Look at Me* (New York, NY: Crowell, 1969), p. 98.

53. Brooks, *In the Mecca*, p. 43.

54. Shange, *Ridin' the Moon in Texas*, p. xii.

55. Wheatley, *Collected Works*, p. 114.

56. See Sander L. Gilman's influential "Black bodies, white bodies: Toward an iconography of female sexuality in late nineteenth-century art, medicine, and literature" for an account of the Hottentot as "representative of the essence of the black" in nineteenth-century Europe (in Henry Louis Gates, Jr. [ed.], *"Race," Writing, and Difference* [Chicago, IL: University of Chicago

Press, 1986], pp. (223–261) [p. 225]). Elizabeth Alexander learned of the Hottentot from this essay (email to the author March 2, 2006). Several Hottentot women were displayed in nineteenth-century Europe. The most famous was Saartjie Baartman, called the "Hottentot Venus"; another Hottentot woman, depicted in the print to which Alexander refers, was also called "the Hottentot Venus." Displayed nude, she "was the prize attraction at a ball given by the Duchess Du Barry in Paris" in 1829 (Gilman, "Black bodies, white bodies," p. 232).

57. Elizabeth Alexander, *The Venus Hottentot* (Charlottesville, VA: University of Virginia Press, 1990), p. 5.

58. Tom Feelings, "Introduction" in Maya Angelou, *Now Sheba Sings the Song*, art by Tom Feelings (New York, NY: Plume, 1987), pp. 5–6 (p. 5).

59. Angelou, *Now Sheba Sings the Song*, p. 33.

60. Rita Dove, *On the Bus with Rosa Parks* (New York, NY: Norton, 1999), pp. 48–49.

61. Ibid., pp. 49–50.

62. Rita Dove, *The Yellow House on the Corner* (Pittsburgh, PA: Carnegie Mellon University Press, 1989), pp. 14, 15.

63. Dove, *On the Bus with Rosa Parks*, p. 69; spacing Dove's.

64. Ibid., p. 70.

65. John James Piatt, "To the Statue on the Capitol: Looking Eastward at Dawn" in Hollander (ed.), *The Gazer's Spirit*, p. 205.

66. Dove, *Museum*, p. 36.

67. Ibid. p. 9.

68. Susan Stewart, *On Longing: Narratives of the Miniature, the Gigantic, the Souvenir, the Collection* (Baltimore, MA: Johns Hopkins University Press, 1984), pp. 152, 153.

69. Rubin and Kitchen, "Riding that current," p. 9.

70. Moore, *Becoming Marianne Moore*, p. 101.

71. Dove, *Museum*, p. 9.

72. Ibid., pp. 9–10.

73. Dove, "Introduction" in Tolson, "*Harlem Gallery*," p. xxiii.

74. Jahan Ramazani, *The Hybrid Muse: Postcolonial Poetry in English* (Chicago, IL: University of Chicago Press, 2001), p. 6.

75. Dove, *Museum*, p. 13.

76. Ibid., p. 10.

77. Rubin and Kitchen, "Riding that current," p. 7.

78. Dove, *Museum*, pp. 18–19.

79. Ibid.

80. Helen Vendler, "An interview with Rita Dove" in Henry Louis Gates, Jr. (ed.), *Reading Black, Reading Feminist: A Critical Anthology* (New York, NY: Meridian, 1990), pp. 481–491 (p. 485).

81. Dove, *Museum*, p. 16.

82. Ibid., p. 21.

83. Frantz Fanon, *Black Skin, White Masks*, trans. Charles Lam Markmann (New York, NY: Grove, 1967), p. 135.

84. Dove, *Museum*, p. 20.

85. Ibid., p. 24.

86. Ibid., p. 54.

87. Ibid., p. 72.

88. Ibid., pp. 27–28.

89. The poem comments on the 1878 oil (*A Vision of Fiammetta*), not the 1866 oil (*Fiammetta*). The interrelation of illustration and ekphrasis is demonstrated once more here. On the frame of the painting three texts are inscribed: the sonnet by Boccaccio that Rossetti's painting illustrates ("On His Last Sight of Fiammetta"), Rossetti's translation of the sonnet, and his sonnet on his own painting. For image and more information, see the Rossetti Archive, www.rossettiarchive.org/docs/s252. rap.html.

90. Rossetti Archive, www.rossettiarchive.org/docs/2–1881.1stedn.rad.html# 1-1879.s252.

91. Dove, *Museum*, p. 28.

92. Bob Marley, "Sun is shining," www.iration.com/wailers/sunisshining (accessed June 20, 2005), quoted by Dove in *Museum*, p. 29.

93. Marley, "Sun is shining."

94. Jill Lloyd, "Christian Schad: Reality and illusion" in Jill Lloyd and Michael Peppiatt (eds.), *Christian Schad and the Neue Sachlichkeit* (New York, NY: Norton, 2003), pp. 15–28 (p. 15).

95. Johnson and Peabody, "A cage of sound," p. 29. See the catalogue of the show, *Christian Schad* (Berlin: Staatliche Kunsthalle Berlin, 1980).

96. Ibid., p. 28.

97. Taleb-Khyar, "Gifts to be earned," p. 76.

98. Dove, *Museum*, p. 41.

99. Pereira, *Rita Dove's Cosmopolitanism*, p. 82; and Therese Steffen, *Crossing Color: Transcultural Space and Place in Rita Dove's Poetry, Fiction, and Drama* (Oxford: Oxford University Press, 2001), p. 91.

100. Lloyd, "Christian Schad," p. 26.

101. Dove, *Museum*, p. 41.

102. Ibid., p. 42.

103. Ibid., p. 41.

104. Ibid., p. 42.

105. Ibid. Ellipsis Dove's.

106. Ibid., p. 41.

107. Ibid., pp. 78, 77.

108. Steffen, *Crossing Color*, p. 90.

109. Ibid., p. 91.

110. Pereira, *Rita Dove's Cosmopolitanism*, p. 80.

111. Dove, *Museum*, p. 43.
112. Ibid., pp. 44, 43.
113. Ibid., pp. 43, 44.
114. Ibid., pp. 43–44.
115. Vendler, "Interview," p. 485. Italics mine.

Bibliography

Abse, Dannie. "Brueghel in Naples." *Poetry Review* 79.2 (1989), 26.

Abse, Dannie and Joan Abse, eds. *Voices in the Gallery*. London: The Tate Gallery, 1986.

Adams, Pat, ed. *With a Poet's Eye: A Tate Gallery Anthology*. London: The Tate Gallery, 1986.

Aisenberg, Katy. *Ravishing Images: Ekphrasis in the Poetry and Prose of William Wordsworth, W. H. Auden and Philip Larkin*. New York, NY: Peter Lang, 1995.

Alexander, Elizabeth. *The Venus Hottentot*. Charlottesville, VA: University of Virginia Press, 1990.

Alpers, Svetlana. "Ekphrasis and aesthetic attitudes in Vasari's *Lives*." *Journal of the Warburg and Courtauld Institutes* 23 (1960), 190–215.

Altieri, Charles. *Painterly Abstraction in Modernist American Poetry: The Contemporaneity of Modernism*. University Park, PA: Pennsylvania State University Press, 1989.

Alvarez, A. *The Savage God: A Study of Suicide*. New York, NY: Random House, 1972.

Anderson, Nathalie. "Ted Hughes and the challenge of gender." In Sagar, *The Challenge of Ted Hughes*, pp. 91–115.

Angelou, Maya. *Now Sheba Sings the Song*. Art by Tom Feelings. New York, NY: Plume, 1987.

Ariès, Philippe. *The Hour of Our Death*. Trans. Helen Weaver. New York, NY: Knopf, 1981.

Ashbery, John. *Self-Portrait in a Convex Mirror*. New York, NY: Viking, 1975.

Ashton, Jennifer. *From Modernism to Postmodernism: American Poetry and Theory in the Twentieth Century*. Cambridge: Cambridge University Press, 2005.

Attridge, Derek. "Innovation, literature, ethics: relating to the other." *PMLA* 114.1 (January, 1999), 20–31.

Auden, W. H. *Another Time*. New York, NY: Random House, 1940.

  "Calm even in catastrophe." In McClatchy, *Poets on Artists*, 127–137.

  ed. *Van Gogh, a Self-Portrait: Letters Revealing His Life as a Painter*. London: Thames & Hudson, 1961.

Auden, W. H. and Christopher Isherwood. *Journey to a War*. New York, NY: Random House, 1939.

Auden, W. H. and Louis MacNeice. *Letters from Iceland*. London: Faber and Faber, 1937.

Bakhtin, M. M. *The Dialogic Imagination.* Ed. Michael Holquist. Trans. Carol Emerson and Michael Holquist. Austin, TX: University of Texas Press, 1981.

Bal, Mieke. *Looking In: The Art of Viewing.* "Introduction" by Norman Bryson. Amsterdam: G + B Arts, 2001.

   Reading "Rembrandt": Beyond the Word–Image Opposition. Cambridge: Cambridge University Press, 1991.

Baskin, Leonard. Letter to George Nicholson. July 3, 1976. Leonard Baskin Collection. British Library, London.

   Letter to Ted Hughes. January 1, 1969. Ted Hughes Collection. Manuscript, Archives, and Rare Book Library. Emory University, Atlanta, GA.

   Letter to Ted Hughes. December 8, 1973. Ted Hughes Collection. Manuscript, Archives, and Rare Book Library. Emory University, Atlanta, GA.

   Letter to Ted Hughes. August 26, 1984. Ted Hughes Collection. Manuscript, Archives, and Rare Book Library. Emory University, Atlanta, GA.

   Sculpture, Drawings & Prints. New York, NY: Braziller, 1970.

Baxandall, Michael. *Patterns of Intention: On the Historical Explanation of Pictures.* New Haven, CT: Yale University Press, 1985.

Bazin, Germain. *The Museum Age.* New York, NY: Universe Books, 1967.

Becker, Andrew Sprague. *The Shield of Achilles and the Poetics of Ekphrasis.* London: Rowman & Littlefield, 1995.

Becker, Ernest. *The Denial of Death.* New York, NY: Free Press, 1973.

Berryman, John. *77 Dream Songs.* New York, NY: Farrar, Straus and Co., 1964.

Bishop, Elizabeth. *The Complete Poems, 1927–1979.* New York, NY: Farrar, Straus and Giroux, 1983.

   One Art. Ed. Robert Giroux. New York, NY: Farrar, Straus and Giroux, 1994.

Bishop, Nick. *Re-making Poetry: Ted Hughes and a New Critical Psychology.* New York, NY: St. Martin's Press, 1991.

Bluemel, Kristin. "The dangers of eccentricity: Stevie Smith's doodles and poetry." *Mosaic* 31.3 (September, 1998), 111–132.

Boime, Albert. "Van Gogh's *Starry Night*: A history of matter and a matter of history." *Arts Magazine* 59:4 (December, 1984), 86–103.

Boland, Eavan. *Outside History: Selected Poems 1980–1990.* New York, NY: Norton, 1990.

Bornstein, George. *Material Modernism: The Politics of the Page.* Cambridge: Cambridge University Press, 2001.

   "What is the text of a poem by Yeats?" In *Palimpsest: Editorial Theory in the Humanities.* Ed. George Bornstein and Ralph Williams. Ann Arbor, MI: University of Michigan Press, 1993, pp. 168–193.

Bourdieu, Pierre and Alain Darbel. *The Love of Art: European Art Museums and Their Public.* Trans. Caroline Beattie and Nick Merriman from *L'Amour de l'art* (1969). Stanford, CA: Stanford University Press, 1990.

Bradshaw, Graham. "Creative mythology in *Cave Birds.*" In Sagar, *The Achievement of Ted Hughes*, 210–238.

Breslin, James. *From Modern to Contemporary: American Poetry, 1945–1965.* Chicago, IL: University of Chicago Press, 1984.

Britzolakis, Christina. *Sylvia Plath and the Theatre of Mourning.* Oxford: Oxford University Press, 1999.

Brooks, Gwendolyn. *In the Mecca.* New York, NY: Harper & Row, 1968.
Report from Part One. Detroit, MI: Broadside, 1972.

Bryant, Marsha. *Auden and Documentary in the 1930s.* Charlottesville, VA: University Press of Virginia, 1997.
"Plath, domesticity, and the art of advertising." *College Literature* 29.3 (Summer, 2002), 17–34.

Bryson, Norman. "Introduction." In Bal, *Looking In,* pp. 1–39.

Cappellazzo, Amy and Elizabeth Licata, eds. *In Company: Robert Creeley's Collaborations.* Chapel Hill, NC: University of North Carolina Press, 1999.

Cappellazzo, Amy, Reine Hauser, Seth McCormick and Elizabeth Licata, "The collaborators talk." In Cappellazzo and Licata, *In Company,* pp. 22–27.

Caprices, Grotesques and Homages: Leonard Baskin and the Gehenna Press – A Library of Congress Exhibition. Washington, DC: Library of Congress, 1994.

Carrier, David. *Artwriting.* Amherst, MA: University of Massachusetts Press, 1987.

Carroll, Anne. *Word, Image, and the New Negro: Representation and Identity in the Harlem Renaissance.* Bloomington, IN: Indiana University Press, 2005.

Castelman, Riva. *A Century of Artist's Books.* New York, NY: Museum of Modern Art, 1994.

Cavalieri, Grace. "Brushed by an angel's wings" (1995). In Ingersoll, *Conversations with Rita Dove,* 136–147.

Caws, Mary Ann. *The Art of Interference: Stressed Readings in Verbal and Visual Texts.* Princeton, NJ: Princeton University Press, 1983.
"Looking: Literature's other." *PMLA* 119.5 (October, 2004), 1293–1314.
ed. *Textual Analysis: Some Readers Reading.* New York, NY: Modern Language Association, 1986.

Chapman, Wayne. "'The Municipal Gallery Re-visited' and its writing." *Yeats Annual* 10 (1993), 159–187.

Char, René. *Les voisinages de Van Gogh.* Paris: Gallimard, 1985.

Christ, Carol T. *Victorian and Modern Poetics.* Chicago, IL: University of Chicago Press, 1984.

Christian Schad. Exhibition catalogue. Berlin: Staatliche Kunsthalle Berlin, 1980.

Clements, Robert J. "Brueghel's *Fall of Icarus*: Eighteen modern literary readings." *Studies in Iconography* 7–8 (1981–1982), 253–268.

Colburn, Steven E., ed. *Anne Sexton: Telling the Tale.* Ann Arbor, MI: University of Michigan Press, 1988.

Costello, Bonnie. *Marianne Moore: Imaginary Possessions.* Cambridge, MA: Harvard University Press, 1981.

Cluver, Claus. "On intersemiotic transposition." *Poetics Today* 10:1 (Spring, 1989), 55–90.

Crane, Susan A. "Curious cabinets and imaginary museums." In *Museums and Memory*. Ed. Susan A. Crane. Stanford, CA: Stanford University Press, 2000, pp. 60–90.

Deane, Seamus. *Celtic Revivals: Essays in Modern Irish Literature, 1880–1890*. Winston-Salem, NC: Wake Forest University Press, 1987 [1985].

Deese, Helen. "Lowell and the visual arts." In *Robert Lowell: Essays on the Poetry*. Ed. Steven Gould Axelrod and Helen Deese. Cambridge: Cambridge University Press, 1986, pp. 180–216.

DeLoss McGraw: As a Poem, So Is a Picture. Exhibition catalogue. Scottsdale, AZ: Scottsdale Center for the Arts, 1997.

Dickie, Margaret. "The maternal gaze: Women modernists and poetic authority." In *Alternative Identities: The Self in Literature, History, Theory*. Ed. Linda Marie Brooks. New York, NY: Garland, 1995, pp. 221–242.

Diggory, Terence. *William Carlos Williams and the Ethics of Painting*. Princeton, NJ: Princeton University Press, 1991.

Dijkstra, Bram. *Cubism, Stieglitz, and the Early Poetry of William Carlos Williams: The Hieroglyphics of a New Speech*. Princeton, NJ: Princeton University Press, 1969.

Dove, Rita. *Grace Notes*. New York, NY: Norton, 1989.

"Introduction." In Tolson, *"Harlem Gallery,"* pp. xi–xxv.

Mother Love. New York, NY: Norton, 1995.

Museum. Pittsburgh, PA:Carnegie Mellon, 1983.

On the Bus with Rosa Parks. New York, NY: Norton, 1999.

The Other Side of the House. Tempe: VARI Studios/Pyracantha Press, School of Art, Arizona State University, 1988.

"Rita Dove on Melvin B. Tolson." In *Poetry Speaks*. Ed. Elise Paschen and Rebekah Presson Mosby. Naperville, IL: Sourcebooks, 2001, pp. 139–40.

"Telling it like it I-S *IS*: Narrative techniques in Melvin Tolson's Harlem Gallery." *New England Review/Bread Loaf Quarterly* 8 (Fall, 1985), 109–117.

Thomas and Beulah. Pittsburgh, PA: Carnegie Mellon University Press, 1986.

The Yellow House on the Corner. Pittsburgh, PA: Carnegie Mellon University Press, 1989.

Downs, Linda. "A recent history of women educators in art museums." In Glaser and Zenetou, *Gender Perspectives*, pp. 92–96.

Drucker, Johanna. "The artist's book as idea and form." In *A Book of the Book: Some Works & Projections about the Book & Writing*. Ed. Jerome Rothenberg and Steven Clay. New York, NY: Granary, 2000, pp. 376–388.

Duarte, João Ferreira. "Auden's Icarus and his fall: Vision, super-vision and revision." In *English Studies in Transition: Papers from the ESSE Inaugural Conference*. Ed. Robert Clark and Piero Boitani. London: Routledge, 1991.

Duncan, Carol. *Civilizing Rituals: Inside Public Art Museums*. New York, NY: Routledge, 1995.

Durcan, Paul. *Crazy About Women*. Dublin: National Gallery of Ireland, 1991.

Give Me Your Hand. London: National Gallery, 1994.

Eaves, Morris. "Graphicality: Multimedia fables for 'textual' critics." In *Reimagining Textuality: Textual Studies in the Late Age of Print.* Ed. Elizabeth Bergmann Loizeaux and Neil Fraistat. Madison: University of Wisconsin Press, 2002, pp. 99–122.

Ede, Lisa and Andrea Lunsford. *Single Text/Plural Authors: Perspectives on Collaborative Writing.* Carbondale, IL:Southern Illinois University Press, 1990.

Elkins, James. *The Object Stares Back: On the Nature of Seeing.* New York, NY: Simon and Schuster, 1996.

   On Pictures and the Words that Fail Them. Cambridge: Cambridge University Press, 1998.

Ellis, Trey. "The new black aesthetic." *Callaloo* 12.1 (1989), 233–251.

Engelberg, Edward. *The Vast Design: Patterns in W. B. Yeats's Aesthetic.* 2nd edn. Washington, DC: Catholic University Press, 1988.

Enzensberger, Hans Magnus. *Mausoleum.* Trans. Joachim Neugroschel. New York, NY: Urizen Books, 1976.

Faas, Ekbert. *Ted Hughes: The Unaccommodated Universe.* Santa Barbara, CA: Black Sparrow, 1980.

Fagles, Robert. *I, Vincent.* Princeton, NJ: Princeton University Press, 1978.

Fairbanks, Arthur. "Introduction." In Philostratus, *Imagines/Callistratus: Descriptions.* Trans. Arthur Fairbanks. New York, NY: Putnam, 1931, pp. xv–xxxii.

Fanon, Frantz. *Black Skin, White Masks.* Trans. Charles Lam Markmann. New York, NY: Grove, 1967.

Feaver, Vicki. "Oi yoi yoi." In Abse and Abse, *Voices in the Gallery,* p. 125.

Feelings, Tom. "Introduction." In Angelou, *Now Sheba Sings the Song,* pp. 5–6.

Feinstein, Elaine. *Ted Hughes: The Life of a Poet.* New York, NY: Norton, 2001.

Feldman, Irving. *All of Us Here.* New York, NY: Viking, 1986.

   Teach Me, Dear Sister. New York, NY: Viking, 1983.

Ferguson, Russell. *In Memory of My Feelings: Frank O'Hara and American Art.* Berkeley, CA: University of California Press (Museum of Contemporary Art, Los Angeles), 1999.

Ferlinghetti, Lawrence. *When I Look at Pictures.* Salt Lake City, UT: Peregrine Books, 1990.

Fern, Alan. "Foreword." In *The Complete Prints of Leonard Baskin.* Ed. Alan Fern and Judith O'Sullivan. Boston, MA: Little Brown, 1984, pp. 7–9.

Fischer, Barbara K., *Museum Meditations: Reframing Ekphrasis in Contemporary American Poetry.* New York, NY: Routledge, 2006.

Fisher, Philip. *Making and Effacing Art: Modern American Art in a Culture of Museums.* New York, NY: Oxford University Press, 1991.

Fles, John, ed. *The Trembling Lamb.* New York, NY: H. Gantt, n.d. [1959?].

Folk Art in America – A Living Tradition: Selections from the Abby Aldrich Rockefeller Folk Art Collection, Williamsburg, Virginia. Atlanta, GA:High Art Museum, 1974.

Freedberg, David. *The Power of Images: Studies in the History and Theory of Response*. Chicago, IL: University of Chicago Press, 1989.

Freeman, Margaret B. *The Unicorn Tapestries*. New York, NY: Metropolitan Museum, 1976.

Fried, Michael. *Absorption and Theatricality: Painting and Beholder in the Age of Diderot*. Berkeley, CA: University of California Press, 1980.

"Art and objecthood." In *Minimal Art: A Critical Anthology*. Ed. Gregory Battock. Berkeley, CA: University of California Press, 1995, pp. 116–147.

Fry, Paul. *A Defense of Poetry: Reflections on the Occasion of Writing*. Stanford, CA: Stanford University Press, 1995.

Fuller, John. *W. H. Auden: A Commentary*. Princeton, NJ: Princeton University Press, 1998.

Gahern, Kathleen McCracken. "Masks and voices: Dramatic personas in the poetry of Paul Durcan." *Canadian Journal of Irish Studies* 13.1 (1987), 107–120.

Gardons, S. S. [W. D. Snodgrass]. "VUILLARD: 'The Mother and Sister of the Artist.'" *Hudson Review* 13.4 (Winter, 1960–1961), 514–516.

Gaston, Paul. *W. D. Snodgrass*. Boston, MA: Twayne, 1978.

Gates, Henry Louis, Jr. "Foreword: In her own write." In Wheatley, *The Collected Works*, pp. vii–xxii.

The Gehenna Press: The Work of Fifty Years. 1942–1992. Dallas, TX: Bridwell Library and Gehenna Press, 1992.

Gelpi, Albert. "Adrienne Rich: The poetics of change." In *Adrienne Rich's Poetry and Prose*. Ed. Barbara Charlesworth Gelpi and Albert Gelpi. Rev. edn. New York, NY: Norton, 1993.

Gifford, Terry and Neil Roberts. *Ted Hughes: A Critical Study*. London: Faber and Faber, 1981.

Gilman, Ernest. *Iconoclasm and Poetry in the English Reformation: Down Went Dagon*. Chicago, IL: University of Chicago Press, 1986.

Gilman, Sander L. "Black bodies, white bodies: Toward an iconography of female sexuality in late nineteenth-century art, medicine, and literature." In *"Race," Writing, and Difference*. Ed. Henry Louis Gates, Jr. Chicago, IL: University of Chicago Press, 1986, pp. 223–261.

Glaser, Jane R. and Artemis A. Zenetou, eds. *Gender Perspectives: Essays on Women in Museums*. Washington, DC: Smithsonian Institution Press, 1994.

Gogh, Vincent Van. *Complete Letters of Vincent Van Gogh*. 3 vols. Greenwich, CT: New York Graphic Society, 1958.

Gorer, Geoffrey. "The pornography of death." In *Death, Grief, and Mourning*. New York, NY: Doubleday, 1965, pp. 192–199.

Graham, W. S. "The Thermal Stair." In Abse and Abse, *Voices in the Gallery*, pp. 145–148.

Gregson, Ian. *Contemporary Poetry and Postmodernism*. New York, NY: St. Martin's, 1996.

Grennan, Eamon. "Prime Durcan: A collage." In Tóibín, *The Kilfenora Teaboy*, pp. 42–74.

Gross, Kenneth. *The Dream of the Moving Statue*. Ithaca, NY: Cornell University Press, 1992.

Gunn, Thom. *Positives*. London: Faber, 1973.

Hagstrum, Jean. *The Sister Arts: The Tradition of Literary Pictorialism and English Poetry from Dryden to Gray*. Chicago, IL: University of Chicago Press, 1987 [1958].

Halpern, Daniel, ed. *Writers on Artists*. San Francisco, CA: North Point, 1988.

Hammacher. A. M. "Van Gogh and the words." In J. B. de la Faille, *The Works of Vincent Van Gogh*. New York, NY: Reynal, 1970, pp. 10–37.

Harper, George Mills. " 'Necessary murder': The Auden circle and the Spanish Civil War." In *On Modern Poetry: Essays Presented to Donald Davie*. Ed. Vereen Bell and Laurence Lerner. Nashville, TN: Vanderbilt University Press, 1988, pp. 67–80.

Hayden, Robert. *Collected Poems*. Ed. Frederick Glaysher. New York, NY: Liveright, 1996.

Heaney, Seamus. *North*. London: Faber and Faber, 1975.
  A Personal Selection. Belfast: Ulster Museum, 1982.
  Sweeney's Flight. London: Faber, 1992.

Hedley, Jane. "Sylvia Plath's ekphrastic poetry." *Raritan* 20.4 (2001), 37–73.

Hedley, Jane, Nick Halpern and Willard Spiegelman, eds. *In the Frame: Women's Ekphrastic Poetry from Marianne Moore to Susan Wheeler*. Newark, DE: University of Delaware Press, 2008.

Heffernan, James. A. W. *Museum of Words: The Poetics of Ekphrasis from Homer to Ashbery*. Chicago, IL: University of Chicago Press, 1993.

Heine, Hilde S. *The Museum in Transition: A Philosophical Perspective*. Washington, DC: Smithsonian Institution Press, 2000.

Henn, T. R. *The Lonely Tower: Studies in the Poetry of W. B. Yeats*. Rev. edn. London: Methuen, 1965.

Herd, David. "Collaboration and the avant-garde." *Critical Review* 35 (1995), 36–63.

Heuving, Jeanne. *Omissions Are Not Accidents: Gender in the Art of Marianne Moore*. Detroit, MI: Wayne State University Press, 1992.

Hines, Thomas Jensen. *Collaborative Form: Studies in the Relations of the Arts*. Kent, OH: Kent State University Press, 1991.

Hirsch, Edward. *For the Sleepwalkers*. Pittsburgh, PA: Carnegie Mellon University Press, 1998.
  ed. *Transforming Vision: Writers on Art*. Boston, New York, Toronto, London: Bulfinch Press [Little, Brown & Co.] for The Art Institute of Chicago, 1994.

Hirschberg, Stuart. *Myth in the Poetry of Ted Hughes: A Guide to the Poems*. Totowa, NJ: Barnes and Noble, 1981.

Hollander, John. *The Gazer's Spirit: Poems Speaking to Silent Works of Art*. Chicago, IL: University of Chicago Press, 1995.

Hollenberg, Donna K. "'History as I desired it': Ekphrasis as postmodern witness in Denise Levertov's late poetry." *Modernism/Modernity* 10.3 (2003), 519–537.

Holley, Margaret. *The Poetry of Marianne Moore: A Study in Voice and Value.* Cambridge: Cambridge University Press, 1987.

Horowitz, Helen Lefkowitz. *Alma Mater: Design and Experience in the Women's Colleges from Their Nineteenth-Century Beginnings to the 1930s.* New York, NY: Knopf, 1984.

Hoy, Philip. "*The Starry Night*: Snodgrass's Van Gogh reconsidered." *Agenda* 34:1 (1996), 22–111.

Hudson, Kenneth. *Museums of Influence.* Cambridge: Cambridge University Press, 1987.

Hughes, Ted. Letter to Leonard Baskin. [1969–1970?] Leonard Baskin Collection. British Library, London.

  Letter to Leonard Baskin. [*c.* 1971–1972.] Leonard Baskin Collection. British Library, London.

  Letter to Leonard Baskin. July 29, 1974. Leonard Baskin Collection, British Library, London.

  Letter to Leonard Baskin. August 15, 1984. Leonard Baskin Collection, British Library, London.

  Letter to Leonard Baskin. March 25, 1995. Leonard Baskin Collection. British Library, London.

  "The hanged man and the dragonfly (note for a panegyric ode on Leonard Baskin's *Collected Prints*)." 1984. In Hughes, *Winter Pollen*, pp. 84–102.

  The Letters of Ted Hughes. Ed. Christopher Reid. London: Faber and Faber, 2007.

  New Selected Poems. New York, NY: Harper & Row, 1982.

  New Selected Poems 1957–1994. London: Faber and Faber, 1995.

  "The poetic self: A centenary tribute to T. S. Eliot." 1988. In Hughes, *Winter Pollen*, pp. 268–292.

  "Poetry in the making: Three extracts." 1967. In Hughes, *Winter Pollen*, pp. 10–24.

  Selected Poems 1957–1994. New York, NY: Farrar, Straus and Giroux, 2002.

  Winter Pollen: Occasional Prose. Ed. William Scammell. New York, NY: Picador, 1995.

Hughes, Ted and Leonard Baskin. *Cave Birds: An Alchemical Cave Drama.* New York, NY: Viking, 1978.

  Cave Birds: Poems. Ilkley: Scolar Press, 1975.

  Crow: From the Life and Songs of the Crow. London: Faber and Faber, 1974.

Hunt, John Dixon. *Self-Portrait in a Convex Mirror: On Poems on Paintings.* London: Bedford College, 1980.

Hutcheon, Linda and Michael Hutcheon. "A convenience of marriage: Collaboration and interdisciplinarity." *PMLA* 116:5 (October, 2001), 1364–1376.

Ibis Communications. "Invasion of England, 1066." www.eyewitnesstohistory.com/bayeux.htm (accessed February 20, 2004).

Ingersoll, Earl, ed. *Conversations with Rita Dove*. Jackson: University of Mississippi Press, 2003.

Jaffe, Irma B. *The Sculpture of Leonard Baskin*. New York, NY: Viking, 1980.

Jarrell, Randall. *The Complete Poems*. New York, NY: Noonday, 1969.

Jay, Martin. *Downcast Eyes: The Denigration of Vision in Twentieth-Century French Thought*. Berkeley, CA: University of California Press, 1993.

Johnson, Gretchen and Richard Peabody. "A cage of sound" (1985). In Ingersoll, *Conversations with Rita Dove*, pp. 15–37.

Jordan, June. *Who Look at Me*. New York, NY: Crowell, 1969.

Joyce, Elisabeth. *Cultural Critique and Abstraction: Marianne Moore and the Avant-Garde*. Lewisburg, PA: Bucknell University Press, 1998.

Kalstone, David. *Five Temperaments: Elizabeth Bishop, Robert Lowell, James Merrill, Adrienne Rich, John Ashbery*. New York, NY: Oxford University Press, 1977.

Karp, Ivan, Christine Mullen Kreamer and Steven D. Lavine, eds. *Museums and Communities: The Politics of Public Culture*. Washington, DC: Smithsonian, 1992.

Kearney, Richard. "Myth and motherland." In *Ireland's Field Day*. Notre Dame, IN: University of Notre Dame Press, 1986 [1983], pp. 61–80.

Keats, John. *The Poems of John Keats*. Ed. Jack Stillinger. Cambridge, MA: Harvard University Press, 1978.

Keaveney, Raymond. "Acknowledgements." In Durcan, *Crazy About Women*, p. vii.

"Introduction." In Raymond Keaveney, Michael Wynne, Adrian Le Harivel, Fionnuala Croke and Sergio Benedetti, *National Gallery of Ireland*. London: Scala, 1998 (1990).

Kehl, D. G., ed. *Poetry and the Visual Arts*. Belmont, CA: Wadsworth, 1975.

Keller, Evelyn Fox and Christine R. Grontkowski. "The mind's eye." In *Feminism and Science*. Ed. Evelyn Fox Keller and Helen E. Longino. Oxford: Oxford University Press, 1996, pp. 187–202.

Kelley, Theresa. "Keats, ekphrasis and history." In *Keats and History*. Ed. Nicholas Roe. Cambridge: Cambridge University Press, 1995, pp. 212–237.

Kennedy, Brian. "*Crazy About Women*: Poems about paintings." In Tóibín, *The Kilfenora Teaboy*, pp. 155–162.

"Foreword." In Durcan, *Crazy About Women*, p. ix.

Klarer, Mario, ed. *Ekphrasis*. Special issue of *Word & Image* 15.1 (1999).

Koch, Kenneth. *Kenneth Koch: Collaborations with Artists*. Ipswich: Ipswich Borough Council, 1993.

Koestenbaum, Wayne. *Double Talk: The Erotics of Male Literary Collaboration*. New York, NY: Routledge, 1989.

Krieger, Murray. *Ekphrasis: The Illusion of the Natural Sign*. Baltimore, MD:Johns Hopkins University Press, 1992.

Laird, Holly. *Women Coauthors*. Urbana, IL: University of Illinois Press, 2000.

Leavell, Linda. *Marianne Moore and the Visual Arts: Prismatic Color.* Baton Rouge, LA: Louisiana State University Press, 1995.

Lehman, David. *The Last Avant-Garde: The Making of the New York School of Poets.* New York, NY: Doubleday, 1998.

Leonardi, Susan and Rebecca Pope. "(Co)labored li(v)es: Love's labors queered." *PMLA* 116:3 (May, 2001), 631–637.

Lerner, Laurence. "What is confessional poetry?" *Critical Quarterly* 29:2 (Summer, 1987), 46–66.

Lessing, Gotthold Ephraim. *Laocoön: An Essay on the Limits of Painting and Poetry.* Trans. Edward Allen McCormick. Baltimore, MD:Johns Hopkins University Press, 1984.

Levertov, Denise. "Light up the cave." In Denise Levertov, *Light Up the Cave.* New York, NY: New Directions, 1981, pp. 80–86.

Levin, Gail, ed. *The Poetry of Solitude: A Tribute to Edward Hopper.* New York, NY: Universe, 1995.

Licata, Elizabeth. "Robert Creeley's collaborations: A history." In Cappellazzo and Licata, *In Company,* pp. 11–21.

Lines = Lignes; Réflexions = Reflections. Los Angeles, CA: Armand Hammer Museum, 1996.

Lloyd, David. *Anomalous States: Irish Writing and the Post-Colonial Moment.* Durham, NC: Duke University Press, 1993.

Lloyd, Jill. "Christian Schad: Reality and illusion." In *Christian Schad and the Neue Sachlichkeit.* Ed. Jill Lloyd and Michael Peppiatt. New York, NY: Norton, 2003, pp. 15–28.

Loeb, Michael. Letter to Leonard Baskin. March 28, 1977. Leonard Baskin Collection. British Library, London.

Loizeaux, Elizabeth Bergmann. "Ekphrasis and textual consciousness." *Word & Image* 15.1 (January, 1999), 76–96.

  "Reading word, image and the body of the book: Ted Hughes' and Leonard Baskin's *Cave Birds.*" *Twentieth Century Literature* 50.1 (Spring, 2004), 18–58.

  Yeats and the Visual Arts. New Brunswick, NJ: Rutgers University Press, 1986. Syracuse, NY: Syracuse University Press, 2003.

Loizeaux, Elizabeth Bergmann and Neil Fraistat, eds. *Reimagining Textuality: Textual Studies in the Late Age of Print.* Madison: University of Wisconsin Press, 2002.

London, Bette. "Introduction: Seeing double." In *Writing Double: Women's Literary Partnerships.* Ithaca, NY: Cornell University Press, 1999, pp. 1–32.

Long, Beverly Whitaker and Timothy Scott Cage. "Contemporary American poetry: A selected bibliography." *Text and Performance Quarterly* 9 (1989), 286–296.

Longenbach, James. *Modern Poetry after Modernism.* Oxford: Oxford University Press, 1997.

  Modernist Poetics of History: Pound, Eliot, and the Sense of the Past. Princeton, NJ: Princeton University Press, 1987.

Longley, Edna. "Paul Durcan and the North: Recollections." In Tóibín, *The Kilfenora Teaboy*, pp. 102–113.

Lowell, Robert. *Collected Poems.* Ed. Frank Bidart and David Gewanter. New York, NY: Farrar, Straus and Giroux, 2003.

Lundquist, Sara. "Reverence and resistance: Barbara Guest, ekphrasis, and the female gaze." *Contemporary Literature* 38.2 (1997), 260–286.

MacLeod, Glen. *Wallace Stevens and Modern Art: From the Armory Show to Abstract Expressionism.* New Haven, CT: Yale University Press, 1993.

Mahon, Derek. "Orpheus ascending: The poetry of Paul Durcan." In Tóibín, *The Kilfenora Teaboy*, pp. 163–170.

   Selected Poems. New York, NY: Viking, 1991.

Malraux, André. *Museum without Walls.* Trans. Stuart Gilbert and Francis Price. New York, NY: Doubleday, 1967.

Marley, Bob. "Sun is shining." www.iration.com/wailers/sunisshining (accessed June 20, 2005).

Martin, Taffy. *Marianne Moore: Subversive Modernist.* Austin, TX: University of Texas Press, 1986.

Martinez, Michele. "Women poets and the sister arts in nineteenth-century England." *Victorian Poetry* 41.4 (Winter, 2003), 621–628.

Maslen, Elizabeth. "Counterpoint: Collaborations between Ted Hughes and three visual artists." *Word & Image* 2.1 (January–March, 1986), 33–44.

Materer, Timothy. *Modernist Alchemy: Poetry and the Occult.* Ithaca, NY: Cornell University Press, 1995.

McCarthy, Kathleen D. *Women's Culture: American Philanthropy and Art, 1830–1930.* Chicago, IL: University of Chicago Press, 1991.

McClatchy, J. D. "Introduction." In McClatchy, *Poets on Painters*, pp. xi–xvii.

   ed. *Poets on Painters.* Berkeley, CA: University of California Press, 1988.

McClellan, Andrew. *Inventing the Louvre: Art, Politics, and the Origins of the Modern Museum in Eighteenth-Century Paris.* Cambridge: Cambridge University Press, 1994.

McCracken, Kathleen. "Canvas and camera translated: Paul Durcan and the visual arts." *The Irish Review* (Fall, 1989), 18–29.

McDiarmid, Lucy. *Auden's Apologies for Poetry.* Princeton, NJ: Princeton University Press, 1990.

   The Irish Art of Controversy. Ithaca, NY: Cornell University Press, 2005.

   Saving Civilization: Yeats, Eliot, and Auden between the Wars. Cambridge: Cambridge University Press, 1984.

McGann, Jerome J. *Black Riders: The Visible Language of Modernism.* Princeton, NJ: Princeton University Press, 1993.

   The Textual Condition. Princeton, NJ: Princeton University Press, 1991.

McGraw, DeLoss. "Two statements on collaborating with W. D. Snodgrass." In *The Poetry of W. D. Snodgrass: Everything Human.* Ed. Stephen Haven. Ann Arbor, MI: University of Michigan Press, 1993, pp. 297–300.

Melchiori, Giorgio. *The Whole Mystery of Art: Pattern into Poetry in the Work of W. B. Yeats.* New York, NY: Macmillan, 1961.

Mendelson, Edward. *Early Auden.* Cambridge, MA: Harvard University Press, 1983.

Merrill, James. "Notes on Corot." In McClatchy, *Poets on Painters*, 311–321.

Merrin, Jeredith. *An Enabling Humility: Marianne Moore, Elizabeth Bishop, and the Uses of Tradition.* New Brunswick, NJ: Rutgers University Press, 1990.

Middlebrook, Diane Wood. *Anne Sexton: A Biography.* Boston, MA: Houghton Mifflin, 1991.

Millay, Edna St. Vincent. *Collected Sonnets.* New York, NY: Harper & Row, 1988.

Miller, Cristanne. *Marianne Moore: Questions of Authority.* Cambridge, MA: Harvard University Press, 1995.

Millett, Kate. *Sexual Politics.* Garden City, New York, NY: Doubleday, 1970.

Mirollo, James V. "Bruegel's *Fall of Icarus* and the poets." In *The Eye of the Poet: Studies in the Reciprocity of the Visual and Literary Arts from the Renaissance to the Present.* Ed. Amy Golahny. Lewisburg, PA: Bucknell University Press, 1996, pp. 131–153.

Mitchell, W. J. T. *Iconology: Image, Text, Ideology.* Chicago, IL: University of Chicago Press, 1986.

Picture Theory: Essays on Verbal and Visual Representation. Chicago, IL: University of Chicago Press, 1994.

Molesworth, Charles. *Marianne Moore: A Literary Life.* New York, NY: Atheneum, 1990.

Moore, Marianne. *Becoming Marianne Moore: The Early Poems, 1907–1924.* Ed. Robin G. Schulze. Berkeley, CA: University of California Press, 2002.

The Complete Poems of Marianne Moore. New York, NY: Macmillan, 1982 [1967].

The Complete Prose of Marianne Moore. Ed. Patricia C. Willis. New York, NY: Viking, 1986.

Mulvey, Laura. *Visual and Other Pleasures.* Bloomington, IN: Indiana University Press, 1989.

Murphy, Maureen. "Back to the Municipal Gallery: W. B. Yeats and modern Ireland." In *Conflicting Identities: Essays on Modern Irish Literature.* Ed. Robbie B. H. Goh. Singapore: UniPress, 1997, pp. 121–143.

Nadell, Martha Jane. *Enter the New Negroes: Images of Race in American Culture.* Cambridge, MA: Harvard University Press, 2004.

Nelson, Deborah. *Pursuing Privacy in Cold War America.* New York, NY: Columbia University Press, 2002.

Nelson, Lynn Harry. www.ku.edu/Kansas/medieval/108/lectures/bayeux_tapestry.html (accessed August 1, 2003).

Nicholson, George. Letter to Leonard Baskin. January 14, 1976. Leonard Baskin Collection. British Library, London.

Nochlin, Linda. *Women, Art, and Power and Other Essays.* New York, NY: Harper & Row, 1988.

North, Michael. *The Final Sculpture: Public Monuments and Modern Poets*. Ithaca, NY: Cornell University Press, 1985.

O'Doherty, Brian. *Inside the White Cube: The Ideology of Gallery Space*. Santa Monica, CA: The Lapis Press, 1986.

O'Hara, Frank. *The Collected Poems of Frank O'Hara*. Ed. Donald Allen. Rev. edn. Berkeley, CA:University of California Press, 1995.

Olson, Tillie. *Silences*. London: Virago, 1978.

Packard, William. "Craft interview with Anne Sexton (1970)." In *Anne Sexton: The Artist and Her Critics*. Ed. J. D. McClatchy. Bloomington, IN: Indiana University Press, 1978, pp. 43–47.

Paul, Catherine. *Poetry in the Museums of Modernism: Yeats, Pound, Moore, Stein*. Ann Arbor, MI: University of Michigan Press, 2002.

Paulson, Ronald. "English iconoclasm in the eighteenth century." In *Space, Time, Image, Sign: Essays on Literature and the Visual Arts*. Ed. James Heffernan. New York, NY: Peter Lang, 1987, pp. 41–62.

Pearce, Lynne. *Woman/Image/Text: Readings in Pre-Raphaelite Art and Literature*. Toronto, ON:University of Toronto Press, 1991.

Pereira, Malin. *Rita Dove's Cosmopolitanism*. Urbana, IL: University of Illinois Press, 2003.

Perloff, Marjorie. *Frank O'Hara: Poet among Painters*. Chicago, IL: University of Chicago Press, 1998 [1977].

  The Futurist Moment: Avant-Garde, Avant Guerre, and the Language of Rupture. Chicago, IL: University of Chicago Press, 1986.

  The Poetics of Indeterminacy: Rimbaud to Cage. Princeton, NJ: Princeton University Press, 1981.

  Radical Artifice: Writing Poetry in the Age of Media. Chicago, IL: University of Chicago Press, 1991.

  21st-Century Modernism: The "New" Poetics. Oxford: Blackwell, 2002.

Phillips, Robert. *The Confessional Poets*. Carbondale, IL: Southern Illinois University, 1973.

Philostratus. *Imagines/Callistratus: Descriptions*. Trans. Arthur Fairbanks. New York, NY: Putnam, 1931.

Piatt, John James. "To the Statue on the Capitol: Looking Eastward at Dawn." In Hollander, *The Gazer's Spirit*, p. 205.

Pickvance, Ronald. *Van Gogh in Saint-Rémy and Auvers*. New York, NY: The Metropolitan Museum of Art/Harry N. Abrams, 1986.

Plath, Sylvia. *Collected Poems*. Ed. Ted Hughes. New York, NY: HarperCollins, 1981.

Pollock, Griselda. "Artists' mythologies and media genius, madness and art history." *Screen* 21:3 (1980), 57–96.

  Vision and Difference: Femininity, Feminism and Histories of Art. London: Routledge, 1988.

Posnock, Ross. *Color and Culture: Black Writers and the Making of the Modern Intellectual*. Cambridge, MA: Harvard University Press, 1998.

Pound, Ezra. *Literary Essays of Ezra Pound.* Ed. T. S. Eliot. New York, NY: New Directions, 1968.

Putnam, Michael C. J. *Virgil's Epic Designs : Ekphrasis in the Aeneid.* New Haven, CT: Yale University Press, 1998.

Rabaté, Jean-Michel. *The Ghosts of Modernity.* Gainesville, FL: University Press of Florida, 1996.

Race, Ethnicity and Culture in the Visual Arts: A Panel Discussion. New York, NY: American Council for the Arts, 1993.

Rainey, Lawrence. *Institutions of Modernism: Literary Elites and Public Culture.* New Haven, CT: Yale University Press, 1998.

Ramazani, Jahan. *The Hybrid Muse: Postcolonial Poetry in English.* Chicago, IL: University of Chicago Press, 2001.

Yeats and the Poetry of Death: Elegy, Self-Elegy and the Sublime. New Haven, CT: Yale University Press, 1990.

Rich, Adrienne. *Blood, Bread, and Poetry: Selected Prose 1979–1985.* New York, NY: Norton, 1986.

Collected Early Poems 1950–1970. New York, NY: Norton, 1993.

Dream of a Common Language: Poems 1974–1977. New York, NY: Norton, 1978.

Necessities of Life: Poems 1962–1965. New York, NY: Norton, 1966.

On Lies, Secrets, and Silence: Selected Prose 1966–1978. New York, NY: Norton, 1979.

A Wild Patience Has Taken Me This Far: Poems 1978–1981. New York, NY: Norton, 1981.

Riffaterre, Michael. "Textuality: W. H. Auden's 'Musée des Beaux Arts.'" In Caws, *Textual Analysis,* pp. 1–13.

Robinson, Edward Stevens. *The Behavior of the Museum Visitor.* Washington, DC: Publications of the American Association of Museums, new series no. 5, 1928.

Rosenbaum, Susan. "Elizabeth Bishop and the miniature museum." *Journal of Modern Literature* 28.2 (2005), 61–99.

Rosenthal, M. L. *The New Poets: American and British Poetry since World War II.* New York, NY: Oxford University Press, 1967.

"Some thoughts on Irving Feldman's poetry." In *The Poetry of Irving Feldman: Nine Essays.* Ed. Harold Schweizer. Lewisburg, PA: Bucknell University Press, 1992, pp. 29–39.

Rosenthal, M. L. and Sally M. Gall. *The Modern Poetic Sequence: The Genius of Modern Poetry.* New York, NY: Oxford University Press, 1983.

Rossetti Archive. www.rossettiarchive.org/docs/s252.rap.html. www.rossettiarchive.org/docs/2–1881.1stedn.rad.html#1–1879.s252.

Rossiter, Margaret W. *Women Scientists in America: Struggles and Strategies to 1940.* Baltimore, MD:Johns Hopkins University Press, 1982.

Rubin, Stan Sanvel and Judith Kitchen. "Riding that current as far as it'll take you" (1985). In Ingersoll, *Conversations with Rita Dove,* 3–14.

Ruby, Jay. *Secure the Shadow: Death and Photography in America*. Cambridge, MA: MIT Press, 1995.

Ruffins, Fath Davis. "Mythos, memory, and history: African American preservation efforts, 1820–1990." In Karp, Kreamer and Lavine, *Museums and Communities*, pp. 506–611.

Sagar, Keith, *The Art of Ted Hughes*. 2nd edn. Cambridge: Cambridge University Press, 1978.

  The Laughter of Foxes: A Study of Ted Hughes. Liverpool: Liverpool University Press, 2000.

  ed. *The Achievement of Ted Hughes*. Athens: University of Georgia Press, 1983.

  ed. *The Challenge of Ted Hughes*. New York, NY: St. Martin's Press, 1994.

Sagar, Keith and Stephen Tabor. *Ted Hughes: A Bibliography 1946–1980*. London: Mansell, 1983.

Sassoon, Siegfried. *Collected Poems 1908–1956*. London: Faber and Faber, 1971 [1961].

Saunders, Susanna Terrell. "Georgiana Goddard King (1871–1939): Educator and pioneer in medieval Spanish art." In Sherman with Holcomb, *Women as Interpreters of the Visual* Arts, pp. 209–238.

Schapiro, Meyer. *Vincent Van Gogh*. New York, NY: Abrams, 1950.

Schweizer, Harold. "Lyric suffering in Auden and Feldman." *English Language Notes* 31.2 (December 1, 1993), 66–74.

Scigaj, Leonard. "The painterly Plath that nobody knows." *Centennial Review* 32.3 (1988), 220–249.

  The Poetry of Ted Hughes: Form and Imagination. Iowa City, IA: University of Iowa Press, 1986.

  Ted Hughes. Boston, MA: Twayne, 1991.

Scott, Grant. *The Sculpted Word: Keats, Ekphrasis, and the Visual Arts*. Hanover, NH: University Press of New England, 1994.

Seidel, Frederick. "Robert Lowell." In *Writers at Work: The "Paris Review" Interviews*, Series 2. Ed. Malcolm Cowley. New York, NY: Viking Press, 1963, pp. 337–368.

Sexton, Anne. *Anne Sexton: A Self-Portrait in Letters*. Ed. Linda Gray Sexton and Lois Ames. Boston, MA:Houghton Mifflin, 1977.

  The Complete Poems. Boston, MA: Houghton Mifflin, 1981.

  Letter to W. D. Snodgrass. February 6, 1961. W. D. Snodgrass papers. University of Delaware Library, Newark, DE.

Shange, Ntozake. *Ridin' the Moon in Texas: Word Paintings*. New York, NY: St. Martin's Press, 1987.

Shelley, Percy Bysshe. "On the Medusa of Leonardo da Vinci, in the Florentine Gallery." Ed. Melissa J. Sites and Neil Fraistat.
  www.rc.umd.edu/editions/shelley/medusa/medusa.html (accessed November 17, 2007).

Sherman, Claire Richter. "Widening horizons (1890–1930)." In Sherman with Holcomb, *Women as Interpreters of the Visual Arts*, pp. 27–59.

Sherman, Claire Richter, with Adele M. Holcomb. "Precursors and pioneers (1820–1890)." In Sherman with Holcomb, *Women as Interpreters of the Visual Arts*, pp. 3–26.

eds. *Women as Interpreters of the Visual Arts, 1820–1979*. Westport, CT: Greenwood, 1981.

Showalter, Elaine. "Towards a feminist poetics." In *Women Writing and Writing about Women*. Ed. Mary Jacobus. New York, NY: Barnes and Noble, 1979, pp. 22–41.

Smith, Mack. *Literary Realism and the Ekphrastic Tradition*. University Park, PA: Pennsylvania State University Press, 1995.

Snodgrass, W. D. [also known as S. S. Gardons]. *After Experience: Poems and Translations*. New York, NY: Harper & Row, 1968.

After-Images: Autobiographical Sketches. Rochester, NY: BOA Editions, 1999.

The Death of Cock Robin. Newark: University of Delaware Press, 1989.

The Führer Bunker: A Cycle of Poems in Progress. Brockport, NY: BOA Editions, 1977.

In Radical Pursuit: Critical Essays and Lectures. New York, NY: Harper & Row, 1975.

Letter to Anne Sexton. "Friday night," n.d. [September, 1958]. W. D. Snodgrass–Anne Sexton Correspondence. The Harry Ransom Humanities Research Center, Austin, TX.

Letter to Anne Sexton. June 23, 1959. W. D. Snodgrass–Anne Sexton Correspondence. The Harry Ransom Humanities Research Center, Austin, TX.

Letter to Anne Sexton. December 10, 1960. W. D. Snodgrass–Anne Sexton Correspondence. The Harry Ransom Humanities Research Center, Austin, TX.

Letter to Anne Sexton. January 26, 1961. W. D. Snodgrass–Anne Sexton Correspondence. The Harry Ransom Humanities Research Center, Austin, TX.

"MANET: 'The Execution of the Emperor Maximilian.'" *Hudson Review* 16.2 (Summer, 1963), 246–248.

"MATISSE: 'The Red Studio.'" *ARTNews Annual* 3 (1960), 90–91.

Telephone interview with Elizabeth Bergmann Loizeaux. October, 2001.

W. D.'s Midnight Carnival. Encinitas, CA: Artra, 1988.

Sontag, Susan. "Looking at the unbearable." In Hirsch, *Transforming Vision*, pp. 91–92.

On Photography. New York, NY: Farrar, Straus and Giroux, 1977.

Spence, Steve. "Van Gogh in Alabama, 1936." *Representations* 75 (Summer, 2001), 33–60.

Spiegelman, Willard. *The Didactic Muse: Scenes of Instruction in Contemporary American Poetry*. Princeton, NJ: Princeton University Press, 1989.

Spitzer, Leo. "The 'Ode on a Grecian Urn,' or content vs. metagrammar." In *Essays on English and American Literature*. Ed. Anna Hatcher. Princeton, NJ: Princeton University Press, 1962, pp. 67–97.

Stafford, Barbara Maria. *Good Looking: Essays on the Virtue of Images.* (Cambridge, MA: MIT Press, 1996).

Stamy, Cynthia. *Marianne Moore and China: Orientalism and a Writing of America.* Oxford: Oxford University Press, 1999.

Steffen, Therese. *Crossing Color: Transcultural Space and Place in Rita Dove's Poetry, Fiction, and Drama.* Oxford: Oxford University Press, 2001.

Stein, Richard. *The Ritual of Interpretation: The Fine Arts as Literature in Ruskin, Rossetti, and Pater.* Cambridge, MA: Harvard University Press, 1975.

Steiner, Wendy. *The Colors of Rhetoric: Problems in the Relation between Modern Literature and Painting.* Chicago, IL: University of Chicago Press, 1982.

Stevens, Wallace. *The Collected Poems of Wallace Stevens.* New York, NY: Knopf, 1971.
  The Necessary Angel: Essays on Reality and the Imagination. New York, NY: Vintage, 1951.

Stewart, Susan. *On Longing: Narratives of the Miniature, the Gigantic, the Souvenir, the Collection.* Baltimore, MD: Johns Hopkins University Press, 1984.

Stillinger, Jack. *Multiple Authorship and the Myth of Solitary Genius.* New York, NY: Oxford University Press, 1991.

Stone, Irving and Jean Irving. *Dear Theo: The Autobiography of Vincent Van Gogh.* Garden City, NY: Doubleday, 1937.

Sullivan, Janet. "Encountering the unicorn: William Carlos Williams and Marianne Moore." *Sagtrieb: A Journal Devoted to Poets in the Imagist/ Objectivist Tradition* 6.3 (Winter, 1987), 147–161.

Swan, Barbara. "A reminiscence." In Colburn, *Anne Sexton: Telling the Tale*, pp. 39–45.

Swanberg, W. A. *Citizen Hearst.* New York, NY: Scribners, 1961.

Swensen, Cole. "Interview." By Jon Thompson. http://english.chass.nscu/freeverse/ Archives/Winter_2003/Interviews/interviews (accessed October 1, 2005).
  Such Rich Hour. Iowa City, IA: University of Iowa Press, 2001.

Taleb-Khyar, Mohamed B. "Gifts to be earned" (1991). In Ingersoll, *Conversations with Rita Dove*, pp. 74–87.

Taylor, Kendall. "Pioneering efforts of early museum women." In Glaser and Zenetou, *Gender Perspectives*, pp. 11–27.

Tillinghast, Richard, ed. *A Visit to the Gallery.* Ann Arbor, MI: University of Michigan Museum of Art, 1997.

Tóibín, Colm. "Portrait of the artist as a spring lamb." In Tóibín, *The Kilfenora Teaboy*, pp. 7–25.
  ed. *The Kilfenora Teaboy: A Study of Paul Durcan.* Dublin: New Island Books, 1996.

Tolson, Melvin B. *"Harlem Gallery" and Other Poems of Melvin B. Tolson.* Ed. Raymond Nelson. Introduction by Rita Dove. Charlottesville, VA: University Press of Virginia, 1999.

Travisano, Thomas. *Midcentury Quartet: Bishop, Lowell, Jarrell, Berryman and the Making of a Postmodern Aesthetic.* Charlottesville, VA: University Press of Virginia, 1999.

Trilling, Lionel. *Beyond Culture: Essays on Literature and Learning.* New York, NY: Viking, 1965.

Valéry, Paul. "The problem of museums." In *The Collected Works of Paul Valéry.* Ed. Jackson Mathews.15 vols. Princeton, NJ: Princeton University Press, 1956–1975. Vol. 12, pp. 202–206.

Van Dyne, Susan R. "The mirrored vision of Adrienne Rich." *Modern Poetry Studies* 8 (1978), 140–173.

Vasseleu, Cathryn. "Illuminating passion: Irigaray's transfiguration of night." In *Vision in Context: Historical and Contemporary Perspective on Sight.* Ed. Teresa Brennan and Martin Jay. New York, NY: Routledge, 1996, pp. 127–137.

Vendler, Helen. "Four elegies." In *Yeats, Sligo and Ireland.* Ed. A. Norman Jeffares. Totowa, NJ: Barnes and Noble, 1980, pp. 216–231.

The Given and the Made. Cambridge, MA: Harvard University Press, 1995.

"An interview with Rita Dove." In *Reading Black, Reading Feminist: A Critical Anthology.* Ed. Henry Louis Gates, Jr. New York, NY: Meridian, 1990, pp. 481–491.

Violi, Paul. Introduction. In *Kenneth Koch: Collaborations with Artists.* Ipswich: Ipswich Borough Council, 1993. Unpaginated.

Vogel, Susan. "Always true to the object, in our fashion." *Exhibiting Cultures: The Poetics and Politics of Museum Display.* Ed Ivan Karp and Steven D. Lavine. Washington, DC: Smithsonian, 1991, pp. 191–204.

Voices and Visions: Program 8 – Marianne Moore. Videocassette. New York, NY: The New York Center for Visual History, 1988.

Wain, John. "The Shipwreck." In Adams, *With a Poet's Eye*, p. 40.

Webb, Ruth. "*Ekphrasis* ancient and modern: The invention of a genre." *Word & Image* 15.1 (1999), 7–18.

Welch, William H. "Contribution of Bryn Mawr College to the higher education of women." *Science* 56 (July 7, 1922), 1–8.

Wells, William. "Two tapestries in the Burrell Collection." *Scottish Art Review* 6.3 (1957), 7–10, 29.

Wheatley, Phillis. *The Collected Works of Phillis Wheatley.* Ed. John C. Shields. New York, NY: Oxford University Press, 1988.

Whelchel, Marianne. "Mining the 'earth-deposits': Women's history in Adrienne Rich's poetry." In *Reading Adrienne Rich: Reviews and Re-visions, 1951–1981.* Ed. Jane Roberta Cooper. Ann Arbor, MI: University of Michigan Press, 1984, pp. 51–71.

White, James. *National Gallery of Ireland.* New York, NY: Praeger, 1968.

Wilbur, Richard. *The Poems of Richard Wilbur.* New York, NY: Harcourt Brace Jovanovich, 1963.

Williams, William Carlos. *The Autobiography of William Carlos Williams.* New York, NY: Random House, 1951.

Collected Poems of William Carlos Williams. Vol. 1. Ed. A. Walton Litz and Christopher MacGowan. New York, NY: New Directions, 1986.

Collected Poems of William Carlos Williams. Vol. 2. Ed. Christopher MacGowan. New York, NY: New Directions, 1988.

Pictures from Brueghel and Other Poems. New York, NY: New Directions, 1962.

Willis, Patricia C. "Charity Overcoming Envy." *Marianne Moore Newsletter* 3.1 (Spring, 1979), 2–6.

"Discoveries: 'The Magician's Retreat.'" *Marianne Moore Newsletter* 1.2 (Fall, 1977), 2–5.

Wilson, Violet A. *Queen Elizabeth's Maids of Honour and Ladies of the Privy Chamber.* London: John Lane, 1922.

Yau, John. "Active participants: Robert Creeley and the visual arts." In Cappellazzo and Licata, *In Company*, 45–82.

Yeats, William Butler. *Autobiographies.* Ed. William H. O'Donnell and Douglas Archibald. New York, NY: Scribner, 1999.

The Poems. Ed. Richard J. Finneran. Rev. edn. New York, NY: Macmillan, 1989.

Senate Speeches. Ed. Donald R. Pearce. Bloomington, IN: Indiana University Press, 1960.

Uncollected Prose. 2 vols. Vol. 1. Ed. John P. Frayne. Vol. 2. Ed. Frayne and Colton Johnson. New York, NY: Columbia University Press, 1970–1976.

Under the Moon: The Unpublished Early Poetry. Ed. George Bornstein. New York, NY: Scribner, 1995.

The Variorum Edition of the Poems of W. B. Yeats. Ed. Peter Allt and Russell K. Alspach. Corrected 3rd printing. New York, NY: Macmillan, 1966.

Zivley, Sherry Lutz. "Sylvia Plath's transformations of modernist paintings." *College Literature* 29.3 (Summer, 2002), 35–56.

Index